The Halved Soul

Judith Pintar is a storyteller and musician. Her academic grounding in folklore and mythology and the inspiration of an Ojibwe medicine woman and storyteller led her to write and design *A Voice From the Earth: The Cards of Winds and Changes*, the successful book and cards pack. She is also well known for her celtic harp compositions and recordings. *At Last the Wind* is her most recent release.

THE
HALVED SOUL

Retelling the Myths of Romantic Love

JUDITH PINTAR

Pandora
An Imprint of HarperCollinsPublishers

Pandora Press
An Imprint of HarperCollins*Publishers*
77–85 Fulham Palace Road,
Hammersmith, London W6 8JB

Published by Pandora Press 1992
1 3 5 7 9 10 8 6 4 2

A catalogue record for this book
is available from the British Library

ISBN 0 04 440868 4

Typeset by Harper Phototypesetters Limited,
Northampton, England
Printed in Great Britain by
Mackays of Chatham, Kent

Contents

Introduction

> One can conceive of very ancient myths, but there are no eternal ones; for it is human history which converts reality into speech, and it alone rules the life and death of mythical language.
>
> ROLAND BARTHES

Cultural myths and social ideals tell us what we can expect from our lives, what lifestyles or possessions we should value and seek to attain. When our lives do not conform to these images we tend to question the worth of our own experiences rather than the validity of the expectations.

Nowhere in our lives do myths operate more powerfully than in our intimate relationships. Romantic Love is the predominant myth of personal love in the Western world. The myth tells us that there is one perfect person out there for each of us. A woman waits for her true love, the "armored knight" who will "sweep her off her feet." A man attains his true love through searching for and, presumably, "sweeping away" the perfect woman. Innocent and idealistic as it seems, the myth of Romantic Love actually perpetuates within us a damaging set of emotions and expectations. Romantic Love teaches a woman that her worth comes from being sexually desired and emotionally needed. At the same time she may lose sight of her own identity when she becomes involved with a man. When she takes his name in marriage she becomes, traditionally, an appendage to *his* life and identity. There is always an element of self-sacrifice involved: according to the myth, once a woman truly loves a man his faults and even his abuses become tolerable. Her faithful acceptance of suffering and pain are considered to be proof of her love.

While the key to Romantic Love for a woman is being needed by a man, for the man it centers around the depth of his need: the greater a man's emotional and sexual hunger, the truer is his love. Because Romantic Love is supposed to be uncontrollable and irrational, jealousy and anger seem to be natural expressions of passion as well. Romantic Love teaches a man that he must identify a perfect woman, then conquer or possess her in order to satisfy his need.

Many of these cultural myths of Romantic Love have found expression in familiar religious, mythical or literary motifs. Adam and Eve had the first "marriage made in heaven," for instance, and the "knight in shining armor" once was named Lancelot. An examination of the historical contexts in which these stories arose reveals the influence that they have had on the development of the romantic myth. Still, it can be difficult to see how these old stories come to affect our personal lives.

The relationship between cultural expectations or "myths" and the old stories which are classified as "myths" is reciprocal. People tell stories to communicate specific social or religious beliefs about human nature. The stories are used, in turn, to disseminate and and to enforce the beliefs. The stories change as we change and we change as our stories change, and that is why we are free to *rewrite* mythical stories to match our own needs and unique experiences. This aggressive attitude towards mythology may seem a little blasphemous. We often assume that the oldest myths must be the truest ones, and that if we go back far enough the "real" meaning of a given myth can be discovered.

Although it is easy to think of mythological stories as ageless and inviolable, it may be more accurate to understand myth as a language of symbols. Just as words and their meanings travel through time and across the globe, mixing with other languages, evolving as the priorities of the speakers change, so do mythical images and stories change dramatically over time to suit the varying needs of religious and cultural mythmakers. In this sense, mythology tells us less about spiritual truth than it does about political influence. While dominant cultural myths do not necessarily reflect the authentic experiences of individuals, they demonstrate that we are capable of accepting and internalizing images which are presented to us, even when they contradict our intuition, experience or common sense.

It is through this process of conversion that we begin to follow and fulfill cultural myths. Roland Barthes said, "In myth, things lose the memory that they once were made." The expectations of an adopted myth can become more powerful than our original feelings and needs. That is why it is so difficult to break free from cultural myths like Romantic Love, and even more difficult to transform them. We may feel that we are following private and spontaneous desires when we are, in fact, seeking relationships we believe we *should* have, inspired by mythic images that we have unconsciously accepted. In order to escape the expectations of the romantic myth, we have to free ourselves from the conviction that Romantic Love is natural and universal. There is a certain tyranny in the use of the term *universal* when it is employed to describe human nature. Patriarchal societies often maintain that whether or not women want to be submissive, it is in their *true nature* to be so. This view vindicates whatever force is necessary to keep an erring woman in her "proper place" in society and in her family. The romantic myth has a very definite prescription for what a "real man" and a "real woman" should be. The influence of these ideas can be seen even within homosexual relationships when individuals choose to identify with one or the other of the traditional gender roles: the stereotypical lesbian distinction between "butch" and "femme," for instance. Images like these are difficult to avoid because they are commonly accepted. But just because a myth is widespread, that does not mean that it is universal. Just because Romantic Love has become habitual, that does not mean that it is natural.

What we really need to do is to turn the romantic myths upside

down, give them a good shake, and see what falls out of them –
to understand what has been hiding inside of them all along.
Fortunately, the cultural myths of Romantic Love are based on
very specific literary and folk motifs which can be examined and
challenged. What if it were possible to think about mythical
characters *not as expressions of universal truths*, but as *individuals*?
What could they tell us about their childhood wounds, their fears,
their mistakes, their illusions? What would happen if we invited
Eve or Guenevere to question the romantic myth by challenging
and retelling their own stories?

To begin with, it might not occur to Eve that she would have
the right to make her own interpretations about her birth, just
as we rarely claim the right to interpret or reject the cultural
myths which intimately affect our lives. Eve might ask:

> *How can my feelings be as true as ancient wisdom? How am I
> supposed to know myself better than the prophets and scholars who
> wrote about me?*

But who can know Eve better than Eve? The story of Adam's rib
and its interpretations have shifted with the social assumptions
and the religious agenda of each era in which it was retold. Eve's
retelling would be as valid as any of these – more so, perhaps,
because it would arise from her own experience.

Imagine then, that you are standing on the vast plain of the
Underworld. In that expanse of twilit land, legendary heroes fight
the wars it seems they have always fought; mythical women,
constant, love those they have always loved; children play
unchanging games. As if in contrast to the changeless world
below, the sky displays a restless Upperearth where history
continuously is made. If you persevere, you can see both worlds
wheeling in their opposite extremes: the Upperearth rushing
through time, the Underworld changing, but slow. You can see
myths created and recast by the history of men and women,
above. You can see men and women influenced in turn by the
myths below.

Throughout this book, the flow of the text will be interspersed with comments and dialogue from the mythical characters of the Underworld. If they can retell their own myths, we may begin to question the romantic myths in our lives as well. Romantic Love has had a great influence on the dynamics of intimate relationships, but we do not have to suffer its expectations of need, impossibility and tragedy; by transforming the myth of Romantic Love we can help ourselves to lead whole lives and engage in relationships which express fullness, possibility and joy.

I

EVE:
Longing for Wholeness

Although the most familiar symptom of Romantic Love is the feeling of overwhelming longing, it can be difficult to identify what exactly we are longing for. We feel a deep separation; we long for reunion. We feel incomplete; we long for wholeness. It is the myth of Romantic Love which interprets these emotions and gives the longing a particular name. According to the romantic myth there was a primal separation between men and women, a separation which now causes us to turn towards each other with incredible desire. This is the myth of the "Halved Soul" and it is the heart of Romantic Love:

> When the Holy One, Blessed be He, first created mankind, he created him with two faces, two sets of genitals, four arms and legs, back to back. Then he split Adam in two, and made two backs, one on each side.[1]

The myth of the Halved Soul has very specific cultural and social ramifications. The bible advises that a man should leave his father and mother to be united with his wife so that the two can become "one flesh." In Jewish folk tradition, a "marriage made in heaven" happens when the two halves of the very same soul come together again. According to the traditional romantic myth, a woman's longing for a man is different from a man's longing for a woman, though the reason for the difference may not be intuitively obvious. The romantic myth declares that a man longs to possess his beloved and that a woman longs to be possessed, not only sexually, but emotionally and spiritually. Romantic Love rests on the assumption that because the primal separation was inequitable, men and women are essentially different, inherently unequal. The source of this idea is not biological but mythical:

> The Lord God caused the man to fall into a deep sleep; and while he was sleeping he took one of the man's ribs and closed up the place with flesh. Then the Lord God made a woman from the rib he had taken out of the man and he brought her to the man. The man said: 'This is bone of my bones and flesh of my flesh; she shall be called woman for she was taken out of man.'[2]

As the mythical "first woman" Eve set the stage for every woman who came after her. But if we want to consider Eve as an individual with her own thoughts and feelings, we would have to wonder how her unusual beginning affected her life and her relationship with Adam. If we could ask Eve about her self-image, what might she say? Very likely she will feel that being born out of a rib is not worth as much as being born something on her own. Jewish folk tradition is humorous but explicit:

> When God was on the point of making Eve, he said:
> 'I will not make her from the head of man,
> lest she carry her head high in arrogant pride;
> not from the eye, lest she be wanton-eyed;
> not from the ear, lest she be an eavesdropper;
> not from the neck, lest she be insolent;
> not from the mouth, lest she be a tattler;
> not from the heart, lest she be inclined to envy;
> not from the hand, lest she be a meddler;
> not from the foot, lest she be a gadabout.
> I will form her from a chaste portion of the body . . .'
> Nevertheless, in spite of the great caution used,
> woman has all the faults God tried to prevent.[3]

In the book of Genesis there are two versions of the origin of humanity. The first maintains that God created Adam and Eve together, "male and female created He them"; the second story describes Eve taken from Adam's side. But rib or no rib, most of the commentary on the scriptures, Jewish and Christian, indicates that Adam was whole and then he was somehow split in two. Adam was there first. Adam was originally androgynous. Adam lost a part of himself and when he gets it back, *he* will be whole. The story never says that when Eve gets Adam back, *she* will be whole. The New Testament teaches that "a man . . . is the image and glory of God; but woman is the glory of man. For man was not made from woman, but woman from man. Neither was man created for woman, but woman for man."[4]

In order to resolve their primal separation, Eve, the fragment, must give herself back to Adam, who waits to receive her. Because of this inequity, emotional implications follow as a matter of course. Eve's longing for Adam inspires her to serve and obey him, while his longing to be whole inspires him to want to possess her, to try to absorb her back into himself. Thus the romantic myth declares that a woman must take responsibility for the feelings and needs of others and, especially, aspire to selfless devotion to a man. As will become increasingly apparent, the romantic myth teaches that men desperately need to receive love and women desperately need to give it, all because *Adam* lost a part of himself and only *Eve* can give it back.

In spite of its sexist assumptions, the story of the Halved Soul is particularly tenacious. This is probably because its image of incompleteness does provide a workable explanation for the longings that many of us experience. In the most famous version of the myth of the Halved Soul, Plato also described the original humanity as dual beings who were split down the middle and who now wander through the world searching for their other halves. He went on to illustrate with great clarity the kind of longing that would result from such a primal separation:

'Do you desire to be wholly one; always day and night to be in one another's company? For if this is what you desire, I am ready to melt you into one and let you grow together so that being two you shall become one, and while you live, live a common life as if you were a single man, and after your death in the world below still be one departed soul instead of two.

'I ask whether this is what you lovingly desire, and whether you are satisfied to attain this?' There is not a man of them who when he heard the proposal would deny or would not acknowledge that this meeting and melting into one another, this becoming one instead of two, was the very expression of his ancient need. And the reason is that human nature was originally one and we were a whole, and the desire and pursuit of the whole is called love.[5]

Philosophers and novelists have been influenced by Plato's story for thousands of years because the idea of "soulmates" does describe one aspect of human interaction: the compulsive longing that underlies Romantic Love. And it is an appealing thought, that there might exist for each of us "one true love," a soulmate who would complete us in such an essential way.

The belief is so prevalent, in fact, that it has come to be explained by a popular psychological truism: people fall in love with the qualities in the opposite sex that they really need in themselves. Plato's version of the myth of the Halved Soul has been used frequently by psychologists to defend Carl Jung's theory of the anima and animus. Erich Fromm, for instance, in *The Art of Loving* explains:

The idea of this polarization is most strikingly expressed in the myth that originally man and woman were one, that they were cut in half . . . The meaning of the myth is clear enough. Sexual polarization leads man to seek union in a specific way, that of union with the other sex. The polarity between the male and female principles exists also *within* each man and each woman.[6]

This use of Plato's fable is elegant but inaccurate. What Plato said was that originally there were *three* different combinations of paired creatures: two women, two men and a man and a woman attached to each other. In effect, the other half of some men is a man; the other half of some women is a woman! Plato was using the story of the Halved Soul, in part, as a mythical explanation for the practice of homosexuality. Plato plainly was aware that the emotions of romantic longing occur between members of the same sex as often as they do between heterosexual men and women.

Still psychology, as religion, is quick to make its own interpretations of myth into universal laws: "The idea that the original human being was male and female is found in numerous traditions. It is a thought expressed most succinctly, perhaps, in Plato's Symposium ... In our century C.G. Jung is the first scientist to observe this psychological fact of human nature."[7] And even more immoderate: "In every person both male and female qualities are present in different degrees ... This law was first expounded by Plato."[8]

Myths can be transformed very easily into facts and laws, but in this case it was not Plato's intention to develop a serious philosophical or psychological paradigm based on the myth of the Halved Soul. He treated the idea with great humor:

> There was a time, I say, when we were one, but now because of the wickedness of mankind God has dispersed us ... If we are not obedient to the gods, there is a danger that we shall be split up again and go about in basso-relievo, like the profile figures having only half a nose.

And this is how Plato describes humanity before the split:

> He could walk upright as men now do, backwards or forwards as he pleased, and he could also roll over and over at a great pace, turning on his four hands and four feet, eight in all, like tumblers going over and over with their legs in the air; this was when he wanted to run fast.

Not only did Plato poke fun at the idea of the Halved Soul, he was offering wry commentary on all lovers who cling desperately to their "other halves," justifying their exaggerated passion and need for each other through the myth.

In the end the psychological myth of the anima and animus can be considered to be another retelling of the Halved Soul, valid to the same extent that the story of the rib is valid. The rib myth reflects the feelings of inferiority that have been the real experience of many women. In the case of the rib it is easy to see that the inferiority was maintained by the same social structure that created it in the first place. But Jungians also have their ideas about what masculinity and femininity are, what "normal" sexuality is, and these assumptions necessarily affect the way they choose to describe human psychology. The idea that men need to accept their femininity, and women their masculinity, does make individuals responsible for their own wholeness, a very important shift. But how can we know what masculinity and femininity *would* be without myths telling us what they *should* be and mythmakers making sure we get it right?

All cultures maintain order through careful expression and application of their myths. A mythic woman like Eve is clay, shaped and reshaped in a storyteller's hands. The story of Eve's creation from Adam's rib traditionally has been used to establish the inferior nature of women, but Eve's inferiority lies in the *interpretation* of the story; it is not necessarily implied by the imagery. Meister Eckhart considered Eve's rib origin to be evidence for the absolute equality of women with men.[9] Historically, of course, this has not been a popular view. The New Testament declares: "A woman must be a learner, listening quietly and with due submission. I do not permit a woman to be a teacher, nor must woman domineer over man; she should be quiet. For Adam was created first and Eve afterwards."[10]

Egyptian physician and advocate of women's rights, Nawal El Saadawi, recalls a childhood conversation she had with her father in which she asked him why all the verses of the Koran used the male gender to refer to Allah. Her father replied that it was not appropriate to speak of Him as a female. She was persistent, inquiring if this meant that women were unworthy, or suffered from some fault or stigma which men did not possess. His response was unambiguous:

> The superiority of males over females is the real reason behind the fact that prophets have always used the male gender when addressing Allah or speaking of Him . . . The first man on earth, Adam, was placed above Eve since he was at the origin of the human race, was more powerful and gave life to her from one of his ribs.'[11]

This interpretation of Genesis, especially the identification of God in masculine terms, has psychological as well as theological implications since it encourages everyone, male and female, to think about the world from an *androcentric* point of view, that is to say, from a male perspective. The use of the generic term "man" and the pronoun "he" to refer to both men and women, for instance, has been claimed to be innocent and inoffensive grammatical shorthand, but the unconscious assumptions of this convention have been very damaging to the self-image of women. Feminist writer Demaris Wehr explains:

> The male is the center of experience, and that experience is normative. The male norm parades as universal, and by that norm women are defined as 'other', not center, as 'object', not subject. Androcentrism drowns or silences women's voices and perceptions by the continual pouring-out of male perceptions into the world. It conveys the message of women's inferiority to them on a subtler, deeper level than does simple negative treatment or belittlement.[12]

Because most of us are unconscious of this sexist lens it has the effect of making social structures of sexism, like the belief in the superiority of males, seem to be natural, just "the way things are." Lady Mary Wortley Montague, a Victorian women's rights activist, wrote of her sex:

We are a lower part of creation. We owe obedience and submission to the superior sex and any woman who suffers her vanity and folly to deny this rebels against the laws of the Creator and the indisputable order of nature.[13]

The power of myth to decide what constitutes nature should not be underestimated. Simone de Beauvoir was one of the first feminist writers to point out that a belief which seems as if it were expressing the "natural order of things" is already on its way to being perceived as divinely ordained. And in fact, myths have their greatest influence, not through social commentary, but through the process in which certain stories are chosen to become scripture in the first place, those myths officially determined to be divinely inspired, sacred and inviolable. It becomes more difficult for women to challenge their social inferiority if they believe it has been sanctioned by God. How is Eve supposed to question her origins if to do so she is rebelling against God's law?

The first thing for Eve to realize is that even "divinely inspired" scriptures are myths. Religious elders decide what is truth and what is heresy for political reasons as often as spiritual ones. The Judaic scriptures were canonized two thousand years ago and the Christian bible has been in its present form for almost seventeen hundred years. It is easy to believe that the inclusion of certain books and the exclusion of others was a graceful and consensual process. Actually there was lively dissension between the rabbis while they sorted their teachings, and the Christian bible remained consistent only after three hundred years of factionalism and debate. There were so many different Christian groups in the first few centuries of Christianity that it is impossible to identify the "original" or the "authentic" Christian myth.

Among the early Christians whose teachings were eventually considered to be heretical there were diverse sects who identified themselves as Gnostics, from the word *gnosis* or knowledge. Although Gnosticism predated Christianity and not all Gnostics became Christian, many of those who did claimed to have secret traditions and writings which had been passed to them from Jesus and his disciples. The Gnostic texts suggest that there was disagreement on every major point that now underlies modern Christianity, including the historical crucifixion of Jesus, the bodily resurrection and the apostolic succession. Some Gnostic writings describe a feminine aspect of God, advocate equal status in the church for women and name Mary Magdalene as Christ's best-loved and most spiritually advanced disciple. [14]

While the Orthodox Church looked at scripture as truth to be obeyed, Gnostic Christians felt free to interpret holy texts, even to rewrite traditions to express their personal insights. To take Gnostic spiritual imagery literally is to miss the point of Gnosticism: "Truth did not come into the world naked, but it came in types and images. The world will not receive truth in any other way." [15] Not surprisingly Gnostics also interpreted the story of the creation of Adam and Eve very differently from the way that early Church fathers chose to view it. Consider this Gnostic explanation of Eve's origins:

> Let us bring a deep sleep over [Adam], and let us teach him in his sleep that she came from his rib so that his wife may obey, and he may be lord over her. [16]

This passage is startling because it demonstrates that the writer was *aware* that mythical images can exert a cultural influence, in this case, the connection between Eve's origins and the social status of women. The implication of this text for Eve, the individual, is that she was not necessarily born from Adam's rib! She does not have to accept the truth of any of the stories that have been told about her. She can choose the story that she needs to be true. What does *Eve*, from her vantage in the Underworld, think about the myth of the Halved Soul?

"I admit I never liked the rib myth," says Eve, "and I'd be glad to get rid of it, but I really like the story of the Halved Soul. Isn't it

obvious? Women have always *waited for men to come along to make them whole. I'm incomplete because I used to be part of Adam."*

It is much easier to discard the story of the rib, with its conspicuous judgment about the worth of women, than to give up the beguiling romance of the "Halved Soul." Eve's experience of romantic longing is justified if Adam is truly her soulmate, her other half. She can gain a certain emotional security by locating her romance in eternity. But how secure is her conviction, really, even in mythical terms? Jewish tradition noted the discrepancy between the two origin stories in Genesis and produced an explanation. The Kabbalah records the tradition that Eve was not Adam's first wife at all, that a woman named Lilith was being described in the first story and Eve in the second:

> When the Holy One, blessed be He, created Adam the first man single, He said: It is not good for the man to be alone and He created a woman from the earth like him, and called her Lilith. [17]

When Adam tried to dominate Lilith she insisted on her equality:

> Instantly they began to quarrel. She said: 'I shall not lie beneath,' and he said, 'I shall not lie beneath but above, for your place is beneath and mine above.' She said to him: 'Both of us are equal for both of us are of earth.' And they did not listen to each other. When Lilith saw this, she uttered the Ineffable Name and flew off into the air of the world.

Adam asked God to bring Lilith back to him:

> Thereupon Adam rose in prayer before his Creator and said: 'Master of the World! The woman whom You gave me fled from me.' Instantly the Holy One, blessed be He, sent three angels after her to bring her back. And the Holy One, blessed be He,

said to Adam: 'If she wants to return, good and well, and if not, she will have to take it upon herself that every day one hundred of her children should die.'

Lilith refused to return to Adam, so the Creator made Eve from Adam's side:

The woman destined to become the true companion of man was taken from Adam's body, for 'only when like is joined unto like' the union is indissoluble.

Lilith's story is disturbing for several reasons, but principally because of the way she has been remembered. Lilith as an individual, the first wife of Adam, became obscured. Her myth degenerated, focusing on her rejection of Adam which was taken as evidence of her evil nature. Eventually she simply merged with other folk traditions and became the demon that kills infants for spite and forces men to have sex with her in the middle of the night.

> *"That's me," Lilith says bitterly. Seeing the startled expression on Eve's face she explains: "No, I don't rape men and I don't kill babies. But that's what the mythmakers said about me. You think they're going to write I lived happily ever after without Adam? I was born equal to Adam and I refused to be less than God made me. Now my children are dead and you can see what they did to my reputation – just because I refused to be Adam's property!"*
>
> *Eve's eyes are open wide. "That's why they made me from Adam's rib? So I wouldn't leave him like you did?"*

The balance of power in Adam's first marriage to Lilith is very different from the dynamics of his second marriage with Eve. The story of Lilith and Adam records the origins of humanity as the creation of two equals, born whole. The tension between them does not come from a longing for wholeness, but a desire for control. Adam seeks to dominate Lilith and she refuses him. She

leaves the garden to preserve her independence. The second
woman, however, was made for Adam. Eve will not refuse Adam
because she is incapable of leaving him; she is part of him. Control
is not an issue between these two, but there is a longing between
Adam and Eve that was not there between Adam and Lilith. There
is an emotional, a *romantic* longing.

*Eve shakes her head. "But Lilith, didn't you miss Adam? How could
you stand to leave the garden?"*

"You left the garden too Eve," answers Lilith.

"But I wasn't alone."

*Lilith laughs shortly. "Do I miss Adam? Not the way you're
thinking. I have longings the same as you do. But for me, they're
spiritual longings – to understand God, maybe even to be God in
some blasphemous way. Of course I have sexual and emotional needs,
but I don't confuse them with my longing for God. How in the world
could Adam be holding the piece of me that would make me whole?"*

*Lilith's tone becomes confidential. "I'll tell you something. I know
for a fact Adam was born with spiritual longing too. Maybe he
confused it with sexual desire. Maybe his longing made him afraid,
so he turned to me, to dominate me, to force me to lie beneath him,
and I refused. My rejection made him feel even more powerless and
he blamed that on me too. Then you got caught up in his confusion.
If Adam would stop trying to own you, Eve, maybe he'd remember
he can be a whole person without you."*

Lilith proposes a model for relationships in which men and
women would be free to love and help each other in a side-by-side
process of healing and growth, if they resist the temptation to seek
wholeness *through each other*. The confusion between spiritual
and sexual longing that occurs in Romantic Love arises, in part,
from a spiritual view which portrays God as a being above and
outside of us whom we can obey or disobey, love or reject.
Judaism, Christianity and Islam all try to help their followers
negotiate a proper *relationship* with God. This attitude toward the
divine is so unconscious that we rarely are aware of it enough

to question it, much less to consider that there might be alternatives. Buddhism, for instance, encourages people to *identify* with the divine, and Native American tribes who acknowledge the spirit in every part of the Earth perceive no profound distinction between human and nonhuman inhabitants of the world.

The unchallenged Western view makes us especially vulnerable to the romantic myth since Romantic Love insists that an intimate relationship with someone *outside* of us can complete us and make us whole. Still, the sense of primal separation is a real experience, an intrinsic part of our human condition. Love and sexuality are obvious metaphors for our longing for wholeness, and can be helpful ones, as long as they are not interpreted literally. The Hindu story of the Halved Soul declares that the longing between men and women is a metaphor for spiritual longing. The imagery is familiar:

> In the beginning, this universe was Viraj, the Self alone, in the shape of a person . . . He desired a mate. He became the size of a man and woman in close embrace and He divided his body into two.[18]

The story goes on to say that from the union of this first couple human beings were born. But commentary on the passage explains that the love of husband for wife and wife for husband, though it may ease the day-to-day loneliness, can never fulfill the deeper need of individuals to realize oneness, not with each other, but with the original divine Self. The significance of this idea becomes clear when it is compared to the sentiments of Romantic Love – a love in which longing for a beloved has *replaced* the longing for God.

Eve speaks slowly, "But if you didn't need Adam to be whole, he doesn't need me either. And where does that leave me? If you were the first woman, then I'm nothing."

"You are Eve, mother of all life," says Lilith. "You were alive before

Adam needed you."

"But Lilith," says Eve miserably, "I've worked so hard to give Adam a good life, to make up for what I did to him."

"What did you do to him that was so terrible?"

"Oh, you know, the serpent and the apple," says Eve. "All the suffering in the world is really my fault."

The story of Adam and Eve, as it is presented in Genesis, establishes not only that woman is inherently less worthy than man, but that she was guilty of the first, most terrible sin. The story is familiar to everyone. When the serpent came to talk to Eve in the garden, he asked her, "Is it true God forbade you to eat from any tree in the garden?" She answered: "We may eat the fruit of any tree in the garden, except for the tree in the middle of the garden; God has forbidden us to eat or even to touch the fruit of that tree; if we do, we'll die."

But the serpent said, "Of course you won't die. God knows that as soon as you eat it, your eyes will open and you will become like gods understanding both good and evil."

Eve saw that the fruit of the tree was good to eat and pleasing to the eye so she took some and ate it. She also gave some to Adam and he ate it too. Then their eyes were opened. They realized that they were naked, so they stitched fig-leaves together and made loincloths.

But when Adam and Eve heard the sound of the Lord God walking in the garden in the cool of the day, they hid from Him among the trees. The Lord God called out to Adam, "Where are you?" Adam said, "I heard the sound of you in the garden. I was afraid because I was naked, so I hid."

God asked, "Who told you that you were naked? Have you been eating of the tree I forbade you to eat?" Adam answered, "It was the woman you put with me; she gave me the fruit and I ate it."

The Lord God asked Eve, "What have you done?" She answered, "The serpent tempted me and I ate."

So God said to Eve: "You will give birth to your children in pain. Your longing will be for your husband, and he will lord it over you." To Adam he said: "Accursed is the soil because of you. With suffering will you get your food every day of your life."

The implications of the story are very clear. By eating the apple from the tree of good and evil Eve chose knowledge instead of obedience. [19] For this act of independence the suffering of the world was laid at her feet. Many theologians took advantage of the mythical opportunity, suggesting that all the women of the world should accept Eve's guilt. Tertullian called women the Devil's Gateway: "Do you not know that every one of you is an Eve? The sentence of God on your sex lives on in this age; the guilt, of necessity, lives on too." [20]

> *"I'm the Devil's Gateway," moans Eve. "All the suffering women go through is my fault."*
>
> *Lilith shakes her head. "You don't have to believe you're the cause of everyone's suffering."*
>
> *"But the story . . ." Eve protests.*
>
> *Lilith laughs. "Which version? The mythmakers, they had a good time with this one."*

Talmudic scholars for the most part explained that Eve's sin, like Adam's, was disobedience. The early Christian fathers agreed. They read the story as evidence of humanity's free will. We have the freedom, as Adam and Eve had, to do good or to do evil. But Gnostics saw something entirely different in the story: no guilt, no disobedience, not even a devil. The act of eating the apple instead symbolized spiritual freedom and consciousness:

> Then the Female Spiritual Principle came as a Snake, the Instructor; and it taught them, saying, "What did he say to you? Was it, 'From every tree in the Garden shall you eat; yet – from the tree of . . . evil and good do not eat'?"
>
> The carnal Woman said, "Not only did he say 'Do not eat,' but even 'Do not touch it; for the day you eat from it, with death you are going to die.'"
>
> And the Snake, the Instructor, said, "With death you shall not

die; for it was out of jealousy that he said this to you. Rather your eyes shall open and you shall come to be like gods, recognizing evil and good." And the Female Instructing Principle was taken away from the snake, and she left it behind, merely a thing of the earth.[21]

Influenced by Gnostic writings, and inclined towards interpreting religious texts as myths, Jung also described Eve's actions as positive and necessary for the growth of the human spirit: "Eve in the garden of Eden could not rest content until she had convinced Adam of the goodness of the forbidden apple. Were it not for the leaping and twinkling of the soul, man would rot away in his greatest passion, idleness."[22] But the most familiar interpretation of Genesis originated in the fourth century, when St. Augustine invented Original Sin. Augustine did not perceive humanity to be free but, rather, constrained by the punishments that Adam and Eve received. Their sin condemned humanity forever afterwards to a state of helpless suffering. To Augustine the pain of childbirth and the inevitability of death were not natural phenomena but the consequence of Original Sin: "Nature, which the first human being harmed, is miserable . . . What passed to women was not the burden of Eve's fertility, but of her transgression."[23] Humanity's helplessness, for Augustine, did not stop at the suffering of physical existence, but included also the inability to choose to do good. Augustine believed that because of Adam's sin men cannot help themselves from sinning; specifically, he was referring to the sin of sexual desire.

Augustine did not believe that a man could use his will to dictate the actions of his libido: "Behold the 'vital fire' which does not obey the soul's decision, but for the most part, rises up against the soul's desire in disorderly and ugly movements."[24] This view of sexuality may have more to say about Augustine's personal sexual history than it does about the intentions of the Genesis mythmakers up to that time. Augustine experienced his own sexuality as painfully out of control and found an explanation for his suffering in the sins of Adam and Eve, rather than in the will of God or the nature of physical creation.[25] With the help of the doctrine of Original Sin he could mediate his own guilt through a demonstration of Eve's guilt, saying in effect, "I am guilty, but it's not my fault."

It is a common psychological pattern which manifests here: if there is some fault to be guilty about, the fault can be blamed. We can always say, as Adam and Eve did, that some other tempted us, that evil is outside of us. The act of assigning blame is exactly the same kind of externalization that supports the myth of the Halved Soul in the first place. The romantic myth supposes that some other is responsible for our emptiness, and so it follows that the actions of someone else could complete us. The desperate longing of Romantic Love requires this kind of outward searching, and it is perilously close to the dynamics of blame. The ramifications of the Augustinian view of Genesis for the romantic myth are dramatic. Because Augustine interpreted Eve's temptation of Adam to be sexual in nature, women seem to be responsible for *causing* the sexual desires of men.

In *The Hidden Face of Eve*, Nawal El Saadawi describes how Islam also upheld Eve's reputation as an instrument of Satan and how the myth was used to establish the basis for women's *fitna*, the power of sexual attractiveness. The romantic myth portrays men to be helpless in the face of overwhelming female seduction, a psychological paradigm which has dramatic consequences in Arab culture:

> Woman was therefore considered by the Arabs as a menace to man and society, and the only way to avoid the harm she could do was to isolate her in the home, where she could have no contact with either one or the other. If for any reason she had to move outside the walls of her prison, all necessary precautions had to be taken so that no one could get a glimpse of her seductiveness.[26]

If men accept the idea that their sexuality cannot be controlled and that women are the source of evil and temptation, they are likely to blame their acts of sexual violence on their victims.

In the Christian world it was Augustine's interpretation of Genesis which most powerfully influenced Western social order, injecting blame and denial into the center of the romantic myth.

> *"Any way you look at it, the serpent didn't lie to you,"* says Lilith to Eve. *"I hate to be the one to point this out, but God said you'd die if you touched the apple. Now that was a lie. The serpent told you you'd gain the knowledge of good and evil by eating from the tree. That's what happened."*
>
> *She pauses to let this sink in, then adds, "And after that, God decided to throw you out of the garden, because he was afraid you'd eat from the tree of life too and live forever."*
>
> *"I don't like God the way you're describing him," says Eve.*
>
> *"Neither did the Gnostics. That's why they made the feminine God supreme. The Creator God, her son, is a childish god who punishes you because he's spiteful and jealous. It's Sophia who speaks through the serpent to tell you the truth."*
>
> *"Wait," interrupts Eve. "Who's Sophia?"*
>
> *Lilith smiles. "She's your mother."*

Augustine wrote unequivocally that man, but not woman, was created in the likeness of god. If God is masculine, then original humanity, made in His image, must also be male. But well before Augustine the Gnostics wondered who the Lord was referring to when He said "in *Our* likeness, male and female," and concluded that it must be a reference to a female God:

> I am the first and the last. I am the honored one and the scorned one. I am the whore, and the holy one. I am the wife and the virgin. I am the mother and the daughter . . . I am knowledge, and ignorance . . . I am shameless; I am ashamed. I am strength, and I am fear. [27]

Passages which celebrated female aspects of divinity were intentionally excluded from canonical scriptures. The effect of this filtering is so all-pervading that it is nearly invisible.

Feminist writers have long suspected a relationship between masculine images of divinity and the social authority of men. Demaris Wehr believes that "the continued use of masculine symbols comfortably masks our society's fear of women's authority and power. Vesting divine power in the masculine reinforces internalized oppression of women, giving it a sacred cast."[28] Even though most people would deny that their use of the pronoun "He" to refer to God means that He has the shape of a man, the masculinization of the divine is more than just semantics. God the father, wrathful or protecting, is a familiar idea. God the mother is an unknown and frightening image. Wehr continues:

> If we allow ourselves to change our religious language to feminine language, and to experience fully all the ambivalent feelings that change elicits, we can begin to comprehend the ambivalence we have toward the full power and authority of female being in general. We will begin to see the degree to which our feelings have been conditioned by the dearth of symbols of female authority in our society.[29]

Through the passionate worship of the Virgin Mary the Catholic Church celebrated those aspects of divine "femininity" which were acceptable within a patriarchal culture: submission, modesty and purity. Protestantism withdrew respect for Mary and the female saints and so denied women even these. From a mythological point of view the Gnostic Trinity seems to make more intuitive sense: God the father, God the *mother* and God the Son; but a religion which sanctions this kind of divine equality also provides an unmistakable challenge to patriarchal assumptions.

Just as Augustine's male God creates man in His image, so does the Gnostic female God empower woman. According to one story, Eve was sent by Sophia, or Wisdom, to awaken life in Adam:

After the day of rest, Sophia sent her daughter Zoe, who is called Eve, as an instructor in order that she might make Adam, who had no soul, arise, so that those whom he should engender might become containers of light. When Eve saw her male counterpart prostrate she had pity upon him, and she said, 'Adam, become alive! Arise upon the earth!' Immediately her word became accomplished fact. For Adam, having arisen, suddenly opened his eyes. When he saw her, he said, 'You will be called Mother of the Living. For it is you who have given me life.'[30]

Told in this way, the myth credits Eve with much more integrity than does the story of a woman created from Adam's rib for his personal use.

"Wait," says Eve. "Which God is the real God?"

"Pick any one you want!" says Lilith. "Should I have to believe in the one that sends his thugs to drag me back to Adam? The one who brags about killing my children because I refused to submit?"

"But what if that's the real God?" asks Eve, with horror.

"The Gnostics said, 'Men make gods, and worship their creations. It would be fitting for the gods to worship men!' If you ask me," she continues, *"I say any God described by a man is going to have the prejudices of a man."*

Eve's eyes are open very wide. "Does that mean God is just a myth? A story?"

Lilith shrugs. "When I decided to leave Adam I pronounced the unpronounceable name of God. I appealed to His justice and mercy, and I was taken to safety by the power of His name. So I have good reason to believe in the unknowable God. But Eve, why in the world should I believe in the God who is spiteful and cruel, the one who demands that half the human race submit to the other half?"

Eve looks furtively around her, wondering if they are going to be struck dead. Nothing happens, but she is still afraid. What if Lilith's ideas turn out to be heretical? But heretical by whose standards? Why should any one of the stories be more true than any other? She cannot deny that her myth has affected the lives of women for thousands of years and that the interpretation of the myth always seems to benefit the ones doing the interpreting. The origins of Adam and Eve have been used as divine proof for the inequality between the sexes. Romantic Love depends on this inequality for many of its expectations and ideals. If Adam had accepted Lilith's need for independence, the implications of their myth could very well have required social equality between men and women. But the mythmakers wrote the story the way they did for a different purpose.

It has been very effective to portray Lilith as a demon. Theologians have been able to say to the women of the world, "You have a choice. You can be submissive and good or you can be independent and evil." According to this thinking, good women are what Eve might have been and should still attempt to be: submissive, weak, unselfish, obedient, yielding and vulnerable. Bad women, like Lilith, are those who refuse the demands of men, who seek equality and choose to be alone rather than to accept a relationship in which they are abused or controlled. The romantic myth teaches women that they are supposed to be excited by powerful men, not to challenge them. They are meant to feel guilty for having independent thoughts and actions. The idea of equality between the sexes and relationships based on a joining of two whole individuals are not a part of the traditional romantic myth. They are ideas that Lilith insisted on, and Adam violently refused, but which Eve never had a chance to consider.

> "Romantic Love comes from your myth, Eve, not from mine," says Lilith. "I'm the 'Devil's Advocate' of Romantic Love. At least, that's what the mythmakers made me. Lilith is the nightmare, she's the evil that lurks outside a woman's rightful place. And where's that? Underneath her father and her husband!"
>
> "Is it true Romantic Love started with me?" asks Eve quietly.
>
> Lilith considers for a moment. "There are a lot of romantic myths,

*but none that tell the story of men and women as completely as
yours does." She laughs shortly. "Except maybe for mine."*

"Am I really allowed to retell the story?"

*"You have as much right as anyone else who's told it. More right,
as far as I'm concerned," says Lilith.*

*Eve is silent for a moment, then claps her hands together once
and nods her head. "All right then."*

The Genesis of Romantic Love

In the beginning God the Mother and God the Father created
humanity in Their own image, Female and Male created They
them. The first woman and the first man were called Lilith and
Adam, and they were equal in the sight of God.

Being spirits cast into physical form, Lilith and Adam
experienced an incredible loneliness and a longing to be part of
God again. Adam's loneliness made him afraid and his fear made
him feel powerless. To make himself appear more powerful he
began to bully the birds and beasts which lived in the world with
him. Eventually he turned to Lilith, intending to master her as
well. Having sex with Lilith had always made Adam feel less
lonely. Lilith liked sex too, but when Adam tried to dominate her
that took all the fun out of it, so she began to refuse Adam's sexual
advances.

Lilith's rejection of Adam sent him into a rage. It wasn't really
about the sex. It was just that she had reminded him that he was
afraid and powerless and he couldn't stand that. When he could
not persuade Lilith, he tried to force her. Lilith could not believe
this kind of violence was part of God's plan, so she uttered the
ineffable name. God listened to her appeal and took her away
from the garden.

Adam sank into a depression and his longing for God became
confused with this new heartache. He saw all the other animals
with their mates, while he had none. He tried to get Lilith to come
back. He cajoled her and threatened her. "What a bitch," he said,
forgetting that he'd had any part in why she had run away. Every

bad thing that happened after that, every mishap and accident, he blamed on her. He was so depressed that he cried until his spleen ached. Then he fell into a deep sleep.

God took this opportunity to send another woman to the garden. She woke Adam. When he opened his eyes he was amazed to see her. "I will call you Eve, that is Life, because you have awakened life in me," he said. Adam fell in love with Eve and forgot that he'd ever had a wife before her. But there was a problem. Where had she come from? He remembered a little bit of a dream that he'd had, a pain in his side, a lingering sense of incompleteness. Eventually he realized what must have happened: Eve was taken from his side when he was asleep! They needed each other, because they had been originally one. *This* woman could never leave him because she was part of him.

Eve didn't remember anything from before she woke Adam and so she believed his story, though it seemed fantastic, because it explained the longing she had experienced from her moment of arrival in the garden. She understood now that it was a longing to be part of Adam again. So Adam and Eve lived in the garden happily together. Eve had sex with Adam whenever he wanted. This made her feel needed, and thus complete, and made him feel powerful, and thus complete – at least until it was over. But they could always do it again. Which they usually did.

Now, there was a tree in the garden from which God had told them not to eat. This was a test for Adam and Eve so God would know when they had matured enough to act independently, and could begin to fulfill the great destiny God had in mind for them. But Adam and Eve had grown lazy in the garden, content to be ignorant, so God sent the serpent to stir things up a bit. Adam didn't talk to beasts because he had decided he was superior to them, but Eve had an affinity for all living things and she liked to talk to anything that would talk to her.

The serpent told her that she wouldn't die if she ate the apple, that she would only gain knowledge. So she took an apple from the forbidden tree and ate it; by that act of independence, not from any property of the apple itself, she gained consciousness.

Adam arrived to find Eve eating the apple. She offered it to him.
He took the apple and ate some, and by this act of will he also
gained consciousness. But now when Adam looked at Eve, he
remembered his first wife, Lilith, and what he had done to make
her run away. He felt ashamed when he saw Eve's naked body,
so he picked some branches to cover their nakedness and they
hid in the bushes when God came looking for them.

God pretended not to know what had happened. "What
happened, Adam?" he asked, when he found them hiding in the
bushes. Now, God was really talking about Adam's treatment of
Lilith, not the apple at all. If Adam had admitted what he had
done right then and there, he could have had a clean beginning
with God. Instead he pointed at Eve. "She tempted me," he said,
meaning the apple (but in his heart, remembering Lilith). Then
God turned to Eve who was too frightened to admit what she had
done. "The serpent tricked me," she said.

God was saddened by the words of Adam and Eve. There was
no need to punish them. He knew that they had created both
suffering and evil by assigning blame outside of themselves. God
simply pointed out what was true: when men suffered they would
always look for someone else to blame. Women would be subject
to their fathers and husbands so that childbearing would be
fettered labor instead of the joy that God had intended. The snake
would be despised as the icon of evil, even though evil was just
an illusion produced by cowardice and denial.

Truly the apple was the fruit of the knowledge of good and evil:
Adam and Eve created evil so they would have something to
blame. And it all came to pass as God predicted that it would.

> When she is finished Eve grins at Lilith and waits for a reaction.
> "That was wonderful," says Lilith.
> "Thanks," says Eve. "And that's just how it happened, too."

Although the source of the longing is different for men and
women, the romantic myth can be characterized principally by
the longing for wholeness. Men and women long for each other,

imagining that sexual and emotional union can make them whole, but the traditional myth informs men that they have been *cheated* both of wholeness and paradise, and that their loss was caused by a woman. As a result, the longing of men is mixed with need and blame. Correspondingly, women are taught that they are *responsible* for men's suffering, and so the longing of women is mixed with self-sacrifice and guilt. The romantic myth incorporates both the blame and the guilt into its definition of love.

ISEULT:
Longing for Love

Although the myth of the Halved Soul has archaic roots, and emotional longing is as old as civilization, Romantic Love as a model for intimate relationship is a relatively recent paradigm, traceable to the literary development of courtly love in Europe in the twelfth and thirteenth centuries:

If this be not love, what is it then?
But if it is love, God, what can love be?
If good, why mortal bitterness to me?
If ill, why is it sweetness that torments?[1]

When Petrarch called love a mortal bitterness, he was describing Romantic Love, a love which celebrates suffering more than joy, longing more than contentment. On the sudden appearance of courtly love C.S. Lewis remarked that "real changes in human sentiment are very rare – there are perhaps three or four on record – but I believe that they occur, and that this is one of them."[2] Whether it was the sentiment which was new or merely the literary expression of it, certainly courtly love promoted a set of social behaviors that were radically different from what male-female relationships had been before.

The ideals of courtly love first appeared in the love poetry of the troubadours of southern France who adored women in almost religious fashion and celebrated adultery as a virtue. The idealization of adultery, which seems shocking at first, was an inevitable outgrowth of the medieval institution of marriage which was concerned not with love, but power. Marriage was a business transaction in which women were transferred like property. According to Lewis, "Marriages had nothing to do with love, and no 'nonsense' about marriage was tolerated ... Any idealization of sexual love in a society where marriage is purely utilitarian, must begin by being an idealization of adultery."[3]

The systematic process of obstructing love in marriage that feudalism began, the Church completed. Sex for reproductive purposes was allowed by the Church within marriage. Sex, per se, was not wrong, but sexual *desire* was wrong, always, even within marriage. The Church taught that it was a sin to sexually desire one's spouse. Saint Jerome said simply, "Any man who loves his wife too much is an adulterer."

It might seem that adultery in the traditional sense should have been considered the worse sin, because it involves sexual desire *and* it occurs outside of marriage. But the Church had nothing to say about passion, and courtly love was more interested in passion than with the fulfillment of desire, more concerned with sexual fidelity than with sexuality itself. In its beginnings courtly love included sexual love as part of its ideal, but by the thirteenth century it had become confused with the devotional cult of the Virgin. The influences between them were reciprocal: religious poetry praising Mary became passionate and romantic while any woman worthy of idealization, by definition, had to be too "pure" to sexually involve herself with her admirers.

The most powerful deterrent to consummation, however, must have been the simple fact that passion was a dangerous undertaking. The punishment for adultery was often torture or death, at least for the offending woman. George Duby, in his study on medieval marriage, explains that "the shame had to be public and established in order to be legitimately avenged. The husband had the right to kill."[4] This dramatic polarization of options, which placed the tragedy of loveless marriage on one hand and the danger of illicit passion on the other, developed through restrictive social conditions; it became a mythical paradigm when it was romanticized by the poets of the times.

Chretien de Troyes, the twelfth-century writer most closely associated with the literary development of courtly love, was the court poet of Marie de Champagne, the daughter of Eleanor of Aquitaine. Encouraged by themes which Marie proposed, Chretien helped to popularize the myths of two pairs of tragic adulterous lovers: Tristan and Iseult, and Guenevere and Lancelot. The danger of disclosure and the threat of punishment were central themes in their stories. But passion, it would seem, was sometimes worth the danger.

> *"Arthur would have burned me at the stake, if Lancelot hadn't rescued me," confesses Guenevere, from her vantage in the Underworld.*
>
> *"Mon cher Tristan saved me, too," adds Iseult. "At first my husband, Mark, was going to burn me, but he changed his mind and decided to give me to the lepers to be their whore."*
>
> *"Of course, they were within their rights by law. I did make love with Lancelot, and you did indeed sleep with Tristan."*
>
> *"Certainement! As often as possible," says Iseult. "But the law of Love answers to a higher court that the laws of Man."*
>
> *"Or even the laws of God," agrees Guenevere.*

According to Guenevere and Iseult, the same sacrifice that individuals have been willing to make out of devotion to their religious faith is owed to the object of romantic passion. Courtly lover and Christian martyr both suffered from the oppression of secular law which governed their lives, and both chose absolute fidelity (to illicit love or outlawed faith), including the willingness to suffer torture and death. Chretien described Lancelot genuflecting at the foot of Guenevere's bed before he entered it, as if it were a shrine. And Gottfried von Strassbourg, a German redactor of the story of Tristan and Iseult, wrote in great detail about their life together in a "holy grotto," making it seem more like a cathedral than the cave in the wilderness it actually was.

These descriptions were not arbitrary images. The pseudo-religious worship of a woman suggested by courtly love is an indication of confusion between the longing for spiritual wholeness and the longing for love.

In his Jungian analysis of the myth of Tristan and Iseult Robert Johnson describes this dynamic of Romantic Love: "When we are "in love" we feel completed, as though a missing part of ourselves had been returned to us; we feel uplifted, as though we were suddenly raised above the level of the ordinary world . . . If we ask where else we have looked for these things, there is a startling and troubling answer: religious experience."[5] The glamor of the religious myth of the Halved Soul is everywhere apparent in the story of Tristan and Iseult. Their longing for each other is powerful and irrational. They quite literally cannot live without each other, nor do they have to, since they die within moments of each other. After their tragic deaths the vines about their graves grow together in both root and branch. Metaphorically, Tristan and Iseult are able to be one being in death as they had longed to be in life. But their tragic ending does not diminish the worth of their romance; rather, the pain and the tragedy become the focal point of their story.

"It's your myth again," says Lilith to Eve. "Only they added tragedy to the love."

Eve looks troubled. "Well, consider the times. Guenevere and Iseult loved the only way they were allowed to love. That is tragic."

"What makes you so sure what they felt was love?" Lilith lets her question hang in the air and Eve extends their conversation to include the other women.

"Tell us Iseult, what does your love for Tristan feel like?" "What do you mean?" Iseult answers angrily. "It feels like love. Mon Dieu, it is love! I have no life apart from Tristan. He tried to kill himself when he thought I was dead. Our need for each other is so great we risk dishonor and death to be together. There, you see, that is love."

Through the poetic sentiments of courtly love, and the stories of Guenevere and Iseult in particular, tragedy and pain became the central feature of romance as they still are to this day. Iseult loves Tristan, a man who is not her husband. Part of the sweetness of their love is the pain itself, the fear each time they are together that it will be the last, the danger that they will be found out. But when they are apart they long to be together again, no matter the danger, no matter the pain.

All this misery in the story of Tristan and Iseult appears for historical as well as mythical reasons as a direct result of conflicts between feudalism and chivalry, between two different codes of honor: duty owed to the laws of man, and those owed to love. In a sense courtly love simply borrowed the structures of feudalism. Where a feudal vassal owed absolute loyalty and obedience to his feudal lord, a knight now considered his idealized lady, who would also have had higher social status, to be his master. He was required by the laws of courtly love to respond to her whims, no matter how spurious or irrational. In Chretien's *Lancelot*, Guenevere snubs Lancelot cruelly, to punish him for his unwillingness to suffer humiliation quickly enough to suit her. Loyalty to his lady might well put a knight in conflict with his political lord, as Tristan was in fact betraying his own King by loving Iseult.

Although Chretien de Troye's redaction of the myth has not survived, other versions of the story of Tristan and Iseult from France and Germany outline the emotions and expectations of Romantic Love in a dramatic way. For instance, the romantic myth requires that the circumstances of the meeting of lovers must be in some way extraordinary. Romeo and Juliet, the most famous star-crossed lovers, were predated by Tristan and Iseult. We find that Iseult lives in Ireland, Tristan in Cornwall, their families mortal enemies. As the story unfolds Tristan kills Iseult's uncle in battle but is wounded with a terrible poison. Believing that only Iseult can heal him, he travels in disguise to Ireland. Iseult saves his life and they become fast friends, until the inevitable revelation, that he is really the murderer of her uncle;

nevertheless, Tristan's life is spared and he goes back to Cornwall.

When King Mark of Cornwall, Tristan's uncle, hears of Iseult's beauty, he decides he wants to marry her and sends Tristan back to Ireland to get her. The match is made and Iseult returns across the Irish Sea with Tristan as her chaperon. But, as fate would have it, Iseult and Tristan accidentally drink a love potion which changes their perspective on things enormously. They are in love, and waste no time consummating their new passion.

> *"In Cornwall, after I married the king, it all became much more dangerous," says Iseult.*
>
> *"You kept on sleeping with Tristan after you were married?" asks Lilith.*
>
> *"You do not understand. I could not help myself. It was the drink. I had to love Tristan," Iseult protests.*
>
> *"So you didn't choose to love him?" asks Lilith.*
>
> *"No, of course not! One does not choose to love. Love is a malady, how do you say, a trick of fate. It was not my fault."*

With the introduction of the love potion, the romantic myth begins to take on some shape. Love is represented as an event which happens to us, but one that we have no freedom to choose. Love is fated. It visits itself upon us like a sudden illness, and its symptoms are much the same: fever, dizziness, weakness, depression. According to the Arab poet Ibn Hazm, "Love is a fatal disease, a state of ecstasy, an infirmity for which we yearn. He who is not afflicted searches for its woes, and he who is seized with its malady no longer seeks to be cured."[6]

So Iseult weeps for days on end, sick with love. But if it hurts so much, why would anyone want to love in such a way? There is one obvious advantage of perceiving love as an illness. If love is something that we choose, something that we can control with the force of our will, then we are accountable for the actions we take on behalf of the love. But if love is a sickness, we are innocent of blame. This view of love as an irrational force which takes precedence over all previous laws or loyalties is reminiscent of

Augustine's view of human sexuality as a curse, something which
cannot be controlled by a force of will because it is intrinsic to
our nature. Original Sin may well have been a liberating view for
Augustine, since it gave him an explanation for his personal
suffering. Iseult says, as Augustine, "I am guilty but it's not my
fault."

*"Now, Iseult," says Guenevere, "surely you feel responsible for
deceiving your husband and for Tristan's exile and for his death?"*

*"Responsible?" asks Iseult, bewildered. "It was the potion, not me,
who chose Tristan. After that I did what I had to do because of the
love. I had no power to resist."*

*Guenevere looks grim. "I'm afraid I have quite different feelings
about this. I also was given in an arranged marriage to a king, and
I fell in love with the knight who was sent to escort me to him. But
there was no love potion. There's nothing and no one I can blame
but myself for all the evil that came about because I loved Lancelot."*

The disparity between the attitudes of Iseult and Guenevere
towards a very similar circumstance of adultery can be attributed
to two different attitudes towards guilt. Iseult is almost righteous
in defense of her love while Guenevere seems to have accepted
the blame in full. Both Guenevere's story and Iseult's originated
in oral traditions from Celtic sources and became popular in
Western Europe during the rise of courtly love. But the myth of
Tristan and Iseult was so heavily influenced by the feudal
traditions that it never really moved past them. Even though the
fifteenth-century Arthurian chronicler Thomas Malory brought
Tristan and Iseult to Camelot, the earlier stories retain their
emotional hold on the myth. In contrast, Guenevere's story
changed profoundly as it was told and retold in the next seven
hundred years, serving various interpretations of Christians,
Victorians and twentieth-century playwrights.

In the end Iseult's adultery comes across as tragically heroic
while Guenevere's is tragically sinful. Iseult escaped blame
through the device of the potion while Guenevere quickly lost

that grace. The Arthurian myth reflects social reckonings of Christianity: the woman is more guilty than the man in a sexual liaison because she is a "temptress." Iseult's story, however, reflects feudal conditions, and so it is not burdened with this kind of moral agenda. Iseult is caught between a man she wants and one who owns her. The historical conflict between the laws of feudalism and the laws of love found their way into her myth.

"So you didn't love Mark?" asks Guenevere.

Iseult shakes her head emphatically. "No, of course not. One does not love one's husband!"

"The thing I don't understand," says Lilith, "is why you married Mark at all. I mean, Iseult, you were already in love with Tristan, you'd even slept with him."

"I had no choice about marrying the king," Iseult insists angrily. "A betrothal is like a contract. Tristan was bound by his honor to bring me to Mark!"

"But you knew before you married him you'd keep on sleeping with Tristan. That's not particularly honorable," says Lilith.

"Well, yes, that is true," Iseult admits. "We had to start lying to Mark at once – on the very wedding night! My maid slept with him the first time instead of me, because, you see, I was no longer a virgin. It was a very exciting charade." She pauses, laughing to herself, remembering.

"I wonder if the maid thought it was such a good time," Lilith says under her breath to Eve.

Tristan and Iseult's story is full of deceptions of the king which make him seem like a fool. In a particularly humorous instance Iseult agrees to a trial to determine her fidelity. She must place her hand in a fire and proclaim her innocence. If she is telling the truth, she will not be burned. Proudly she swears that she has never lain with any man except her husband and, of course, the poor pilgrim who caught her when she fell that day in plain sight of a gathered crowd. The pilgrim was, by their own design, Tristan in disguise. To the letter of her oath Iseult has spoken the truth. Her hand is magically unburned and she is set free.

This mockery of the justice of her society is dramatic, yet the situation was created by her obedience to feudal law in the first place. In the same way that loyalty to a feudal lord would have to come before honor, the laws of courtly love, based on the feudal system, required that a lover put his love ahead of anything else, including ethics or honesty or secular law. The idea that love could be above the law, or at least outside of its jurisdiction, would have been very important in medieval society where transgressions of love brought punishments of death. If love is considered to be a religion, then a lover could justify illicit behavior by claiming obedience to a higher, spiritual law. If love is considered to be a sickness, then it must obey its own correspondingly natural laws.

Defining justice through a hierarchy of laws involves determining which law is "higher" than which and under what circumstances. The parents of a child who dies because they refuse to seek medical assistance may be charged with murder, but if their actions were in response to the teachings of their religious faith, they will plead their innocence. The belief that religious laws supersede secular laws is full of philosophical and political ambiguities. But if love is considered to be a sickness, it will run into no such complications because natural laws are unarguably beyond conscious control. Crimes of passion have often been judged less severely, both by public opinion and by statute, than premeditated crimes committed for gain because of the common belief that our emotions cannot be controlled, and so we should not be held accountable for what we do when our emotions "take over."

A woman who continues to stay with a husband who beats her may explain that she "can't help it," she just loves him too much to leave. If the man later kills his wife in a possessive rage, he very likely will claim to have acted out of his great love for her. This murderer's pathological jealousy and his victim's distorted devotion even may have been the gauge with which they judged the validity of their love for each other! Romantic Love advises us that if it hurts, it must be love. If love does not have that violent intensity, it cannot possibly be "true love"; it certainly is not romantic. How much we suffer for the one we love becomes the measure of how much we love. Even more disturbing, how much our beloved suffers on our behalf is supposed to demonstrate how much we are loved.[7]

The attachment to the suffering and the romanticization of tragedy is so ingrained in the myth of Tristan and Iseult that without it there would not be much of a story. But that fact in itself is deeply suspect. The pain that is supposed to be proof of their love has little to do with resolving the story in any loving way. They anguish over and prolong the conditions that make their relationship hurt the most.

Lilith asks curiously, "Why didn't you tell Mark the truth before you married him? Or why didn't you run away with Tristan when you had the chance? Mark even let you be with Tristan for a couple of months in the wilderness, but when Mark forgave you, you went back to him and let Tristan go into exile!"

"Yes, yes," says Iseult impatiently. "What are you trying to say, that I do not love Tristan? But I risked death again and again to make love with him. I suffered for him. When I heard he married another woman in Brittany, I thought my heart would break from grief."

"You wanted Tristan to stay faithful to you, even in exile, even after you chose to go back to Mark?" asks Eve.

"Bien sur! I remained true to him always. I never let myself be happy with Mark. Of course I did not want him to be happy without me. Tell them Guenevere, tell them how it is to be in love."

Guenevere speaks slowly, unwillingly. "I'm not sure I wanted Lancelot to be unhappy without me. I suppose I hoped his love for me would be enough to make him happy. Perhaps it wasn't. Perhaps I betrayed him too."

Iseult dismisses Guenevere's remarks with a wave and turns an angry face towards Lilith. "If it is not love which Tristan and I feel for each other, what is it then?"

In 1940, in a book entitled *Love in the Western World*, Denis de Rougement first disrupted the complacency of the myth of Romantic Love by daring to suggest that Tristan and Iseult never loved each other. This idea is not very shocking today since the reign of Romantic Love has been eroding steadily in recent years, aided by various popular writings. But de Rougement's ideas about Romantic Love did not find a sympathetic public until the 1970s, the previous decades being far too committed, culturally, to traditional sex roles and relationships.

De Rougement understood what a controversial and emotionally charged subject he had taken on, and he seemed to have a premonition of the backlash before it occurred. "The Romance of Tristan is 'sacred' for us precisely to the extent that it seems 'sacrilegious' on my part to attempt to analyze it," he warned. [8]

And he was right. In an introduction to a translation of Strassbourg's *Tristan and Isolde*, indignation at de Rougement's assertion is lavish: "One is actually invited to believe that Tristan and Isolt did not love each other and that they never missed a chance of parting. This of the most famous lovers of medieval romance, who over and over again risked death to meet in secret embrace!" [9]

The criticism is ironic since de Rougement perceived this romantic definition of love, the willingness to risk death on behalf of passion, to be an error: hysterical sentiment mistaken for love. Romantic Love differs in principle from other kinds of love, between a parent and child or between friends, for instance, in which we want the best for those we love. Ordinary love like this makes us feel well and happy, not sick and suffering. There is no glamor in being apart from our friends; we simply miss them. There is no idealization of tragedy when it occurs in our families; we simply grieve. So what are we to make of Tristan and Iseult who value their longing and their tragedy above the experience of being together?

De Rougement is unequivocal: "Tristan and Iseult do not love one another. They say they don't and everything goes to prove it. *What they love is love and being in love* . . . Their need of one another is in order to be aflame, and they do not need one another as they are. What they need is not one another's presence, but one another's absence. *Thus the partings of the lovers are dictated by their passion itself.*"[10] The basis for his argument is the striking lack of compassion and concern Tristan and Iseult have for each other, when they offer and expect suffering as evidence of love. Each time they have an opportunity to transcend the impossibility of their situation, they seem to deliberately sabotage their chances in favor of the more difficult, the more painful, the more *romantic* circumstances of their longing.

Lilith suggests cautiously, "Maybe, Iseult, you love the tragedy or the excitement – the idea of Tristan, not actually Tristan himself."

"And I suppose you think also Tristan is in love with the idea of me?" asks Iseult indignantly.

When Lilith does not reply, Iseult says impatiently, "Tristan loves me. He died from love and then I died from grief!"

Lilith shakes her head. "No, Iseult. You died for love because you wouldn't live for it."

"You speak in riddles," protests Iseult. "What are you talking about?"

When we feel romantic longing for someone, we say that we have "fallen" in love. Everyone would agree that Romantic Love differs from ordinary love in this aspect, that we do not fall in love with our children or our friends. There is a definite connection between falling in love and sexual attraction. Although we are not always in love with those who attract us, we are almost always attracted to those with whom we feel we are in love. We might say to an admirer that we are dismissing, "I love you, but I'm sorry, I'm just not *in love* with you." Romantic Love requires the feeling of being in love to satisfy its own definitions.

Although the union of romantic lovers is often idealized as a fusion of two people who become one, such a blurring of the boundaries between individuals in a relationship can actually prevent real love from occurring. In an essay on marriage, the poet Rainer Maria Rilke beautifully describes how "falling" in love actually can bring about a loss of love: "When a person abandons himself, he is no longer anything, and when two people both give themselves up in order to come close to each other, there is no longer any ground beneath them and their being together is a continual falling."[11]

But there is a persistent mystery about being in love. We consider the state to be sacred and superior to ordinary loving. What lovers receive from their heightened longing may be described as a mystical experience perhaps, but their ecstatic oneness must ignore temporal concerns, and thus it has less power to affect the real world (though, of course, it does not seem so at the time). In *The Road Less Traveled*, M. Scott Peck makes a clear distinction between the sensation of being in love and the opportunity for growth that mature love can afford: "Once the precious moment of falling in love has passed and the boundaries have snapped back into place, the individual may be disillusioned, but is usually none the larger for the experience. When limits are extended or stretched, however, they tend to stay stretched. Real love is a permanently self-enlarging experience. Falling in love is not."[12]

Romantic Love is supposed to be powerful and magical and yet it lacks much of the strength of ordinary love to heal and to inspire change. Robert Johnson also expressed this contradiction: "Most people think that being 'in love' is a much more intimate, much more meaningful relationship than 'mere' friendship. Why then do couples refuse each other the selfless love, the kindness and good will, that they give readily to their friends?"[13] The obvious answer is that *Romantic Love is not inherently loving*. A romantic relationship does not necessarily include love as one of its priorities. So what *is* love, if Romantic Love is what love is not?

Surprisingly, literature, theology and psychology have all offered a consistent definition of love which stands in stark contrast to the romantic myth. This is how D.H. Lawrence described his relationship with his cow Susan, in terms of love:

She knows my touch and she goes very still and peaceful, being milked. I, too, I know her smell and her warmth and her feel. And I share some of her cowy silence, when I milk her. There is a sort of relation between us. And this relation is part of the mystery of love: the individuality on each side, mine and Susan's suspended in the relationship. [14]

Lawrence was not proposing a sentimental or anthropomorphic attachment to the cow, but rather an awareness of and a respect for *cow-ness* which is distinct from his own *human-ness*. This relation of love arises from an awareness of the beloved not as an *object*, nor as an extension of the self, but as a distinct *other*. The theology of Martin Buber is also based on this notion of love. When Buber characterizes the many points of view he can choose to take when observing a tree, he includes the awareness of relationship: "It can also happen, if will and grace are joined, that as I contemplate the tree I am drawn into a relation, and the tree ceases to be an It." [15]

The natures of human and tree, as human and cow, do not have to be identical to be in relationship with each other; they are not the same and they cannot be the same. *But neither must human and tree be two halves of one whole.* Respect for the distinctions and the equality between the self and other is crucial for love to occur. It may be easier to see the significance of this principle of love when it is directed towards a cow or a tree than to see it working between people. It is customary to perceive the non-human inhabitants of the planet as extensions of ourselves, possessions to be used and destroyed when they no longer serve, but few of us would admit to objectifying people the way we might objectify a cow or a tree. And yet this is exactly what we do when we make generalizations based on class, race or gender. This is what really occurs in families where adults abuse their children. And this objectified view of other people is a central characteristic of Romantic Love.

The myth of the Halved Soul, as a model for relationship, requires the projection of an identity onto another person. To name someone a "soulmate" seems to be proof of love, but it also can be a glorified claim of ownership. The intense longing for union with a beloved that is the mark of Romantic Love is often deficient in simple respect – the kind of respect for the integrity of the other that D.H. Lawrence had for his cow!

Erich Fromm defined mature love as "union under the condition of preserving one's integrity, one's individuality."[16] Unfortunately, romantic lovers often celebrate the union and forget the integrity. Women may submerge their identities within their relationships, saying to the beloved, as Eve, "I am you," while men draw others into themselves, saying as Adam, "You are me." But mature love requires two individuals to respect the inherent separation between them, without seeking to absorb the other into themselves or giving up their identity to the other. This union provides not a merging but a balance. As Rilke has said, real companionship can only occur between two "neighboring solitudes," individuals who have made peace with their separation. It is the love between two whole individuals which gives the greatest opportunity for emotional sharing and growth. Unfortunately most people do not choose their intimate relationships on the basis of personal growth or self awareness; they choose relationships which promise the most *feeling*. How does Iseult know that she loves Tristan? It feels like love, she says. There is both self-deception and laziness in this definition. Iseult knows she is in love because it fulfills her expectations of what love should feel like. And if those expectations involve pain or tragedy or wildly improbable idealizations of the beloved, real love, mature love, will always be beyond her reach.

The critics of Romantic Love agree that action, rather than feeling, is the central element of mature love. El Saadawi, for instance, explains that Romantic Love "is fundamentally a sick emotion, since it is deprived of the quality of action. It is a love that sustains itself through deprivation and lives on emotional reactions rather than on action."[17] And Peck offers a dramatic example of the emotional self-deception that can occur when someone confuses the *action of love* with the *feeling of love*. He describes an alcoholic man, whose family is desperately in need of him, crying in a bar, explaining to the bartender how much he loves his children. This man's feelings for his family have no positive effect on their lives at all. According to Peck, "it is easy and not at all unpleasant to find evidence of love in one's feelings. It may be difficult and painful to search for evidence of love in one's actions."[18]

To be in love is a state which is suffered or undergone; to love is an act which is chosen. Iseult and Tristan are afflicted: they suffer from the sickness of being in love with each other. They never chose to love in the first place, since the potion enchanted them against their will. In some versions of the story the potion actually has limited effect and the romance cannot last forever. Iseult and Tristan are given several opportunities to be together, but they never are able to make the crucial leap from the feelings of passion and enchantment and longing, to the actions of real loving. It is on the level of choice and commitment that the traditional romantic myth will always fall apart.

Lilith purses her lips, thoughtfully. "The woman Tristan married when he went into exile, her name was Iseult, too, wasn't it?"

"Iseult of the White Hands," says Iseult, "a coincidence which confused Tristan for a little while. But still they lived a chaste marriage. When he was in bed with her, he thought only of me. He could not love her, he could not perform with her, because of me."

"That interpretation would work," says Lilith, "if you were a historical character. But in mythical terms, La Belle Iseult and Iseult of the White Hands are probably the same person."

"What in the world are you saying?"

"Isn't it obvious? Tristan could not love Iseult, his own wife, but only Iseult, Mark's wife. Tristan preferred impossible love to possible love."

"No, no, it is just the times," Iseult declares. "A man could not passionately love his wife!"

Lilith interrupts her: "But imagine a world where it's acceptable for a man to love his wife passionately. What would it mean then

if Tristan ignored the Iseult right next to him because he was obsessed
with the Iseult he couldn't have?"

Love as it was defined by the courtly poets has little in common
with the relationships described by Rilke and Buber. As women
became symbols of men's spiritual longing, they necessarily
ceased to be considered as individuals. Poets of the times praised
women they had never spoken to, women they had, perhaps,
"seen from afar." Because of this idealization, the awareness of
I and Thou was lost. The "other" was never respected as an
integral individual, but only as an abstract representation of
"Passion" or "Modesty" or "Beauty" or "Love" itself, as these
things were understood by men.

It is commonly believed that the idealization of women
encouraged by courtly love caused a sudden improvement in the
social status of women, since they were considered to be precious
and fragile and thus "put upon the pedestal" by men. But feminist
studies have demonstrated that the perception of women as "the
weaker vessel" has damaging social implications: the belief that
women need male protection keeps women tied both socially and
economically to men, and deprives them of the resources they
need to establish and control their own lives. But even in the
twelfth century, this chivalrous attitude towards women did not
cause men suddenly to respect women as a class. According to
the laws of courtly love, as described by Andreas Capellanus, the
chaplain of Marie de Champagne, an idealized woman had to be
of equal or higher rank than the man. To make a peasant girl yield
to his sexual desires a knight was counseled to use *"modica
coactio,"* a little force![19] Courtly love still taught women to be
obedient to the wishes of men, including the acceptance of any
cruelty.

Jung called sentimentality "the superstructure erected upon
brutality," and that reflection could be made of the institution of
courtly love which promoted sentimental attachment, but very
little love. Men loved other men's wives rather than their own,
because they never intended to know or respect a flesh and blood

woman at all; courtly love directed them to glorify and adore some untouchable stranger. While women were being adored, they lost their individual identities, becoming instead symbols of men's spiritual aspirations and their emotional and sexual needs.

This phenomenon occurs with dramatic regularity in the modern Arab world in the countries in which marriage laws are still based on a feudal model. These Arab men have the legal sanction to own, abuse and abandon their wives with few consequences. Marriages are arranged as financial transactions, and adultery by a woman, even the suspicion of it, may still be punished with death. Not surprisingly the romantic model, with all of its twisted contradictions, is prevalent. A woman who feels Romantic Love or who becomes the object of it shows herself to be unworthy and may be rejected as a marriage partner:

> Arab songs and literature unceasingly swamp her senses with associations and feelings related to love. Yet if she responds to the call of love, then punishment and reprobation is swift and merciless . . . No man will marry her, even the man with whom she is in love. He will explain to her that he cannot trust a girl who allows herself to love a man before marrying him, even if he is himself that man. [20]

In the Middle East, as indeed everywhere, a man romances a woman and then leaves her to whatever fate her society decrees for "soiled" women: poverty, prostitution or death. Romantic Love produces similar contradictions, even in the supposed freedom and equality of modern Western societies, because the power of myth is always greater than the historical context where it first emerges. Twentieth-century women find themselves drawn to impossible, romantic men. They love men the twelfth century has directed them to love, through the timeless authority of Iseult's story. In turn, men idealize the women they cannot have, even though society has changed completely since the Middle Ages.

The history of loveless marriage has transformed into the myth of loveless marriage, a myth which, for the most part, is no longer based on feudal social conditions. Iseult is afraid of marriage of duty, where a woman is property. She is afraid that Tristan would not even want her as a wife. In modern terms a woman might be afraid of commitment without romance, a traditional inequitable marriage where the needs of a man comes first. Or she may be afraid to discover that when it comes down to it, a man only wants her for sex, not for intimacy, not for long-term commitment.

How realistic are Iseult's fears? "Will the lover with all his desires gratified continue to be in love with his Iseult once she has been wed? . . . Would he still love her if she were his wife?" De Rougement thinks not: "It is unbelievable that Tristan should ever be in a position to marry Iseult. She typifies the woman a man does not marry; for once she became his wife she would no longer be what she is, and he would no longer love her."[21] Tristan preferred impossible love to possible love and that preference is at the center of Romantic Love. The association of passionate love with an illusory rather than an actual woman is the motivating force that keeps Tristan and Iseult's romance illicit. Their love could not possibly survive any other way, at least not love the way they have defined it. Romance and love are in this sense a contradiction in terms. De Rougement defines Iseult as a romanticization of impossibility itself: "She is the woman-from-whom-one-is-parted: So Iseult had to be the Impossible, for every possible love recalls us to its bonds."[22]

We often fall in love with people with whom we could not possibly have a relationship, people who are, for one reason or another, out of our reach. We may become enamored of a person we have never met, a movie star or other public figure. We might fall in love with someone who is married or become attracted to a person who has a different sexual orientation from our own. Whatever the particular excuse, the exhausting repetition of romantic relationships which come to nothing is a familiar pattern both in literature and in the world.

Everyone knows about Don Juan, the dashing fellow who was

a soulmate to thousands of women. Don Juan's behavior suggested to de Rougement the uselessness of romantic longing, "the constant quest of the one woman whom desire in its untiring self-deception is never able to find."[23] Don Juan cannot find the perfect woman because his desire to find her is a lie. There is no woman in the world for Don Juan because no possible woman would suffice.

Still, Don Juan is popular with the ladies. That is because he has a secret to his romantic success. His admirers are amazed by his apparent sensitivity, his ability to become intimate quickly and deeply with strangers. The vulnerability is an illusion, of course, because Don Juan is always in complete control. He is excited by the desire he inspires in others, but he never feels that desire himself. Lawrence said that Don Juan is only Don Juan because he lacks desire:

> He had broken with his own integrity, and was a mess to start with . . . He mashed and trampled everything up, and desired no woman, so he ran after every one of them, with an itch instead of a steady flame. And tortured by his own *itch*, he inflamed his itch more and more. That's Don Juan, the man who couldn't desire a woman. He shouldn't have tried. He should have gone into a monastery at fifteen.[24]

Every Don Juan knows that if he does not need anyone, he will not be hurt. He will mercilessly dismiss his following of enchanted women the moment they stay longer than he wants them to stay. His lovers have no power and no say because Don Juan is not likewise enchanted. He is in complete control and he does not need anyone at all. That is his big secret, and that is what makes him so irresistible. Unfortunately, it is a lie. The truth is that Don Juan does not like pain and he is very good at avoiding it. He says that hurting others causes him pain, but undoubtedly it hurts less than wanting someone and being rejected himself. In fact Don Juan is not squeamish about hurting women, and may even take pride in his ability to be cruel. But he likes to *think* that he does not like hurting women. "I didn't tell you the truth because I didn't want to hurt you," he will say to a lover he has betrayed. But lies of omission only hide his cowardice behind a face of compassion.

It would be an error to blame the failure of relationships on men as if women are always available for intimacy and commitment while men inevitably run away. Tristan and Iseult are equally unavailable to each other. The very fact that women are attracted to and set their sights on Don Juan types in the first place is evidence of their own reluctance to enter into possible relationships. There are dozens of recent books which give testimony to the tendency of women to fall in love with men who "can't love" or who are in some other way emotionally unavailable, or in the worst cases, abusive. But there are plenty of Donna Juanas in the world too, each with their own following of romantic lovers who would swear that she must be their one true soulmate. She only seems to be so, of course, because of her chronic unavailability.

Don and Donna are both very good at telling people, "I love you." They cannot understand why it is so hard for other people to say. They believe that they could love anyone and on good days they love everyone. But they never love anyone any more or less than they love anyone else. They are excellent at beginning relationships, but cannot let them develop. They can love many, but they cannot love one. To love just one person would require deepening, would require them to really want to know another person. But Don and Donna have never met anyone as interesting as themselves. That is the real reason (they tell themselves) why they never choose just one person to love: they simply have not met the "right person" yet. The "right person" must be wiser, more attractive, more interesting and more unattainable than they are. When they meet this soulmate, they are confident that they magically will be capable of loving at a deep and lasting level.

Inevitably, Donna Juana could only fall in love with Don Juan, the one person who does not want her! And Don Juan eventually will meet his match in some unattainable Donna Juana, who is after all, just another way for him to love himself. When that happens the truth will be revealed, that they are as empty and needy and loveless as everyone else. Longing for a perfect soulmate can be a fancy way of avoiding commitment; unfortunately, it is also very effective.

Tristan and Iseult have been considered to be archetypal romantic lovers, anima and animus engaged in impossible longing for each other. But this interpretation must ignore the peculiar historical contexts from which their story arose. Before the French adopted the myth, the Welsh told it differently.[25] While still revealing dissatisfaction with marriages made for political reasons and without personal affection, the Welsh story contains no idealization of the tragedy. Instead Tristan and Iseult trick Mark into giving her up forever. She and Tristan are able to be together in the end. It was courtly love which first disdained the happy ending.

Eve, who has been listening quietly to Iseult's story, finally speaks: "Iseult, you don't have to be a victim of your myth. If you don't like it, you can change it. Don't marry Mark at all. Run away with Tristan. Don't marry him either if it bothers you, but choose a happy life together."

"It will not make an exciting story," says Iseult sadly.

"Make it exciting," says Eve, "but make it a love story."

Iseult is silent, and after a few moments, she smiles. "I always prefer my story in French, but if you would like to hear it, I will translate for you."

The Untouched Flask

There lives in Ireland a girl named Iseult whose life is happy since she is the daughter of a king. One day her pleasant life is interrupted by terrible news. Her uncle Morholt has been killed by Tristan, King Mark's heir, of Cornwall. She does not care much for her uncle, who is a brute, but her mother is very sad about the death of her brother. The King is just sad to lose the money that Morholt taxed from their neighbors. The very same week, another strange thing happens. A boat washes up on the shore of Ireland carrying a handsome man, almost dead from his wounds.

Iseult, who is a skillful healer as well as being very beautiful, brings the man back to health. Afterwards, he says his name is Tantris. Friendship and love grow between the two young people. But one day Iseult's mother finds Tantris' sword and discovers that a splinter missing from it matches exactly the splinter taken from Morholt's skull. So she knows Tantris to be, in truth, Tristan, the murderer of her brother. She is going to kill him while he is naked in his bath! But the King stops her, because of the great friendship that has grown between Tristan and their family. Tristan is allowed to go free. Iseult misses Tristan, but she nurses her anger to spite the grief. No one suspects that she still cares for him.

Within the year Tristan returns to Ireland with a proposal of marriage from Mark, the King of Cornwall. Her father weighs the political gain against the happiness of his wife and daughter. Of course he decides to give Iseult to the old king across the water. Iseult's mother is sad about losing beautiful Iseult, and very worried, so she makes a love potion for Iseult to drink in the marriage bed, a tranquilizer/aphrodisiac, to help her through the first horrible night.

This story is almost the same as the old one," says Iseult, interrupting herself. "But listen. Here it changes."

On the journey to Cornwall, Tristan and Iseult have many conversations. She hates to admit she is falling in love with him. How could it be so, how could she love the murderer of her uncle? She is always irritable with him, but he never seems to go away when she tells him. But, of course, after they make love and it is so wonderful, it becomes obvious what is really happening between them. As the shores of Cornwall draw near, Iseult cries, "I do not want to marry Mark, even if he is a king and very rich, too!"

"Well," says Tristan, "I would not want to marry him either." After they cry together, they make love, which makes them cry more. Then they think of a plan. When the boat arrives in Cornwall there is a lot of rejoicing in honor of La Belle Iseult. No one has ever seen such a beautiful woman and everyone is very happy. Tristan and Iseult wait until the festivities are over to meet with King Mark all alone. There they tell him that a terrible accident has occurred. They sipped together a love potion. Now, regrettably, they love each other so much, they cannot pretend otherwise. Iseult tells Mark she will honor the betrothal and marry him, but he can never trust her, because her heart will always belong to Tristan. Tristan tells the King he will also honor the betrothal and give up Iseult, but the King will have to banish him or kill him to keep him away from her.

Mark loves Tristan like a son, but his feelings are badly hurt. They have made him feel like an old man, unattractive and very lonely. So he thinks he will have Tristan killed in the morning, before anyone else finds out about his shame. But that night Mark has a dream in which he is married to Iseult and she deceives him again and again, so that he has to burn her in a fire. From this dream he wakes up crying.

In the morning King Mark calls Tristan and Iseult to his room and tells them he is very sad about what happened, but he does not want to turn his sadness into tragedy. He says he will not marry Iseult, that she is free to marry Tristan if that is what she wants. However, since his heart is lonely at the sight of their love, he sends them away to Brittany, where they are married. And it is a very beautiful wedding. In a few years time (after he marries a woman closer to his own age), Mark calls them back home, making Tristan his heir. Mark dies, surrounded by Tristan and Iseult and their children, who all love the King like a father.

"Tristan and Iseult keep the unopened love potion by their bed in case they ever get tired of each other. But they never open the flask, even though they live to be very old. Voilà!" says Iseult happily. "That is a much better ending."

Tristan and Iseult are free to make a different choice from the one their myth most often provides for them, as are we all. But love must first transform from an involuntary state which we suffer to a conscious act which we choose. The biggest obstacle to this kind of transformation is the unpleasant but crucial realization that romantic expectations have very little to do with creating and maintaining loving relationships. Men and women have different reasons for being afraid of commitment, stemming from very different developmental and social circumstances, but the results are the same: relationships which have nowhere to grow because they are not based on love at all, but only on the longing for love.

3

GUENEVERE:
Longing for Perfection

Based on the images of Adam's loss and Eve's guilt, the myth of the Halved Soul carries the invisible message that women are responsible, not only for the suffering of men, but also for men's sexual desire. And so Woman, the temptress, is the *more guilty* of the two in an adulterous affair and her shame is a staple of the romantic story line.

> He, the King,
> Calls me polluted: shall I kill myself?
> What help in that? I cannot kill my sin,
> If soul be soul; nor can I kill my shame;
> No, nor by living can I live it down.
> The days will grow to weeks, the weeks to months,
> The months will add themselves and make the years,
> The years will roll into the centuries,
> And mine will ever be a name of scorn.[1]

Tennyson is probably the most eloquent of all the Arthurian storytellers, but for Guenevere he is also the harshest. Guenevere's love for Lancelot became more carnal and more selfish as Arthur became more noble each time their story was retold through the centuries. Guenevere's popularity as a mythical character has survived for fifteen hundred years, not because of her love, but because of her guilt.

"I suppose it's my turn now," Guenevere says irritably to Lilith.

"Your turn for what?"

"Oh, don't act so innocent, Lilith," snaps Guenevere. "It's time for my tearful confession."

"Maybe it would help if you told us why you feel so guilty."

"I should think it would be obvious," says Guenevere between clenched teeth. "I betrayed husband, king and country by loving Lancelot. My guilt is well established."

"You feel the guilt the storytellers want you to feel."

"No," says Guenevere. "I feel the guilt I deserve to feel."

The only fact about Guenevere upon which all stories seem to agree is her exceptional beauty. In the Celtic tradition recorded in the Welsh Mabinogi, *Gwenhwyfar* appears as one of the "beautiful ladies of the isle of Britain" and is noted among Arthur's prized possessions. There is scant mention of Arthur in historical literature before 1135, when Geoffrey of Monmouth completed his *History of the Kings of Britain*. According to this account Arthur appointed his beautiful wife Guenevere to be regent, along with his nephew Mordred, when he went off on a campaign. While Arthur was gone Mordred betrayed him, setting the crown of Britain on his own head and linking himself in "unhallowed union" with the Queen. The question of Guenevere's complicity in this betrayal is unclear. Arthur and Mordred have a series of battles and in the midst of it all Guenevere retires to Caernarvon to "lead a chaste life amongst the nuns."[2]

Geoffrey's Latin history was translated into French verse and elaborated by Jerseyman Wace in 1155. Wace decided that Guenevere *had* committed wilful adultery, reporting that the Queen slept with Mordred even before Arthur's departure. He does allow, however, that she repented of her acts and retired to a convent. Lancelot's first adulterous appearance in literature, though undoubtedly not in oral traditions, was in Chretien de Troye's Arthurian romance, written in the late twelfth century. In Chretien's story, the faithful knight Lancelot rescues and avenges Guenevere who has been kidnapped by Meleagant. During the course of the rescue Guenevere and Lancelot manage to spend a night together. Since Chretien's story was meant to showcase the tenets of courtly love, the adultery between Lancelot and the queen is depicted without sin or shame and seems to have no ultimately tragic consequences for the characters. Guenevere is allowed to be as righteous and shameless in her adultery as Iseult. After Chretien's popularization of the myth, however, Arthurian romance swiftly transformed into a psychological study of sin and guilt which focused on the relationship between Lancelot and Guenevere.

The Prose Lancelot, a sequence of three lengthy romances written by different French authors in the early thirteenth century, demonstrates the impact of Christianity on the story. The middle romance of the cycle, *The Quest of the Holy Grail*, presents Lancelot's life as a Christian morality play in which he struggles between sin and chaste redemption. Guenevere appears, predictably, as a two-dimensional figure of seduction and wile. In contrast, the third romance, *The Death of King Arthur*, is free of intense religious agenda. Lancelot's struggle is still presented in terms of his spiritual growth, but it involves much more than his relationship with the queen. Lancelot's love for Guenevere comes across as genuine, not simply carnal, as it does in Christian accounts, but neither is it inflated with courtly rhetoric as it was, for instance, in Chretien's work. Guenevere is portrayed in a very human light, and her love for Lancelot even seems to makes sense, considering her loveless union with the aged king. Arthur, in fact, comes off looking the worst of the three in *The Death of King Arthur*. He is indecisive, pathetic and cruel. Certainly Guenevere's conflict has not yet become an emotional one, but is still a matter of feudal, and to a lesser extent Christian, law.

This romance records Mordred's betrayal of the king and his attempts to "marry" the queen, but it is here represented unambiguously, as a deceitful and forcible violation. Even so, according to *The Death of King Arthur*, when Guenevere finally manages to flee to the convent having successfully rejected

Mordred's schemes, she does so not only to escape Mordred, but Arthur as well:

> My lord the king is going to fight in this battle, and if Mordred wins he will kill me; on the other hand, if my lord has the honour of the battle, nothing will prevent him from thinking that Mordred has slept with me, because of the great force he has used to try to capture me. I am sure that the king will kill me as soon as he can get his hands on me.'[3]

Arthur was granted his more familiar virtues of gentleness and honor by the fifteenth century when Sir Thomas Malory wrote *Le Morte D'Arthur*, perhaps the most famous compendium of Arthurian tales, which would inspire T.H. White's *The Once and Future King* and the Broadway musical *Camelot*. But even in Malory's account Arthur's gentleness does not extend to his wife: he is still eager to burn her on mere suspicion of her adultery. What Malory's romance served to communicate once and for all was that Guenevere was responsible for Arthur's death. Technically, Mordred was still the engineer of Arthur's defeat, but Malory made it clear that the king was vulnerable to treachery only because he was distracted by Guenevere's infidelity.

In *Le Morte D'Arthur* after the death of the King, Guenevere indicts her love for Lancelot when she bids him farewell: "As well as I have loved thee, mine heart will not serve me to see thee for through thee and me is the flower of kings and knights destroyed."[4] As Arthur became more idealized in the literature, Guenevere's association with treacherous adultery became complete and unforgiving. In the nineteenth century Tennyson was able to blame Guenevere for everyone's downfall.

"I was guilty," says Guenevere with bitterness. Lilith looks at Guenevere curiously. "Can't you see that your guilt evolved along with the myth?"

Guenevere shakes her head. "You're just clouding the issue, Lilith. No one tricked me into sleeping with Lancelot. I betrayed my husband of my own free will."

But in emotional terms, what did Guenevere actually betray? When she was betrothed it was Lancelot, not Arthur, who came to escort her to her wedding at Camelot. When she was kidnapped by Meleagant it was Lancelot, not Arthur, who undertook to rescue her. Certainly there is enough material to make a case for a valid love between Guenevere and Lancelot blooming in the waste of a loveless marriage. In contrast to Tennyson's interpretation of the tale, William Morris, the pre-Raphaelite artist and poet, took this more compassionate view of the Queen and wrote "The Defence of Guenevere" in her defense, and in her voice:

> I was bought
> By Arthur's great name and his little love,
> Must I give up for ever then, I thought,
> That which I deemed would ever round me move
> Glorifying all things; for a little word,
> Scarce ever meant at all, must I now prove
> Stone-cold for ever?

Morris does not have to stray very widely from tradition to tell the story in this way. There is little in the earlier Arthurian redactions to suggest that Arthur ever loved Guenevere at all. He treats her as a possession which he can destroy at will if her value is tarnished by adultery – or by rape.

Guenevere's voice is like ice. "Arthur always acted according to law and custom. I'm the one who didn't."

"You are confusing me, Guenevere," says Iseult. "It seems very simple. Do as I have done. Write your story so that you can be with Lancelot. Do not marry Arthur at all!"

"But I'm not the same as you, Iseult," insists Guenevere. "You never loved Mark, but I really do love Arthur."

Iseult shakes her head, and Guenevere tries to explain:

"Lancelot was the best knight in the world but I never wanted him for my husband. Arthur is my husband and I love him too much ever to leave him."

"So you love Arthur, that is very nice, but he does not love you!"
says Iseult.

Guenevere protests, *"Iseult, that's not fair! I always thought*
Lancelot's passion for me was true love. So, of course, Arthur seemed
cold to me. I didn't understand him until it was too late."

Tennyson's work, *The Idylls of the King*, was chiefly responsible
for making Guenevere's conflict an emotional rather than a legal
or a religious one. Tennyson granted Arthur a nobility that made
him worthy of Guenevere's love, not just her marital obedience.
He decided that Guenevere would ultimately love Arthur *more*
than she loved Lancelot, or at least, in a higher way:

> Blessed be the King, who hath forgiven
> My wickedness to him, and left me hope
> That in mine own heart I can live down sin
> And be his mate hereafter in the heavens
> Before high God. Ah great and gentle lord . . .
> I yearn'd for warmth and colour which I found
> In Lancelot – now I see thee what thou art,
> Thou art the highest and most human too,
> Not Lancelot, nor another. Is there none
> Will tell the King I loved him tho' so late?

Tennyson made the story twice as tragic and twice as romantic,
by letting Guenevere fall in love with her own husband the
moment that she lost him forever. Guenevere's story was made
to fit a psychological dilemma that goes far past the
straightforward adultery of courtly love. Since the nineteenth
century Guenevere has been presented as a woman hopelessly
and tragically caught between *two* men that she loves. This could
be described, perhaps, as the quintessential romantic plot. In one
of the most popular films ever made, *Casablanca*, Humphrey
Bogart's character plays a heart-breaking Lancelot to Ingrid
Bergman's Guenevere. Likewise, in Margaret Mitchell's *Gone With
the Wind*, Scarlett O'Hara, after a long obsession with another

man, finally realizes that she loves her husband Rhett Butler, but only after he has "fallen out of love" with her.

"All right then," says Iseult. "Stay with your husband and stop running around with the knight."

Guenevere shakes her head. "Please don't judge me for this, Iseult. Your retelling was so simple for you, but I feel split in half." Guenevere holds out her two open hands. "I gave Lancelot my body and Arthur my heart. The only way I could be faithful to both of them was never to choose between them."

Definitions of faithfulness in the Arthurian story are various and creative. Lancelot refused to return the love of a lady, the fair Elaine, out of "faithfulness" to Guenevere, even after Elaine bore him a son, Galahad. Of course he still slept with Elaine, but he went mad with guilt afterwards. His insanity was meant to demonstrate, apparently, the depth of his love for the Queen. But what about Arthur? Did he live up to the kind of fidelity he expected of his wife? In most versions of Arthur's story the fall of Camelot comes about because Arthur was betrayed by Mordred – his son by his own sister, Morgana. Arthur's sin for this incestuous adultery is addressed in the more religious redactions, but his guilt is mediated in a very clever way. Arthur claims he was tricked into sleeping with Morgana because she disguised herself as Guenevere. Whenever Lancelot sleeps with Elaine he gives the same explanation. As a result everyone's sexual exploits seem to be Guenevere's fault, or more exactly, they are the fault of Guenevere's extraordinary beauty. Her fame rests on the fact that the most valiant knight and the greatest king both wanted her, but then she is blamed for exactly the same thing.

In Tennyson's retelling Guenevere's retreat to the convent lost the innocent necessity that had characterized it when she was merely fleeing Mordred's sexual attack. It became instead a vehicle for penance, a chance for her to accept fully her guilt:

So let me, if you do not shudder at me
Nor shun to call me sister, dwell with you;
Wear black and white, and be a nun like you,
Fast with your fasts, not feasting with your feasts . . .
And so wear out in almsdeed and in prayer
The sombre close of that voluptuous day,
Which wrought the ruin of my lord the King.

Guenevere's symbolic act of "taking the veil" demonstrates that she has accepted that her beauty is part and parcel of her guilt. Most women, like Guenevere, are raised to believe that their value lies in how well they can attract men. Yet this very attractiveness is the quality for which women often are condemned. Arab women in some Islamic nations are taught that their beauty gives them power over men, so they must be veiled. If a woman goes onto the street with her fingers showing through her sleeves, she may be assaulted or even killed. And yet her culture does not support the modesty it enforces, but encourages her to pursue the qualities for which she is meant to feel so guilty. El Saadawi addresses this contradiction:

> I do not understand how it can be possible for the Arab girl to cover up her hair and her body, and hide her seductiveness, if she is surrounded at every moment of the day by advertisements inciting her to be attractive, to seduce men, to soften her skin with creams and to make her lips red and full. [5]

Much as the veiling of Islamic women is to protect men from female seductiveness, Guenevere's retreat from the world puts her where her beauty and desirability can do no further harm. The same double-bind exists in the Western world; it only seems less dramatic because it is more familiar. Until very recently in criminal court, a rapist's typical defense would include the argument that his victim's clothing and demeanor were "seductive" and so she was "asking" to be raped. But from the moment of birth girls are overloaded with messages and suggestions about how to be beautiful and attractive to men. The seductive expression on a young girl's face is not likely to be a display of her own desire; it is a *look* she has learned to wear.

Lilith laughs. "Guenevere, why do you think they wrote the story the way they did? Why do the storytellers always send you to the convent?"

"I went to the convent willingly," says Guenevere angrily, "so that I could redeem my carnality and learn to love Arthur more purely."

"Like the Virgin?" asks Lilith.

"Of course," Guenevere says coldly. "Through Her holy example."

"But don't you get it, Guenevere?" asks Lilith, shaking her head. "Her example doesn't offer to heal you. It supports your guilt. And what's more . . ."

But Guenevere interrupts her. "I've had enough of this! How dare you try to educate me about my religion!" She almost spits out the words: "You – you're a Jew – and a witch!"

There is silence for one long moment, then Lilith asks in an even voice, "Is that one category or two?"

"And she's a lesbian," adds Iseult, gleefully.

Lilith laughs out loud. She laughs so hard that tears come into her eyes. Then she winks at Iseult with exaggerated debauch. "Well, Iseult, you'll be glad to know I'm not a witch."

But Eve is furious. "Guenevere, if you're angry at yourself, fine. If you want to stew in guilt forever, go right ahead, but you don't have the right to blame anyone else for what you feel. You're not angry at Lilith anyway. You're jealous!"

"Jealous?" says Guenevere with scorn. "Of her?"

"Yes," says Eve. "You're jealous because Lilith is free of the need for a man. She's free of guilt. She's even free of Christian sin."

"You're a fine one to lecture me on sin," smirks Guenevere.

Eve shakes her head. "You can't make me ashamed, no matter what you say. But you – you're accepting the blame from the men who wrote all those books!

Guenevere feels guilty because she was unable to fulfill the desires of the men who wanted her. Their desires appear to be her responsibility because the myth makes it clear that it is her attractiveness which enticed them. [6] Arthur wanted Guenevere, so she became his wife. Then Lancelot wanted her, so she became his lover. Guenevere thinks she betrayed Arthur because she could not stay faithful to him. She thinks she betrayed Lancelot because she could not give him enough either. By this logic, perhaps she betrayed Meleagant by escaping from him. And did she betray Mordred, too, by not letting him rape her?

> *Guenevere looks down. "You don't understand," she says miserably. "They all died, and I was left alive . . ."*
>
> *Her words are swallowed up in the clap like thunder and the flash like lightning that explodes through the Underworld. A statuesque blond, sporting wings at the shoulders and wearing an armored breast-plate and a sheathed sword appears in the Underworld among the other ladies. The newcomer casts them all a haughty glance. Eve and Iseult, at least, seem to be cowering.*
>
> *"Great," mutters Lilith. "This is all we need."*
>
> *Brunehilde snarls at Lilith, "I have nothing to say to you, demon-spawned she-wolf. I came to help the Queen." She turns an intense glare towards Guenevere.*
>
> *Guenevere stammers uncomfortably. "Thank you but I'm sure there's nothing you could possibly do to help, Brunehilde."*
>
> *"You're talking about love, and love is something I know all about," says Brunehilde. "Lucky for you I'm here."*

Brunehilde, the large-breasted Valkyrie of Wagnerian fame, is a colorful and violent character from Norse mythology. According to the legend, she was held captive behind a wall of flames by Odin, the chief of the Norse Gods. Only the bravest man could release her, and win her hand in marriage, by riding through the fire. A man named Gunnar intended to perform this feat, but when he (or his horse, depending on which version of the story you prefer) refused to budge past the flames, Sigurd, his brother-in-law, agreed to ride in his place. Disguised as Gunnar, Sigurd rode through the flames and rescued Brunehilde in Gunnar's name.

Everything was fine until the day Brunehilde was washing her hair in the river with Gunnar's sister Gudrun, the wife of Sigurd. Brunehilde insisted on washing upstream of Gudrun, since *her* husband Gunnar was the bravest man, having ridden through the flames to win her. But Gudrun only laughed, saying that *she* should wash upstream from Brunehilde because *her* husband was the bravest. She boasted how Sigurd had disguised himself as Gunnar when Gunnar was afraid to ride into the fire. Brunehilde was outraged to discover that she had married the wrong man. That night she told her husband she would leave him and take away her dowry if he did not murder Sigurd, the man who had so horribly deceived her. Under this pressure Gunnar arranged to have Sigurd killed. And so the hero died, betrayed by his own kin. But he did not die alone: Brunehilde killed her slaves, all of her bondsmaids and then, because of her great love for Sigurd, she killed herself. They laid her beside him and burned them on one pyre. Brunehilde and Sigurd were able to be together in death as they had not been in life. [7]

"Let's see if we understand your story," says Lilith, not in the least intimidated by the Valkyrie. She scratches her head lethargically. "You love Sigurd because he was the one, not your husband, who rode through the flames to rescue you."

"Yes," says Brunehilde.

"And you love Sigurd so much that you couldn't stand for him to be married to anyone else."

"That's it," says Brunehilde.

"So you had him murdered, and then you killed yourself so the two of you could be together in the afterlife."

"Of course," says Brunehilde with a satisfied smack of her lips and looks around to see the reaction.

No one speaks. Eve smiles politely. Iseult coughs.

"What do you mean by that?" roars Brunehilde at the unfortunate Iseult.

"Pardon Madame," says Iseult. "I only – I am not sure – I think I do not understand your story."

"She doesn't understand why you killed Sigurd," says Eve.

"Because I loved him!" There is another long silence.

Eventually Guenevere sighs impatiently. "Oh, why are we all sitting here pretending Brunehilde is talking about love, when it's blatantly obvious she's some kind of psychopath."

Brunehilde turns wide eyes towards Guenevere. Her voice is low and ominously gentle: "Excuse me, Your Majesty, but why do you think you are so different from me?"

Guenevere says nothing, but her face is very white.

Brunehilde continues: "I heard you killed both the men you loved."

"What – what are you saying?" stammers Guenevere.

Brunehilde replies pleasantly, "When Lancelot was dead and Arthur was dead and all his ridiculous English knights too, someone stayed hiding in her rat-hole, didn't she?"

"Please . . ." says Guenevere, her eyes filling with tears.

"Oh yes, you should feel superior to me, Your Majesty. Your husband and your lover died because of you, but you were too much of a coward to kill yourself."

"Yes," says Guenevere, weeping now openly.

"It's not too late, Queen. That's why I'm here." In one quick move Brunehilde is standing behind Guenevere's bowed head, her hand on the hilt of her sword.

In the next moment Lilith is there too, blocking Brunehilde from the weeping queen.

"I think," says Lilith calmly, "it's time for you to leave."

In the place where Lilith had been standing, now there is a wolf, lip curled, teeth bared, poised to leap.

Brunehilde pulls her sword from its sheath. In a horrible flurry of fur and feathers, both wolf and Valkyrie disappear.

Guenevere feels so guilty, she is so sure that she is to blame for everything in her life that when Brunehilde tries to convince her that she deserves to die, she accepts the judgment. In contrast,

Lilith never accepted her guilt. She left Adam because she refused to believe that she would deserve cruelty and violence from anyone, an understanding which gives her access to all of her strength and resources when she needs them, to protect herself and others.

When Lilith reappears she is breathing heavily but smiling. She looks at the row of worried faces. "What, did you think I couldn't handle Brunehilde? She's mostly bravado. I just chased her back to Valhalla. She'll probably be brooding there for a while."

"Is there any hope for her?" asks Eve.

"It depends on what you're hoping for," Lilith replies. "You mean you hope she'll stop murdering people?"

"Yes, that," says Eve, "but is there any hope for her to change her story, like I did, and Iseult."

Lilith considers this. "It would be hard for Brunehilde to do that, but not impossible, I guess. You could see how desperate she is. She needs to believe she murdered Sigurd because she loves him."

Guenevere is silent, staring at her hands. She is obviously struggling for words. Lilith waits.

"I'm not sure what to say," stammers Guenevere. "I behaved monstrously and I hope you'll forgive me."

"No offense taken," says Lilith lightly. "I'm not always the easiest person to get along with."

Guenevere continues, "Well, I am sorry, and very grateful. For getting rid of Brunehilde, I mean. I couldn't have done it myself."

"I'm not a victim," says Lilith simply, "but you're going to have to decide whether you're going to be one or not. Brunehilde can't tell you and we can't tell you either."

"I will tell her," says Iseult, angrily. "I love you, my friend, but I cannot believe you were listening to that – shit Brunehilde was saying!"

"I believed her," says Guenevere, "because I've thought it so often myself."

Tennyson allowed Guenevere to reach for Arthur's love after

death; if Guenevere resists death, if she hides from it, then she is not really worthy of the love that she longs for, and for which she is being given a second chance. Arthur said to her:

> Hereafter in that world where all are pure
> We two may meet before high God, and thou
> Wilt spring to me, and claim me thine, and know
> I am thine husband – not a smaller soul,
> Not Lancelot, nor another. Leave me that,
> I charge thee, my last hope.

The mythic idea that one can find perfect love only in death can be traced to the cultural influences of the medieval Christian Church. The chastity of the Virgin Mary presented women with a terrible double-bind. Through Mary's example the destiny of all women officially became Motherhood. The Church expected women to be submissive wives and mothers. But the Virgin managed it without being "defiled" by sexual intercourse. An ordinary medieval woman was left with only two choices: she could fail her destiny by refusing motherhood or she could defile herself by accepting it.[8] In effect the Church demanded that a woman be both a wife and a virgin to fulfill her spiritual duty. Being "married to Christ" in a convent could give her that, but not as well as death or martyrdom could. And so Guenevere could only escape these contradictions of her faith by looking for a pure marriage: a marriage without consummation.

"Death was your perfect consummation, isn't that right Guenevere?" Lilith asks.

Guenevere nods.

"But that doesn't make any sense," protests Eve.

Lilith nods. "Well, it wouldn't to you, Eve. It's not in your myth. But I suspect Iseult understands."

"Perhaps I understand a little," admits Iseult. "Death was, for Tristan and me, the only escape. Dead, we would be far beyond husbands and marriage. But beyond sex? Mon Dieu! Is there no sex in heaven?"

Eve's romantic myth is about longing for wholeness, as Judaism originally defined it, while Guenevere's is about longing for perfection, as defined by Christianity. Iseult can relate to a romantic view of death but for emotional rather than religious reasons. In Wagner's operatic version of her story, Iseult's potion was meant to poison Tristan. The accidental drinking of the potion of love is a foreshadowing of the death that will eventually come to them both, "the *other* death, the death that will alone fulfil their love."[9] Both Iseult's story, in which she dies of longing, and Guenevere's story, where death offers the opportunity for a perfect marriage, contain the seeds for Brunehilde's monstrous tragedy of murder and suicide.

> *Eve looks bewildered. "But death sounded so stupid in Brunehilde's story. Her love for Sigurd was more like hate. Guenevere, you thought so yourself!"*
>
> *"I know," says Guenevere, "but it has a sick perfection. That's why Brunehilde is so proud. My story falls short."*
>
> *"Yours is more insidious," Lilith says. "You feel guilty just for being alive."*
>
> *"That's it," says Guenevere. "I feel too guilty to live."*

Since we assume that romance is about love, we rarely pause to look more closely at the motivations and behaviors underlying the emotions. The romantic myth arises from an image of men's loss and women's guilt; unfortunately, the inevitable outcome of a myth which is based on guilt is violence. The vocabulary of Romantic Love is unabashedly violent, the maneuverings of lovers like a plan of war, one side aggressive, the other defensive:

> A lover *besieged* his lady. He delivered *amorous assaults* on her virtue. He *pressed her closely*. He *pursued* her. He sought to *overcome* the final *defenses* of her modesty, and *to take them by surprise*. In the end the lady *surrendered to his mercy*.[10]

Dominance and submission as sexual roles correspond with the romantic idea that a man needs to possess the woman he loves, and that the woman longs to be possessed. According to the myth of the Halved Soul, Adam needs to reclaim the part of himself that he has lost, while Eve tries her best to give herself back to Adam. Although a woman cannot actually become a rib, she can submit metaphorically, becoming an extension of a man, not only socially and economically, but sexually as well.

In patriarchal societies male dominance is imposed on women, but women must be educated continually about the reasons for their low status, through myths like Genesis which provide an authoritative explanation for female guilt. All oppressive societies depend on myths which claim that the oppressed group is inferior or evil. Apartheid in South Africa thrives on a myth of white "supremacy," for instance, and Nazi propaganda emphasized the moral corruption of the Jews. In the case of patriarchal myths about women, both judgments apply. Evil and inferior, women must try to make up for what they have done wrong simply by being born female.

Romantic Love teaches women that they should *want* to be dominated by a man, that it is *normal* for women to be submissive. It is clear that what women are supposed to be has been modeled on what *men want* women to be. George Bernard Shaw said simply, "A woman is not considered womanly unless she is of use to a man." The myth of the Virgin Mary explains what women have to do to enter heaven: be obedient, modest and submissive. But submissive to whom? To the laws and values created by men. Simone de Beauvoir observed, "For the first time in human history the mother kneels before her son; she freely accepts her inferiority. This is the supreme masculine victory, consummated in the cult of the Virgin."[11] The Koran is even more explicit: "A woman, who at the moment of death enjoys the full approval of her husband, will find her place in Paradise."

Why exactly men want women to be submissive is a different and very complicated issue. Oppressive societies are fearful places. Racist whites successfully use fear of blacks to spread their hatred, and the Nazis were terrified by the "taint" of Jewish blood; likewise, fear can be found behind the blaming anger that men feel for women. Fear, and the hatred which hides it, provide the basis for patterns of dominance and submission, both in society and in sexual relationships. But why should men be afraid of women? Genesis provides a mythical explanation:

> The myth of Adam and Eve is the story of man's fear of woman. Were it not for this fear, no one would have thought of attributing evil, sin and devilry to Eve . . . Woman, who was able through her power and sorcery and seductive beauty to lead Adam into a trap, to make him drop in one fell blow from the high heavens to the menial earth, and to be the cause of his destruction, his downfall and his death, must indeed be an awesome and fearful creature.[12]

If we assume that the fear came first, and the myth was devised in order to explain it, rather than the other way around, what is the real source of the fear men feel for women? The best clue can be found in what qualities men require of women in order *not* to be afraid: virginity, purity, vulnerability, powerlessness and submission. These are the attributes of a child, not an adult woman. It is not surprising to discover that the "women" idealized and immortalized by Petrarch and Dante were pre-pubescent girls, or that Victorian England was famous for its sexual obsession with children; Ruskin, for instance, fell in love at the age of 39 with a 9-year-old girl.[13] It is the mature physical and carnal female which is the source of the fear for men although, perversely, it is just as often the virginal child who becomes the target for male violence.

Augustine defined virginity as "incorruptible flesh," making the connection between the moral corruption of sexuality and the physical corruption of the grave. The Christian myth allows the Christ and the Virgin to escape both, through their sexual chastity and bodily ascension into heaven. The sexual abstinence of convent life traditionally included a desire to attain *both* of these marks of purity: "As a symptom of sin, putrefaction is concupiscence's twin; and a woman who conquered one penalty of the Fall could overcome the other." [14]

The obvious connection between sexuality and death is flesh. The fear of women may be, most simply, the terror of physical existence and the fear of death. Ernest Becker, in *The Denial of Death*, proposes this explanation for the psychological source of men's horror and fear of women. Becker describes a child's terror of his mother, which eventually develops into fear for his own physical vulnerability:

> The real threat of the mother comes to be connected with her sheer physicalness ... After the child gets hints about the mother's having babies, sees them being nursed, gets a good look at the toiletful of menstrual blood that seems to leave the witch quite intact and unconcerned, there is no question about her immersion in stark body-meanings and body-fallibilities. The mother must exude determinism, and the child expresses his horror at his complete dependency on what is physically vulnerable. [15]

Even as Becker recognizes the connection between men's fear of women and of death, he reveals his underlying sexist assumptions. He goes on to say that children perceive men to be "more neutral physically, more cleanly powerful," but the truth is that men are just as much creatures of flesh as women. By proposing that disgust is the natural, matter-of-course reaction to breast-feeding and menstrual blood, Becker assumes that men's fear of women is a universal psychological principle, rather than a socially conditioned one. The idea that fear of women comes first and *causes* the fear of death is just another version of Original Sin where Eve's sexuality brings about Adam's mortality!

The point Becker misses, perhaps because he is guilty of it himself, is that men are able to deny their own physicalness when they project it onto women, claiming that carnality is some exclusive quality of the female sex. Because the sexuality of women is supposed to be corrupt in a way that male sexuality is not, virginity and chastity become obligatory virtues for women, when they rarely are for men. But a woman's physical virginity has symbolic significance only to the men who require it of her. A woman who has been raped knows that her hymen is the least thing that she has lost. In some Arab countries, family members may kill a child who loses her virginity, even if she was raped, even if it was an incestuous rape, because *she* has brought shame to her family. The rapist is rarely identified or punished.

Such a system of justice seems so unfair that it stretches credulity, but it is entirely consistent with a myth of male dominance and female submission. A man can rape as an expression of his moral right and a woman can be raped and even killed as a natural consequence of her intrinsic carnality. The metaphor of sexual possession and murder is very disturbing, but it is inherent in a sexuality based on fear. Romantic Love does not admit to this fear, of course, but the dominance and the submission encouraged by the myth give it away. The inherent violence of Romantic Love is hidden, encoded in the rhetoric of romance. The primary sexual myth of Romantic Love is that a man wants to "possess" a woman carnally and that a woman wants to be "taken." But when a man's dominance is fueled by fear and a woman's submission enforced by guilt, the result is a dynamic which has much less to do with sexual desire than it does with power.

It is the idealization of the beloved which makes it possible to mistake darker emotions for love. Only objects can be possessed, not individuals. De Rougement says of Tristan and Iseult, "They love one another, but each loves the other *from the standpoint of self and not from the other's standpoint* . . . at times there pierces through their excessive passion a kind of hatred of the beloved."[16] This confusion between idealization and love, and between possession and death, is well illustrated by another medieval tradition: the myth of the virgin and the unicorn.

The image of the "hunting" of a unicorn by a virgin was made famous in the bestiary, *Physiologus*, and was by the fourteenth-century a well-established allegory for love. The unicorn itself became a symbol of power and perfection, so much so that it was sometimes taken to represent the Christ. Pope Gregory the Great made the connection explicit: just as the unicorn cannot resist the lure of the virgin, even if it risks being hunted and captured by men, so Christ suckled at the breast of Mary and then was doomed to die. Although the religious interpretations emphasized the betrayal, while secular versions eroticized the imagery, the idea that only a virgin can draw a unicorn made final the link between virginity, purity and perfection.

In his retelling of the unicorn myth, "The Silken Swift," Theodore Sturgeon reverses the traditional images.[17] The unicorn comes to the woman who is pure of heart, though tarnished by rape, rather than the woman who is technically a virgin but who hates men, who torments and teases them. Sturgeon's morality play makes an important point that should never have to be made: a woman who is not a virgin can still be pure. Not surprisingly, purity is never an issue for the man in Sturgeon's story. He would never be judged in those terms. It is still the seductress who is blamed and the rapist who is set free.

"Possessing and being possessed," says Lilith. "Brunehilde played both parts in her story. She murdered Sigurd and then she killed herself."

Eve looks like she is going to cry. "I still don't understand what death has to do with love."

"It's not about love, that's the point," says Lilith. She muses. "The hunting of the unicorn. Such an innocent story, but do you know what it's about, Eve?"

Eve shakes her head, not sure she really wants to know.

The Hunting of the Unicorn

One slanting ray of moonlight falls with absolute grace from the sky to the forest floor. Footsteps approach the graceful light: lovers are walking by moonlight, hands clasped in promise of love as yet unfulfilled. Beneath their gaze, the moonlight grows in power and gentleness until it lifts a strangely crowned head. It is a unicorn, and its eyes are full of night. In that darkness is a center point of light too bright for human eyes to bear. In a moment the young couple would be blinded, but a cloud moves across the moon. Though nothing has actually changed, they are alone again in the forest, the sky containing a darkness which is merely dark. He turns to her and finds her dull and shadowed. She looks at him and cannot make sense of his features. When they walk back through the forest they do not notice that their clasped hands have broken apart.

In the days that follow they do not eat, they barely sleep, and in their dreams they are always searching for something, though they have forgotten what it is. They clutch at their brief memories of the unicorn like the tokens of a lost love. But they are to be married, so they carry through with the preparations. He kisses her white throat and thinks of the grace of the unicorn. She bears his caress and thinks of the unicorn's power. These thoughts distract them and eventually they are ashamed. They begin to avoid each other in awkward conspiracy.

At the next fullness of the moon they walk again through the forest, but their hands are not clasped and their eyes search the shadows in hunger. Everything is different this time. There is a wind. She is offended by the sound of his breathing. He is irritated by the gracelessness of her step. But then – one slanting ray of moonlight falls with absolute grace from the sky to the forest floor. Their eyes see only what it is not. Disappointment rises in her throat and makes her cry out like a hungry bird. It is an ugly sound. He turns and strikes her with the violence of frustrated desire. And though the silence between them now is deep, there is no stillness in it. He walks away and leaves her, weeping, to follow.

The time of their wedding approaches. By now they cannot abide the ugliness and imperfection in each other. But he approaches her with a plan. She agrees. It is a simple thing. He desires to possess perfection, she to be possessed by it. They can cooperate. She is a virgin; only she can draw the unicorn. He is a man; only he can arrange the hunt. So the hunt becomes a part of their wedding ceremonies. Their families indulge them, relieved to see the strange tension between the two replaced by this frantic anticipation. There is a golden bridle made, and a golden sword. When the moon is full, they dress in white and lead a moonlit procession to the unicorn's wood. There is no wind. The guests fidget, bored or distracted. She sits in a pool of moonlight, the bridle resting in her lap. He stands behind her, his hand upon his sword.

And then – one slanting ray of moonlight falls with absolute grace from the sky to the forest floor. The guests grow still. They see her lift the bridle and hold out her hands as though entreating a lover. They see him standing in front of her, his sword held ready. They do not see the unicorn (its eyes full of night) approach her, and kneel, and place its head in her lap. They do not see his sword thrust deep into the body of the unicorn. But they are rushing at him in horror and holding back his arms, preventing the sword from reaching her heart. There is a spot of blood where it has pierced her dress and skin. She is covering her face with her hands. The guests try to comfort her, but she lifts her head and her eyes blaze in anger. "Why did you stop him? Why did you stop him?" He has dropped his sword and is weeping where it has fallen. The guests are frightened and uncertain. Eventually they take the golden bridle and the golden sword and leave the two where they are.

One slanting ray of moonlight falls with absolute grace from the sky to the forest floor. They raise their heads and see the unicorn. Within its eyes of night there are stars. They find that they can stand, but they move no closer to the unicorn. Very deliberately they turn their backs. Very slowly they walk away. Their hands are clasped. Their steps are full of grace. Behind them and without their eyes to give it form, the unicorn turns back to light.

Iseult had listened very closely to the story of the unicorn. Now her face is troubled. "I can see what is wrong with idealizing a man, but how can one prevent it? It is natural for the beloved to seem perfect and beautiful."

"How about letting moonlight be just moonlight?" Eve suggests. "I mean, let the beloved be a person, not a symbol."

Lilith nods. "For Brunehilde, it was Sigurd's bravery, for Lancelot it was Guenevere's beauty. Can you see how arbitrary those attachments are? That's what people call fate, like your love potion, Iseult, just as accidental."

Guenevere looks helplessly at Lilith. "So what are you saying? That Lancelot and I made unicorns of each other?"

"Yes," Lilith answers. "And Tennyson and Malory and everyone else who used your myth to talk about love. Even William Morris idealized you while he was defending you."

Mature love rarely becomes an obsession because it exists in the world, but Romantic Love, like the unicorn, only exists in twilit unreality. It is no coincidence that the moment the lovers see the unicorn in the moonlight they cease loving each other. This is what occurs in Romantic Love when the beloved is made to symbolize some idealization of a perfect woman or man; no one can live up to such an expectation and disappointment is inevitable. Tanith Lee, in her retelling of the unicorn myth, "The Hunting of Death: the Unicorn," eloquently illustrates this cycle of idealization, disappointment and tragedy. Lee describes the feelings of a musician about his own mortal imperfection: "What he could make could never match the essence of what he had felt. The creation was like a mockery of the stirring and the dream within him. He almost hated himself, he almost hated the gift of music."[18]

These feelings provide the content for his idealization of the unicorn. He thinks to himself:

Here it is, here it approaches you, that which you require, that which for ever and ever you have pursued not knowing it, the wellspring within yourself you cannot tap, the jewel in your mind you cannot uncover. And in that moment the miracle of the unicorn seemed to be that if he could only lay his skin against the skin of it, even so small an area of skin as a finger's tip, everything that burned and smoked within him would be, at last, his to use.[19]

But when the unicorn is finally hunted, captured and caged, the musician feels only disgust for it: "He hated it because it had failed him. It had proved attainable, and vulnerable. It had let itself be dirtied. It was inadequate, as was he."[20] For romantic lovers resentment, even hatred, can arise for the merely human, because love is reserved for the ideal.

Lancelot refused possible love by rejecting Elaine, the mother of his child, in favor of his impossible love for the Queen and their relationship of tragedy and suffering. Ordinary human love was not enough for Lancelot. If Guenevere had been Lancelot's wife, rather than his lover, she probably would have been as unrequited as Elaine. His attachment to Guenevere did not contribute to her happiness, nor did it lead to his growth or wholeness; he was obsessed with her, and so it was a fantasy, a projection, a kind of madness.

But what happens if a woman accepts sexual idealization as a part of her identity? She can come to believe she *needs* to be the object of some man's desire in order to have worth. Ultimately, tragically, she may feel she has to be idealized, to be possessed, perhaps even to be *negated*, in order to be fulfilled. That is what the unicorn story reveals: not that women naturally want to be raped or killed, or that all men have the desire to rape and kill, but that idealization has very little to do with love. Idealization leads as a matter of course to violence, because disappointment is inevitable, and the fall is very hard.

"I'm sorry," says Guenevere. "I see the point of your story, Lilith, how Lancelot and I idealized each other. I can even see how I romanticized death. But what am I supposed to do about it? Are you trying to tell me that if I had been faithful to Arthur, he would have loved me more and treated me better?"

Lilith shakes her head. "I think Arthur probably wanted to burn you for adultery because you stopped being a symbol for him. He couldn't think of you as his pure and faithful queen anymore."

"You became something imperfect," says Eve. "Something real."

"Which is why you looked for redemption and a pure marriage in heaven," Lilith continues, "desperately trying to live up to Arthur's ideal of perfection, even if you had to die to do it."

"So what do I do instead?" asks Guenevere. "I'm trapped in my myth, trapped by Lancelot's needs and Arthur's needs, by Mordred's and Meleagant's, maybe even by Malory's and Tennyson's."

"But why do you feel that you are responsible for all these men?" asks Iseult.

Guenevere shrugs. "Because they love me."

"Guenevere," says Lilith kindly. "Are you willing to consider that maybe they don't? Idealize you, yes. Blame you, yes. But love you? Probably not."

Guenevere is shocked. "But if Lancelot and Arthur don't love me, then I don't have anything. I'm not anything."

"Do you honestly believe that?" asks Eve incredulously. "Do you really believe that all you are is something for them to desire?"

Guenevere is silent, considering. Her lips are pressed together in a hard line. Finally she says, "If there's more to me than that, I have no idea what it could be."

Guenevere's inability to assess her identity beyond her worth as an object of male esteem is the most common experience of women living in a patriarchal culture. Even in contemporary Western society, where women finally are free to pursue any professional goal they desire, they are not necessarily encouraged to do so and few social structures support women in nontraditional choices. It is no coincidence that most versions of the Arthurian story allow Guenevere only one escape from the emotional and social double-binds within which she finds herself, and that is the convent.

The cloistered religious communities of the Church offered women in the Middle Ages one of the few alternatives to the traditional roles of wife and mother. The religious lifestyle could procure for a woman an education, relative freedom of thought and an independence unavailable to other women, except perhaps to those born into very wealthy families. The history of the Church is full of female saints who took the opportunity the Church provided to make extraordinary contributions in fields such as teaching, nursing and social work.

In the Victorian era the unique privileges and responsibilities of convent life provided an alternative to the world of the secular woman whose status under the law was the same as that of children and the mentally impaired. While a nun was allowed to consider the possibility of a vocation which did not involve fulfilling the physical and emotional needs of a man, a wife's duties to her husband and family were narrow and set in stone. Of course a nun was required to sacrifice her physicality and sexuality in exchange for this freedom, so ultimately the Church provided no real alternative to the secular oppression of women. Marina Warner, in *Alone of All Her Sex*, explains: "the foundations of the ethic of sexual chastity are laid in fear and loathing of the female body's functions, in identification of evil with the flesh and flesh with woman . . . Thus the little hard-won independence of the nuns was gained at other women's cost, for belief in the inferiority of their state underpinned it."[21]

The association of purity with virginity must, by definition, reject ordinary sexuality as corrupt. When this belief is projected onto women, at the same time excluding male sexuality from its judgment, the result is the classic double standard of Romantic Love: guilty submissive women trying to fulfill the desires of fearful dominant men.

> *Guenevere looks up after a long silence. "All right," she says tentatively, "I've begun to write a poem."*
>
> *"'The Idylls of the Queen'?" suggests Eve.*
>
> *Guenevere smiles. "I wouldn't presume."*
>
> *"Maybe you should presume," says Lilith. "It's your story."*
>
> *"Can we hear what you've written?" asks Eve.*
>
> *Guenevere nods shyly and begins.*

The Idylls of the Queen

Queen Guenevere confessed to Arthur this:
"Lancelot, your faithful knight, favors me
With all the praise and tenderness I crave."
The king looked down. "You do not love me then?"
"I do," she said, "but love is not enough;
Because you are my king you have not been
The friend and dear companion that I lack."
"And Lancelot . . ." he said, afraid to know.
"Then you would rather be *his* wife than mine?"
She shook her head. "Lancelot, too, must choose
A love more real than what he loves in me.
'Awake,' I said to him. 'Find love; go free.'
My freedom waits for me in convent halls,
Where lingering, I'm free to think, or read,
Or willingly to pray." "You want to be
A nun?" he asked, confused. She laughed, "Oh no,
I just want to be myself! I love you
Arthur, but I could live without you, too.
I've told you what I need; now you may choose."

"Will Lancelot marry Elaine?" asks Iseult breathlessly.
"I don't have the faintest idea," Guenevere replies.
"But what will Arthur choose?"
"I don't know," says Guenevere happily. "But it doesn't matter
what Arthur decides. I didn't choose him over Lancelot. I chose
myself over either one."

The sheer tenacity of the myth of Romantic Love makes it clear
that, for the most part, women are still perceived by men to be
objects of their own need and desire and that women themselves
have a very difficult time releasing themselves from that kind of
objectification. Women need to be set free from both the
expectation of sexual purity and the corresponding
condemnation of carnality that are inherent in the myth of

Romantic Love. Even more importantly, women must be allowed to assess their worth on a scale which measures qualities other than sexual attractiveness, purity and shame.

4

BEAUTY:
Longing for Rescue

As we examine the experiences and relationships of Eve, Iseult and Guenevere it becomes evident that the myth of Romantic Love contributes little to a psychology of healthy relationships. It does, however, outline in extraordinary detail the desires, illusions and distortions of wounded individuals. The implicit need for emotional healing is revealed by nothing so much as the stories themselves, and particularly by one stubbornly recurring motif: the longing for rescue.

Brunehilde was obsessed with the man who saved her from the wall of flames. Tristan saved Iseult from death, and Lancelot saved Guenevere more than once, from kidnapping, rape and death. Every time a man desired Guenevere, as Meleagant or Mordred did, he just took her and then another man had to come along and save her by killing the one who had stolen her. She was always glad to be rescued, but she never had the choice not to be taken in the first place. If "desire to be swept away" were a universal feminine principle, then male brutality and female victimization would have to be considered "natural" as well. After all, a knight in shining armor can only rescue a woman who is in some danger, otherwise the rescue has no meaning.

It seems far more likely that this aspect of the myth of Romantic Love evolved in response to inequitable social conditions and to the resulting patterns of abuse. The appearance of women waiting to be rescued in so many myths points more to centuries of violence against women than it does to any universal truth.

Women need to be rescued because they are rarely encouraged
to protect themselves in any way other than through negotiating
relationships with powerful men. Romantic Love encourages
women in the *habit* of helplessness.

A young girl is taught to dream about the man that she will
marry, the man that will provide her with a new name and an
adult identity. She fantasizes that he will "take her away from all
this," meaning the limitations and frustrations of childhood and
her father's house. The powerlessness of women to make their
own life choices is a crucial part of the romantic myth. In
contrast, the myth teaches a young boy to dream about the man
that he will be, the name he will make for himself and the adult
identity he will establish. He may think about the women he will
marry someday, but he never fantasizes about how she will give
him her name!

It is not for any biological reason that adolescent boys' sexuality
has very different emotional content from girls' sexuality. Sexual
experience is a mark of achievement for a boy, while it is mark
of identity for a girl. A teenage boy might tell his friends "what
he got" from a girl with whom he had sexual intercourse. The
girl, meanwhile, confides in her friends her anxiety about "who
she is" now: is she his girlfriend or is she a slut? His sexual
achievement is perceived as a positive thing, a sign of his
manhood, while her new sexual identity is almost always a
negative change, a loss of status – unless she firmly (or better yet
legally) belongs to the one who "took" her. Romantic books and
films bombard us with images of women living peripherally to
the world of men, powerful only if they are attractive to powerful
men, successful only if they are attached to successful men. All
the progressive education in the world which tries to teach girls
that they can grow up to be anything they want to be, not just
wives and mothers, is wasted if the myths of Romantic Love still
declare that a woman's worth comes from being admired, desired,
rescued and owned by a man.

The popular film, *An Officer and a Gentleman*, for instance,
centers around the romance between a man in military pilot's

training and a woman who wants to be a pilot's wife. During the course of the film the man goes through tremendous physical and emotional challenges to emerge victorious and transformed. At the end of the film, just when you think he has abandoned the woman, he comes back and "rescues" her from the factory where she works, literally sweeping her up in his arms and carrying her out of the building to the envy and wild applause of her co-workers. This is her moment, her victory.

The film makes it very clear that unless the pilot takes her with him into his glamorous new life she will live and die a miserable laborer. Neither she nor the other women who are desperate to become pilots' wives ever consider becoming pilots themselves, nor do they try to escape the mediocrity of their lives in any other way. What lesson does a girl take from watching this film? She learns that a man's victory arises from personal achievement, while a woman's victory comes from being rescued by a man.

There would be no problem with this model of the world and human relationships if it actually satisfied the people involved. The truth is, a woman who is rescued by a man probably will need to be rescued by another man at a later date. Getting married to escape a difficult family situation is a classic example of a romantic rescue. Unfortunately childhood patterns often follow a woman into her married life as, unconsciously, she chooses a man as domineering or inconsistent, undependable or abusive as the parents she tried to escape. Without some kind of healing or personal transformation her subsequent relationship is not likely to be any better, especially if the next man "rescues" her from the one before.

"What I don't understand is why it always comes down to a choice between men," says Guenevere, plaintively. "You're either stuck with the one who takes you or the one who rescues you. Unless some other man comes along to rescue you from your rescuer!"

Lilith laughs. "That's the problem. The man who saves you also gets to claim you. And for women in traditional myths not choosing a man isn't an option, unless they want to get a reputation like mine!"

One of the tales in the Welsh mythic cycle, the *Mabinogi*, recounts the fate of Blodeuedd, a woman who was made from flowers. Blodeuedd was created by the magician Gwydion for his nephew, Lleu Llaw Gyfes. Lleu had been cursed and could never marry a mortal woman. To get around the curse Blodeuedd was made especially for Lleu, to be his wife:

> So they took the flowers of oak, broom, and meadowsweet, and from these they created the fairest and most beautiful maiden anyone ever saw. And they baptized her in the way they did then, and named her Blodeuedd. At the feast they slept together.[1]

Some time after Blodeuedd and Lleu were married, when Lleu was away from their castle, a hunter named Gronw Pebyr came riding by. Blodeuedd invited him in.

> He removed his gear and they went to sit down. What Blodeuedd did was to look at him, and as she gazed, her entire being was filled with love of him. And he noticed her, too, and the same feeling was awakened in him as awakened in her. He could not conceal being in love with her, and he told her; she rejoiced exceedingly, and that night they talked of the love and affection they felt for one another. Nor did they put off past that night embracing each other; they slept together the same night.[2]

Blodeuedd and Gronw *fell in love*, and for the next few nights he stayed with her. Her husband was returning soon and she was distraught. Since her marriage could not be dissolved, Gronw offered her the only possible solution: he would murder Lleu, take over the castle and claim her. The problem was that Lleu was invincible, except under strange and extreme conditions. Eventually Blodeuedd tricked her husband into standing with one foot on the edge of bathtub and the other on the back of a billy goat, the only position in which he could be killed. Gronw shot Lleu with a poison spear, then took over his castle, his land and his wife. But Gwydion found his wounded nephew and restored him to health. Gwydion punished Gronw with death, but Blodeuedd's fate was different:

> Gwydion overtook her then, and said to her, "I won't kill you, I'll do worse: I'll let you go in the form of a bird. And because of the shame you brought upon Lleu Llaw Gyffes, you shall not dare show your face ever in the light of day for fear of the other birds. There shall be enmity between you and all the rest of the birds. It shall be natural for them to persecute you and dishonor you wherever they find you. You shall not lose your name, however, you shall always be called Blodeuwedd." What *blodeuwedd* is, is "owl" in the language of the present day. And from that cause the owl is hated by birds; the owl is still called "flower-face" (*blodeu-wedd*). [3]

Blodeuedd provides a good example of a woman in a loveless marriage, longing for rescue. She attempts to escape her marriage in the only way that her culture (and Romantic Love) allows her, by falling in love with a man who has the means to kill her husband. Since her rescuer does not actually succeed in rescuing her, Blodeuedd's life does not seem very romantic, but then, Blodeuedd is meant to be the villain in this story. Her crime is not so much the attempted murder of her husband, as her desire to get away from him. She becomes an outcast, much like Lilith, simply because she wanted to be free.

> *"I'd like you to meet Blodeuedd," says Lilith dramatically. An owl swoops out of nowhere to land on Lilith's outstretched arm. The owl finds a comfortable perch on Lilith's shoulder, and turns its wide eyes from face to face.*
>
> *Eve is the first to recover. She acknowledges Blodeuedd with a nod. "The least they could have done is turn you back into flowers," she says.*

"So you don't feel the same way about Blodeuedd's crime that you did about Brunehilde's?" Lilith asks.

Eve shakes her head. "It isn't the same at all. I can't explain why."

Blodeuedd's myth is presented from the point of view of her husband and her husband's uncle. Gwydion never asked Blodeuedd if she wanted to marry Lleu or even if she wanted to be a woman at all. She was made and given and that was that: "At the feast they slept together." Blodeuedd is supposed to submit to her marriage without complaint. By resisting her fate she commits a crime against the authority of her husband and his family. It is Gwydion, Lleu's uncle, who punishes her in the end, not because of her crime per se, but because of the *shame* she has caused their family.

Not surprisingly, Blodeuedd's personal feelings about her origins, her marriage or her fate are all irrelevant to the myth. The lesson that was communicated through this cultural myth is that women belong to the men who choose them. Any woman who attempts to make that choice for herself is an evil creature who should be shunned. Fortunately, Blodeuedd's own emotional experience can be discovered in folk traditions which use similar motifs. There is one traditional Scottish folktale in particular in which the woman in the story is trapped in a marriage she cannot escape, powerless to protect her identity from the force of male desire and control. In the tale, a fisherman casts his nets by the sea and chances to see a silkie: a creature who is a seal by day, but a beautiful human being at night.

The fisherman watches the silkie remove her seal skin and put it on the rocks. He stares at her and thinks he has never seen anything more fair. When she is out of sight he steals her seal skin and hides it in his own house, then he returns to find the silkie weeping on the shore. He asks her why she is crying. She tells him that her heart is broken because her seal skin is gone. Without it she can never return to the sea and she does not know how to live on the land. The fisherman comforts her, inviting her to come home with him to be his wife. Since she has no other choice, she goes with him and marries him and raises his children – until the day she finds her skin hidden behind a wall in her house. She never hesitates, but takes the skin to the sea and becomes a seal again, returning to her home which had never ceased its calling.

This folktale is remarkable for its honest appraisal of the fisherman, his desire and his deceit. He rescues the woman from a danger that he created for her in the first place! In societies where a woman's worth is dependent on her chastity, a woman who is seduced might feel, like the silkie, that she does not know how to live without the part of herself that the man has taken from her. She might marry her seducer because she feels that she must. In the old American tradition of the "shotgun marriage" a man was forced, by the family of a girl he seduced, into marrying her, making an "honest woman" out of her. The assumption was that the girl would want to marry the man, but of course this was not necessarily the case. Like the silkie who has lost her skin, a woman who "loses her reputation" has no choice but to find a husband to make her loss (and perhaps her child) legitimate in the eyes of her society.

Marrying a woman who has been raped to the one who raped her is a very old solution to the problem:

> If a man meets a virgin who is not betrothed and seizes her and lies with her and is caught in the act, the man who has lain with her must give the girl's father fifty silver shekels; she shall be his wife since he has violated her.[4]

Even today in some Arab countries a rapist is required by law to marry the woman he has abused. The feelings of the woman about the rape or the marriage are irrelevant to the law or her family's concern. She has dishonored her family by letting herself be "taken" without first being "owned." After the marriage her husband can rape her freely and legally, as part of his marital right.[5]

The idea that the rape of a virgin shames her family implies that the crime is an offense against the father of the woman, not the woman herself. This judgment rests on the belief that a woman is essentially property. If a woman is raped by someone other than her husband she becomes "damaged goods." Only if rape is viewed as vandalism does the punishment fit the crime: "you broke it, you buy it." But the real irony is that the rapist who marries his victim is in fact *rescuing* her. No other man would ever marry her now, and without a marriage, even today, an Arab woman is superfluous in her society. And the situation has been much worse:

> At the end of the forties, when the Swedish ethnologist Hilda Granqvist did a study on child rearing in Jordan, she heard reports of a European woman who had come to Trans-Jordan to help seduced or raped girls. They did not understand her. "Fallen women?" they asked with surprise. "There are none. We don't let them live." [6]

Guenevere feared that Arthur would have her killed, even on suspicion that she had been raped by Mordred, because her reputation (and thus her worth) was just as diminished by rape as if she had been "unfaithful" of her own free will. Iseult and Guenevere were only allowed to prove their innocence "by fire," an image which has a dramatic history in many cultures. In Hindu mythology the god Rama had a wife named Sita who was carried off by the demon king Ravana. Rama eventually defeated Ravana in a great battle, and rescued his wife. He brought her home, but then repudiated her, calling her "a sacrificial offering polluted by a dog." He had fought the war and claimed her only to restore the honor of his family! His wife's honor could not be cleansed so easily. Sita claimed that Ravana had never raped her, that he had touched her only when he actually carried her off, but no one was going to take her word for this. So a funeral pyre was built for Sita to throw herself into – to see if the gods would rescue her from death by fire. Only this miracle would prove her innocence.

What is dramatically obvious from these examples is that women traditionally have not been measured by the same standards that apply to men. Men are able to rescue women for the same reason that they can victimize them in the first place: because women have been deprived of the right to decide their own fates. The story of the silkie bears striking resemblance to a Japanese tale in which the fisherman does not even bother with deceit. His manipulation of the woman he desires is apparent from the beginning.

In this story a fisherman casts his nets into a placid lake and sees, not a silkie, but a crane, dancing upon the farther shore. Drawing his boat near he realizes that the crane is not a living bird, but a robe of feathers hanging upon a branch of a tree. He steps onto the shore and takes the robe. It is the most beautiful cloth he had ever seen. But a woman rises from the water and beseeches the man to return to her the robe of feathers. When he will not, she begins to weep. She explains to him that without her robe of feathers she cannot return to the heavens. The man tells her that if she will live with him as his wife, he will return her robe to her. So the woman enters the boat of the fisherman. She goes to his house and becomes his wife. But he hides the robe of feathers so that she can never leave him. Seven years pass. She bears him two daughters and a son and raises them – until the day she finds her robe of feathers hidden beneath the store of millet. Donning the robe she becomes a white-plumed crane. She flies into the heavens, dancing.[7]

The fishermen in these stories are drawn to the strange beauty of the silkie and the crane. They feel desire but it is mixed with insecurity. Perhaps because of this fear they cripple their wives by hiding the sources of their power, the seal-skin, the robe of feathers, transforming them into wounded, submissive women. In the end, just as the men feared all along, the women leave when they rediscover their own power. But the violation the women experienced at the hands of their husbands would hardly have encouraged them to stay.

The idea that women are the property of their husbands, with no freedom or identity of their own, is one part of the romantic myth which has had tragic repercussions in many marriages. It is no coincidence that men who rape or murder their wives are more likely to do so after their wives have expressed their independence, or have tried to separate from them:

> The fact that rape is used by some men out of a desire for reconciliation provides us with an astonishing insight into patriarchal thinking. Somehow intercourse, even if forced, is seen as an act of repossession that the victim is expected to honor.[8]

Diana Russell's shocking but important work, *Rape in Marriage*, reveals that forced sexual encounters within marriage may be the least-disclosed criminal act of violence. The reason is simple: for most countries in the world, rape in marriage is not a crime. Lobbying against laws which prohibit marital rape, California State Senator Bob Wilson asked in 1979, "But if you can't rape your wife, who can you rape?"[9] This attitude has had a long history. Deuteronomy's declaration of law is tragically ironic: *she shall be his wife since he has violated her*. As of 1990 Russell reports that in most nations of the world, non-Western and Western, and in eight American states, men have the legal right to rape their wives; that is to say there is no law which forbids it. In a few progressive countries and in 26 American states marital rape may be prosecuted if it meets certain requirements: if the wife reports the rape within a certain period of time, and if she was capable of giving consent. In other words, a woman who was *unable* to consent to intercourse with her husband because she is mentally impaired or was under the influence of drugs or alcohol, by the definitions of the law, *was not raped*.

These attitudes are changing, slowly; the United Kingdom recognized marital rape as a criminal act in 1991. But the cultural and religious belief that marriage gives men "conjugal rights" is so prevalent that simply passing laws which prohibit rape in marriage does not prevent it from happening. Although marital rape became illegal in Australia in 1980, in the following five years not one case unassociated with other acts of violence was successfully prosecuted. The lack of attention given to criminal acts of *sexual* violence in marriage is unconscionable considering the fact that women who are raped as well as battered by their husbands have a significantly greater chance of being murdered by their husbands than battered women who are not also raped.[10]

> *Eve says thoughtfully, "Adam didn't want me to leave him like you did, Lilith. So he tried to convince me I didn't have any identity apart from him. I was just his rib."*
>
> *"It's the same for me," says Guenevere. "When I was Arthur's faithful queen, I had value to him. Whenever his ownership was in doubt, he threatened to kill me. Lancelot always saved me, but he had a stake in me too. I never had any worth of my own."*
>
> *"Or maybe it just got hidden, like the robe of feathers," says Eve.*
>
> *"I have to think about that," says Guenevere.*

The romantic myth would have women believe that they have no identity until a man gives one to them. The longing that the silkie and the crane experience is a longing to be who they are, to escape what they have been forced to be. These stories describe the *loss of identity* that a woman experiences when she is possessed by a man, and her apparent powerlessness to choose her own life path for herself. Marital rape is an extreme but tragically common byproduct of the myth of female powerlessness.

Although the "sexual revolution" freed many women from the horrendous burden of protecting their virginity as their most prized possession, and the double standard of sexual behavior for men and women is not so marked as it has been, what is still prevalent is the passive longing for rescue that Romantic Love encourages in women. Men can go out and "*find* the right woman," but women are supposed to "*wait* for the right man" to come along and claim them. Because men establish identity through action, while women establish identity through relationship, a romantic scenario in which a man rescues a woman seems to satisfy a deep emotional need in them both. What happens after they have found each other may be another story entirely.

> *"I do not think I like it,"* says Iseult, *"that women should have to wait to be rescued."*
>
> *"But sometimes men need to be rescued, too,"* says a new voice in the crowd. Startled, everyone turns to see who has joined them.
>
> *"I'm sorry if I spoke out of turn,"* murmurs an embarrassed young woman. *"I'm not really a myth. I'm just a folktale."*
>
> Guenevere laughs. *"Don't let that bother you. We're glad you're here, Beauty."*
>
> *"All I meant to say,"* repeats Beauty shyly, *"is that women aren't the only ones who need to be rescued. That's what my story is about. I rescued my father. And I rescued the Beast."*

The story of Beauty and the Beast is a familiar one. An old man who lives in a forest with his three daughters decides to take a trip to the city. He asks his daughters what gifts he should bring back for them. The eldest daughter begs for clothes, the second for jewels and his youngest daughter, Beauty, asks for a single blue rose. In the city the old man finds a dress for his eldest daughter and a necklace of gems for his second daughter, but nowhere can he find a blue rose for his daughter, Beauty. On the journey home the old man loses his way in the forest, but a sudden clearing opens in front of him. As he enters the clearing he sees a thorny branch and upon the branch, a blue rose.

As soon as the rose snaps into his hand, a voice speaks from behind him, condemning him to death. The old man turns to face the Beast: he has the shape of a man but the face of a lion. His teeth are sharp and his fingernails like claws, but he is dressed in princely clothes. The old man begs for mercy, explaining that he has stolen the rose for the love of his daughter, Beauty. The Beast proposes a compromise. The old man will not have to die if Beauty will agree to live in the enchanted garden. When Beauty hears the tale, she assures her father that he will not have to die; she will go to live with the Beast.

Although she is afraid of the Beast, Beauty is determined to abide his company. The garden is a wondrously beautiful place, and gradually she grows to enjoy the time they spend together, walking and conversing in the garden. But every night the Beast asks Beauty the same question: "Will you marry me?" Every night Beauty replies that she cannot.

Although Beauty is happy in the garden, she misses her family and asks the Beast to let her visit them. At first the Beast refuses, but lets her go after she promises to return in seven days. In her father's house, the days pass too quickly and Beauty's sisters beg her to stay. "But if you're not his wife," they argue, "then why do you have to return? If you love us, stay here with us. Father misses you so much." Until that moment, Beauty had never allowed herself to consider staying away from the garden. But now she begins to cry, agreeing to stay with her family just a few days more. She cannot bear the thought of leaving so soon, not knowing when the Beast will let her return.

But as soon as the seven days have passed, Beauty begins to feel uneasy. She cannot sleep because her dreams are filled with images of the Beast lying on the ground in pain. Awake, she fancies she hears his voice calling her name. Her heart is filled with pity for his suffering and she berates herself for her selfishness and cruelty. She rushes back to the garden and finds him, as in her dream, lying on the ground. His eyes are closed. She touches his hand and it is cold.

Stirred by her touch, the Beast begins to speak. He tells Beauty that she has come too late: he is dying. Beauty's heart is filled with pity and remorse. She asks the Beast if there is anything she can do for him. The Beast's voice has grown so faint, that she has to lean her ear close to his mouth in order to hear his words: "No, Beauty. Only the thing you will never do."

She is terrified, but she knows now what she has to do. She tells the Beast that she will make love with him. At this whispered promise of marriage, the Beast opens his eyes. He puts his arms around Beauty and pulls her close to him. Even as he kisses her he begins to change. Where the Beast had been, now there is as handsome and princely a man as Beauty had ever seen.

"The Beast explained to me that he had been under an enchantment," says Beauty, "made to look like a Beast until some woman would agree to marry him. Only then could he turn back to his own true shape. He was a Prince, and heir to . . ."

Beauty stops speaking suddenly, because the owl has made a strange noise, less like a hoot, than a sigh. In the next moment, standing between Lilith and Beauty in the place of the owl, is a very young dark-haired woman.

"It is making me dizzy, all this coming and going," Iseult whispers to Eve.

Eve nods but her attention is taken entirely by Blodeuedd whose present form is the most fragile example of humanity she has ever seen. Blodeuedd sits perfectly still, rather like a hillside flower in the absence of wind or an animal frozen the instant before flight.

Blodeuedd's voice, unexpectedly, is low and very human: "I know your story, Beauty. But I would tell it differently."

Eve smiles. "Please tell us, Blodeuedd."

"Yes," says Beauty. "Please do."

Beast and the Beauty

An old man lived in the center of the great forest with his three sons. His wife had long since died and the man feared to lose his children to their restlessness and longings. With wives, he thought, they might find their hearts filled and choose to root there in the shadows of his forest home. "I'm going to the city to bring you home your heart's desire," he said to his sons each one by one. But his youngest son, who was troubled with a poet's heart, said, "If you would bring my true love to me, bring me a woman who is fine and fair and fey as a blue rose."

"A blue rose has never grown upon this earth," the old man protested. "Nevertheless," said the poet, "that is my desire."

In the city the old man found two sisters, poor but proud, who agreed to wed his eldest sons. Nowhere did he see a woman as fine and fair and fey as a blue rose. Sadly, but hardly surprised, the old man headed home. When the forest is kind, it leaves the ground clear in places which men call paths. But this day the forest moved the shadows and turned the paths, and a sudden clearing opened before the old man. As he entered the clearing he saw a thorny branch and upon the branch, a single, perfect blue rose. Now the old man knew that this was an enchantment, but love for his son was stronger than caution. He plucked the rose from its branch. As soon as the rose snapped into his hand, a voice spoke from among the trees. "Thief," said a woman's voice, low and powerful. "You have stolen my rose."

The old man answered most humbly. "Forgive me, but I wished only to bring a gift home for my son to ease his heart's desire."

An animal sound rose up from the forest. The old man thought it might be laughter and his heart chilled. "An expensive gift. The price I ask is this same son. You may bring him the rose; he will return it here to me."

That night, while two brothers slept in sweet contentment, the poet gazed at the strange enchantment of the blue rose which he held gently as a lover between his two hands. The next morning he journeyed to the garden. How long he walked there, he could not say. From the moment that he first entered, time lost some meaning that once it had. He ate there. Perhaps he slept. But if he dreamed, he dreamed only of the garden. After a time he remembered that he had a voice and spoke words of praise for the beauty of that place.

"Where are you?" he beseeched. "You for whom all this beauty has been made? I smell your perfume. I taste your fruit. May I not see you?" Then She was there. He had half feared to see some terrible thing hidden among all that beauty but terrible she was not, only strange. Her skin was fair, her features fine and her bearing fey as any blue rose which grew about her. Her voice was low and strong. "I appear before you because you have asked, as I am ever bound to do."

It hardly needs to be said that the poet's heart was lost all in one moment to the woman who stood before him. From that time on they were together in the garden sharing sweet fruits and heavy wine. Though she never told him that she loved him, he knew she must, for every evening she put one question to him in a voice which seemed to hide some longing or deep despair. "And would you leave me?" Thinking to reassure the pain he did not understand, each night he would reply, "No, my beauty, no, I will never leave you." The woman would smile then (she never wept), and the poet fancied that she was comforted.

Time passed in the garden and the poet sorely missed his family, and so he begged leave to visit them. The woman's reply to the poet's request was simple and as familiar to him as the twilight. "And would you leave me?" But the poet answered her that in seven days time he would return.

The house of the old man was filled with light as the poet approached, a stranger. But so many arms drew him to the hearth and into their own warm embrace that he almost felt that he had never left at all. The days passed quickly, so full of food and laughter that few questions were asked about his life in the dreaming garden. Not until he was packing to leave did one of his brothers find the poet alone so he could speak to him as man to man. He asked, with a low secret laugh, about the woman to whom his younger brother was in such a hurry to return.

The poet was offended by his brother's tone, "I never have touched her."

"Is she hideous then, as we have feared, some terrible beast?" asked the brother, his voice filled with fear, and love.

"She is the rarest beauty the Earth has known."

"Well then, is she so large and strong that you fear to approach her, or is she well protected?"

"No," said the poet. "She is slight and all alone there in the garden."

"Then do you not desire her?" the brother asked, in some confusion. In truth, during the long dream he had shared with the woman, the poet's love for the woman had so consumed him that he had not thought once to act upon it. But in the daylight with his brother's questions and mocking laughter in his ears, he thought of Beauty and the thought filled him with desire. He smiled in a way his brother could understand, then he was clapped on the back and sent on his way.

"Beauty," the poet called as he entered the garden, and She was there. Her strangeness made her so desirable, he wondered if he had ever really looked at her before.

"Come here," the poet said, surprised at the tone of his own voice, sure that she would turn and leave, more amazed that she approached. Then she yielded to him, yielded to his arms that roughly pulled her to him. He closed his eyes and kissed her. Her lips were cold.

The poet opened his eyes. What he saw there chilled his desire. He saw no woman's eyes filled with love or passion, but an animal's eyes, an animal trapped beyond hope of freedom. He remembered the first words she had spoken to him. "I appear before you because you have asked, as I am ever bound to do."

He pushed her away from himself, horrified, not at her, but at himself who had understood so little. "I will leave you, Beauty," he said. "I will leave you now." The poet was moving away from the woman when he heard an animal noise behind him. Startled, he turned to see a lioness crouched there, eyes fierce and wild, poised to spring.

As in a dream he accepted what he saw without understanding. "I am to die then," he thought. The lion sprang at him, mouth gaping, but he did not die. Instead he felt the breath of the lion on his face. A quick succession of images appeared in his mind and he understood: cruel enchantment had changed lion into woman, to dwell among men until some man might desire her but let her go. One great leap more and Beauty was over the wall.

When Blodeuedd finishes speaking there is a long silence. Finally Eve says, "I think I understand. If only Lleu could have realized how unhappy you were and how much you needed to be free, maybe you could have turned back into your original form."

"Yes," says Blodeuedd. "I waited and prayed for him to understand and let me go."

"What about Gronw?" Iseult asks. "Did you love him?"

"I cared for him. I slept with him. Did I have a choice? I had

to accept whatever man desired me. Until I was set free."

Beauty finds that she is crying. "That can't be right."

Eve says, "Blodeuedd, I know it feels like you're in prison and you need a man to set you free, but maybe you only feel that way because Romantic Love tells you you're supposed to."

Blodeuedd's face is clouded. "But I do need to be rescued."

Guenevere nods. "I couldn't end my relationship with Lancelot while he was so in love with me."

"Why not?" asks Lilith.

"Well, I suppose – I don't know why. I just couldn't."

"Because she didn't have the right," says Blodeuedd.

"Yes," agrees Guenevere. "I thought I had no right to say no. I thought my body belonged to the men who loved me, and I suppose, ultimately, to whoever wanted me the most."

"But what about what you want?" asks Iseult. "By choosing Tristan I get the man I want instead of the one they gave me to."

Guenevere shrugs. "How was I supposed to know what I wanted? I was my father's daughter, then Arthur's wife and Lancelot's Queen. Poor Blodeuedd was taken and made into something else completely. She didn't even look like herself anymore."

"It's not right," Beauty says again, turning to Lilith.

Lilith answers cryptically, "But nothing prevented the woman in Blodeuedd's story from turning back into a lion all on her own, whenever she wanted to."

"Well, why didn't she then?" demands Guenevere.

There is silence for a moment, then Eve suddenly speaks:

"Because she didn't know she could, Guenevere! Because she'd been told that she couldn't and it didn't occur to her it might have been a lie!"

Blodeuedd's eyes open very wide.

Women feel powerless because they have been told that they are powerless, told and told and told until they believe it as some kind of objective truth. Many women feel, like Blodeuedd, that they are not free to define their own identities and choose their own relationships. It is also common for women to feel, like

Guenevere, that they have no right to make and enforce their own sexual boundaries. But the powerlessness of women is the same kind of lie as the one engineered by the man who hid a seal skin to prevent a silkie from returning to the sea. The husband in the silkie story could not prevent his wife from changing shape; he could only deceive her. A woman in an abusive relationship is not actually as helpless as her abuser would like her to think; she just believes that she is and he exploits that belief. Her power has been hidden, but it is never far away. Once she discovers it again she is free to protect herself, to set new boundaries or to leave.

As suddenly as she had appeared, Blodeuedd, the woman, is gone. An owl circles around their heads twice and soars away. There is an explosion in the sky above them, followed by a whirling blizzard of white.

"What is it?" asks Beauty. She holds out her hand to catch the stars falling from the sky.

"Is it snow?" asks Iseult.

"No," says Eve, happily. "It's flowers."

The air is filled with the rush of petals, oak and broom; the scent of meadowsweet lingers.

The discovery of power, for a woman, is very often a discovery of personal identity. But it can only happen if she gives up longing for rescue by a man, the part of the romantic myth which depends on female helplessness. The classic romantic heroine sits in her tower, waiting for a man to storm the castle. It never occurs to her that she can rescue herself. Or perhaps it has occurred to her, but it is not romantic enough to suit her expectations. Either way, the limpid helplessness of the princess in the tower is a construct of the romantic myth which prevents her from choosing the life, the identity and the relationship she wants for herself.

Beauty studies a tiny petal that has landed in her hand. "I understand about Blodeuedd," she says, "but what does this mean

*for my story? Could the Beast have turned into a prince without
my sacrifice?"*

"Of course," says Lilith.

Beauty looks up. "But then, why didn't he?"

*Guenevere answers suddenly: "I know why! Men want to be rescued
too. Women think men can save them from physical danger, but
men expect women to save them in a different way."*

In the box-office hit *Pretty Woman*, a heartless businessman
"rescues" a beautiful prostitute, chiefly by rehabilitating her
social graces and improving her wardrobe. It is, as the characters
admit, a Cinderella story. At the very end of the film, however,
the ex-prostitute reveals to the no-longer-heartless businessman
that she also has rescued him. This revelation is meant to be a
twist on the traditional myth of Romantic Love, an attempt to
equalize the characters and transform the sexist assumptions in
the plot, but in fact, all the filmmakers did was to tell the story
of Beauty and the Beast. The Beast is powerless to turn into the
Prince without the selfless love of Beauty to set him free from
beastliness. She must love him for himself and accept him
sexually. When she finds it within herself to make the sacrifice
and marry the Beast he becomes a Prince, establishing the moral
that a woman's unselfish love will have its own rewards. It all
sounds very romantic. What is less romantic is the alcoholic who,
after beating his wife says, "If you would stop nagging me about
drinking, I wouldn't need to drink," or "If you'd just accept me
as I am, I wouldn't hit you." These are also examples of the Beast
waiting for Beauty's sacrifice to turn him into a Prince.

But we cannot make others love us more or treat us better by
accepting mistreatment and calling it unselfish love. A woman
cannot "save" a man any more than a man can set a woman free.
She has to do it for herself. And so does he.

*Guenevere continues. "I always thought that if I had been faithful
to Arthur, he would have treated me better. But it's not necessarily
true."*

Beauty shakes her head, suddenly defensive. "Are you telling me I should have walked away from the Beast, let him die? Isn't it a good thing to feel pity and compassion?"

Lilith laughs bitterly. "Where was your father's compassion for you when he gave you to the Beast? Where was the Beast's pity when he made you a prisoner to begin with? Why did they expect you to love them so unselfishly, when they never loved you that way at all?"

"Well, because I'm a woman," says Beauty.

Lilith raises an eyebrow, and doesn't bother to reply.

The same gender stereotyping which deprives women of identity and action denies men the qualities of emotional sensitivity and compassion: a "masculine" man does not cry or remember to send anniversary cards. The longing for rescue that a man feels is the longing for a woman to provide him with the emotional life that he lacks. What he actually needs is to develop these qualities in himself, but the romantic myth does not give him that option. The Beast is supposed to be incapable of becoming a Prince without the unselfish love of a woman to transform him. And if he dies untransformed it is, of course, the fault of the woman for not loving him enough.

These assumptions make it a simple matter for men to manipulate women. The myth of the Halved Soul which underlies Romantic Love reinforces images of male loss and female guilt. Women will sacrifice their time, their health and their bodies to "rescue" men, not only because it seems like a good thing to do, but because they would feel terribly bad if they did not. As a result a woman may sleep with a man simply because he is so pathetic; in effect he uses his emotional need and her predisposition towards guilt to get what he wants from her. Beauty is emotionally blackmailed very easily, first by her father and then by the Beast. The pity that the Beast arouses in Beauty causes her to deny her own sexual feelings in order to rescue him.

A woman may feel that she *must* stay in an abusive marriage, because her husband needs her so much. She is "all that he has."

Perhaps he has threatened to kill himself if she leaves him. He believes, and so does she, that his death would be her fault. The romantic myth maintains that her unselfish love can heal him: the more she loves him, the better he will treat her. But these assumptions are not borne out by the statistics. An alcoholic will never stop drinking because of how quietly his wife accepts his abusive behavior or how often she sacrifices her own needs to suit him. Abusers manipulate the pity of those around them.

In his novel *The Great Divorce*, C.S. Lewis makes an important distinction between the *passion* and the *action* of pity. The passion of pity, "the pity that has cheated many a woman out of her virginity," is a weapon of blackmail, used by makers of misery in the world against the compassionate. In contrast, the action of pity, Lewis says, "changes darkness into light and evil into good. But it will not, at the cunning tears of Hell, impose on good the tyranny of evil."[11] The action of pity encourages a woman to allow her alcoholic husband to feel the consequences of his actions, without "rescuing" him from them. The action of pity allows a woman to feel love for a man and compassion for his needs, but to set up sexual boundaries which protect her as well. The action of pity offers support, but does not rescue.

Beauty looks shaken. "I think I'm angry," she says.

"You are not sure?" asks Iseult.

"Well, I mean, I'm supposed to be a loving, unselfish character. I never knew anyone was taking advantage of me. It makes me mad."

"So what are you going to do about it?" asks Lilith.

Beauty shrugs. "What can I do?"

"Absolutely anything you want!" laughs Eve.

"Anything? Really?"

Eve nods and Beauty is silent for a moment. Then she laughs too. "I think I might enjoy this," she says, and begins:

Beauty, No Beast

An old man lived in the center of the great forest with his three daughters. Now this woodsman's wife had passed from the world before him and so he gave his whole heart to his children, but especially to his youngest daughter, Beauty. One day the old man decided to go the city and he asked his daughters what gifts he could bring them. The eldest daughter begged for new clothes, the second daughter for jewels, but his youngest daughter Beauty asked only for a single blue rose.

"But a blue rose has never grown on this Earth," he protested.

"I know that father," Beauty said. "I was just being poetic. I mean that I don't need anything special and anything you bring me would be very nice."

To Beauty's great surprise when her father returned, not only did he have a dress for his eldest daughter and jewels for his second daughter, but he also carried in his hand a perfect blue rose. Beauty would have been delighted, except for the expression of great sorrow on her father's face. He explained what had happened on his journey, how he had stolen the rose because of his love for her, and how a Beast had declared his punishment for the crime: he must die unless his youngest daughter Beauty would consent willingly to live with the Beast.

"Well, how long would I have to live in the garden?" asked Beauty. Her father looked uncomfortable, but he answered, "Forever, I think."

"Let me get this straight," said Beauty. "You committed a crime, and you want me to go to prison for you?"

"Or else I have to die." explained her father.

Beauty looked at her father suspiciously. "Does this Beast want anything from me while I'm in his garden?"

Her father looked uncomfortable. "I think he wants . . ." her father coughed. "I think he wants to "marry" you."

"So you're saying you want me to have sex with a monster."

"I don't think he'd force you. You can probably live safely enough in his garden."

Beauty shook her head. "I'm sorry that you felt you had to steal this rose for me. I thinks it's time for me to leave your house and live my own life. You're free to live yours, father."

Beauty's father looked frightened. "What if I told you that the Beast is probably a prince, and if you consent to sleep with him, your reward will be very great."

"You can tell him that when he's a Prince he should look me up. Then I'll think about it."

"What about your duty to your father?" he asked Beauty, angry now.

"Well," said Beauty, "if prostituting myself is your idea of duty, I guess I'm going to fail my duty. But if you're afraid to go talk to the Beast, I'd be willing to do that for you."

Beauty kissed her sisters, packed her clothes and left her father's house, stopping in to see the Beast in his garden the next day. As her father had predicted, the Beast asked Beauty to marry him.

Beauty shook her head. "Blackmail is definitely the wrong way to get yourself a girl. I'm not going to marry you and I can't stay here with you either."

"But if you leave I'll die," the Beast protested. "The only thing that can save me is for you to accept me exactly as I am."

"What *exactly* does that mean?" asked Beauty.

"You have to make love with me," explained the Beast. "Or else I'll die," he added for good measure.

"That sounds pathetic enough," said Beauty. "But pity is a bad way to start a relationship." She shook her head. "I don't think you'll die without me, anyway. Stop waylaying old men on the road, stop trying to blackmail young girls into having sex with you and I guarantee you'll start looking more like a prince!" Beauty walked away before he could think of a reply.

"And get yourself a haircut," she called back to the Beast as she left his beautiful garden. All the wide world was ahead of her.

"Can she do that to her story?" asks Guenevere.

"Why not?" says Eve. "You left the men in your story too, Guenevere."

"I know, but I was nicer to them about it."

"Beauty wasn't being cruel," says Eve, "just honest."

"That's what I meant," says Guenevere. "She didn't try to make it any easier for them. I'd feel guilty if I were that blunt."

Lilith laughs. "How do you feel Beauty? Guilty?"

"Ha!" says Beauty. "Never again."

The longing for rescue in the romantic myth is testimony to the need for healing in both men and women. Women's longing for rescue reflects the nature of female wounding, the systematic deprivation of identity, action and power. Men's longing for rescue reveals a very different kind of wounding which arises from the peculiar requirements of traditional masculinity.

A woman waits to be rescued by a man who will provide her with the identity she lacks, while a man waits to be rescued by a woman who will compensate for the emotional life he lacks, but neither rescue has an effect on the wound it is trying to heal. Men and women can support each other but they cannot, through their presence alone, make the other's healing unnecessary.

5

PSYCHE AND EROS:
The Sacrifice

Romantic Love arises in response to our various emotional longings: for wholeness, for love, for perfection, for rescue. Myths of religion, psychology and science have considered both the longing and the violence of Romantic Love to arise from *universal* qualities of human nature and have proposed theories based on this assumption. As we have seen, the phenomenon of Romantic Love logically follows the religious myth of the Halved Soul: if Adam truly lost a part of himself when Eve was created, and then was cheated of paradise because of her, it makes sense that men should try to "get something" back from women and that women should need to give "it" back, even if "it" is themselves. Psychological myths have strengthened the divine authority of Genesis by placing their own reputation behind it. Jungians interpret the primal conflict between Adam and Eve as a conflict between the archetypal masculine and feminine within us: "primal guilt lies between them, an interrupted state of enmity."[1] According to Jung, because masculinity and femininity are eternally attracted and opposed, men and women love each other *because* they hate each other: "a vehement attraction is needed only when an equally strong resistance keeps them apart." This idea in turn is used to explain the violence of Romantic Love: "Although man and woman unite they nevertheless represent irreconcilable opposites which, when activated, degenerate into deadly hostility."[2]

If romantic longing is natural, then psychologists justifiably can claim that it must have its source in our psychic make-up. Jungians are critical of Romantic Love, but they still perceive it to be a *natural* consequence of the innate and inequitable split within our psyches. Although men and women comprise some attributes which are distinctly "masculine" and other traits which are described as "feminine," according to Jung men and women do not have these traits in equal measure. Men have an image inside them of the archetypal woman, but it is an *inferior* woman. Likewise women have an image of the archetypal male, but it is an *inferior* man:

> The conscious side of woman corresponds to the emotional side of man, not to his "mind." Mind makes up the "soul," or better, the "animus" of woman, and just as the anima of a man consists of inferior relatedness . . . so the animus of woman consists of inferior judgments. [3]

Freud also perceived the sexual difficulties between men and women to be an inescapable condition, one which arises as a matter of course from our biological and psychic development. The dynamic of Romantic Love which manifests as the sexual dominance of men and submission of women makes sense if you accept the Freudian assessment of male sexuality as inherently sadistic. Freud believed that the sexuality of most men contains "an element of aggressiveness – a desire to subjugate," and that female sexuality is correspondingly masochistic. The implications of his belief are fairly horrifying:

> We know very well that the female's acceptance of having no penis is the delicate point in the development of female sexuality. In order to reach the transition from girl to woman, from frigidity to object eroticism, from homosexuality to heterosexuality, the woman must be subjected to violence: be raped, subjugated, castrated. [4]

Psychological assessments of the opposing nature of the sexes have lately been given additional credibility by sociobiologists who claim that the sexual and emotional patterns of Romantic Love are inevitable because men are *biologically* more aggressive than women, while women are *biologically* more loving: "Women follow their own physiological imperatives ... In this and every other society [men] look to women for gentleness, kindness, and love."[5] In *Myths of Gender: Biological Theories About Men and Women*, biologist Anne Fausto-Sterling reports that in spite of the lack of substantial scientific evidence for claims of genetic and hormonal inequality between the sexes, the arguments of sociobiologists are popularly believed.[6]

If we give credence to these various myths of the Halved Soul, we will be forced to conclude that Eve is the *lesser* half of the first halved soul, that Iseult is a projection of Tristan's anima, that Beauty's sacrifice to the Beast is an inevitable expression of *her* maternal estrogen and *his* beastly testosterone, and that Guenevere is a masochist: no doubt she *enjoyed* being abducted by all those men. What these models have in common is their attempt to determine *universal* distinctions between men and woman, but they also reveal their prejudices about what a normal woman *should* be, should feel and should want. Consider Lilith, the anti-hero of Romantic Love. Jewish traditions may declare her to be evil for refusing to submit to Adam, but some Christians would worry more that her refusal indicates that she is a lesbian and, thus, an abomination. While Jungians might explain that Lilith is unable to be truly feminine because she is "animus-driven," and Freudians would diagnose a serious case of penis envy, I suspect the sociobiologists would have the last word, claiming that her testosterone levels are simply too high.

The important thing to note here is that none of the experts would diagnose anything wrong at all with Lilith's refusal to be submissive, if she were a man. Romantic Love can be described as a *myth of gender*. It promises healing, an end to our emotional longings, *by proposing solutions which involve accepting or enhancing certain aspects of traditional femininity or masculinity.* The Christian myth, for instance, would allow Lilith to repent both her obstinacy and her lesbianism by submitting to a man, or at least, to male authority, while a Jungian might advise her to integrate her animus, so that she would be able to feel more feminine. A Freudian would assure her that she will never be sexually mature until she shifts from homosexual (clitoral) orgasms to heterosexual (vaginal) ones, while an energetic sociobiologist might just cut through all of these abstract considerations and dose her with some female hormones.

Many people desperately want there to be innate differences between the sexes; this is true even among feminists. In her book *Jung and Feminism*, Demaris Wehr explains that many women find in Jungian psychology an appreciation of "feminine" qualities, like receptivity and intuitiveness, which have long been under-valued. They feel vindicated after all these years, and they are not likely to want to give up these qualities to men now that they finally have value. Women are finding real power in femininity at last and they are, understandably, no more inclined to share these "feminine" powers with men than men have wanted to share their "masculine" power with women.[7]

It is important to point out that, in spite of their explicit sexism, Jungian psychology, Christianity and indeed Freudian psychoanalysis are all systems which have helped people heal. Wehr explains how women have been helped by Jung:

> Although his starting point leaves women in a deficit position with regard to natural female authority, logic, and rationality, the schema does allow women to claim those qualities via their "masculine side." That is clearly more liberating than not claiming them at all.[8]

Jungian psychology may be better than nothing, but it is certainly not as good as it could be. We are susceptible to the myth of the Halved Soul, in all of its forms, because even its sexist assumptions seem to us to be natural, *true* in some essential way. Wehr continues:

> The fact that the "feminine" represents Jung's (and many men's)

experience of what he calls "feminine" would not trouble such women because our entire society shares his androcentric perspective. Likewise, because women habitually internalize sexism, it is easy for women not to notice Jung's sexism.

Myths of the Halved Soul are appealing because they explain our problem and offer to heal us. In the story of Beauty and the Beast, for instance, we are told that if a woman loves and sacrifices enough she will win her prince, a man who needs the unselfish love of a woman to free him from his beastliness. The story has a happy ending; indeed many of us look towards Romantic Love with great optimism, hoping that a romantic relationship will make us whole. The motif of healing within the folktale of Beauty and the Beast appears in another famous love story: the myth of Psyche and Eros.

The first appearance of this myth in literature is the tale of "Cupid and Psyche" found in *The Golden Ass*, an entertaining and stylistically daring novel written in Latin by Lucius Apuleis Platonicus, a contemporary of Augustine. C.S. Lewis retold the story in his novel, *Till We Have Faces*, adding a strain of Christianity by interpreting Eros, the "god of love," as the Christ. Erich Neumann and later Robert Johnson interpreted "Psyche and Amor" as a Jungian fable, seeing the myth principally as a metaphor for female transformation, the story of women's "journey." The corresponding myth for men, according to Johnson, is the Arthurian quest for the Holy Grail.

Psyche is a mortal woman who is so beautiful that Aphrodite demands that she be sacrificed to the Beast on the mountain. But instead of dying she is saved by Eros, the god of Love, and becomes his bride. Her happiness is short-lived, however, and she ends up alone and desolate. She must perform a series of impossible tasks before she can be reconciled to Eros once more. All interpretations of the myth of Psyche and Eros agree that it is a myth of transformation and healing, but the limitation of both the Christian and the Jungian interpretations of the myth is the assumption that human beings (and women in particular) are in need of transformation *because there is something wrong with them to begin with.*

Both religion and psychology have traditionally offered healing to individuals only on these terms. Experts and authorities have concocted theory after theory to explain the wrong: Augustine declared that we are born evil, Jung maintained that we are divided and Freud that we are all sick. Each model recognizes the basis for our longings as universal, diagnoses the problem and proposes a method of treatment, a treatment which invariably requires acceptance of its own particular mythical assumptions. Christian salvation comes only after a believer accepts her intrinsic sinfulness, for instance, while Freudian psychoanalysis "works" only after a patient accepts that he wanted to kill his father so that he could sleep with his mother. It could be said that Freud updated Original Sin, but to do so he needed to establish a credibility equal to divine authority. He accomplished it by interpreting all dream symbolism as expressions of the unconscious *as he defined it*, symbols which we are all supposed to carry because we share basic drives, traumas and fantasies. Jung eventually rejected the sexually repressed unconscious as imagined by Freud in favor of a collective unconscious of mythic images, but he also insisted upon symbols which could be universally applied. Unfortunately, the search for universals in myth works directly against the discovery of contextual or individual truth.

Part of the problem is that we have been enchanted by the *idea* of universal myths. Perhaps because we are so captivated by archetypes we generally let the sexist assumptions that are inherent within them go by without challenge. The existence of archetypes only seems intuitively true because they reflect back to us our dominant cultural myths. This dynamic becomes more obvious when we attempt to consider mythical characters, not as examples of essential archetypes, but as individuals. We fly in the face of a very powerful lobby, perhaps the most powerful interest group that there is: the portion of society which *demands* that gender differences between the sexes be innate, hard-wired and inescapable.

The tyranny of this attitude reveals itself in the early history of psychiatry which diagnosed such mental illnesses in women as "moral insanity" and "hysteria": illnesses of gender. By modern standards they are ludicrous. A nineteenth-century German woman who demonstrated independent thoughts and actions, those which did not fulfill cultural expectations for women, or which simply contradicted the wishes of her father or husband, could be committed to an asylum as "morally insane." As recently as 1860 the commitment laws of the state of Illinois declared that "married women . . . may be entered or detained in the hospital at the request of the husband of the woman . . . without the evidence of insanity required in other cases." [9]

Because the dominant myth of the day sets the standards for sanity, the cause of mental distress will always appear to be the illness of the patient, rather than the illness of the family or society, regardless of the specific history of the individual. It is only recently that symptoms such as depression, addiction and other self-destructive or maladaptive behaviors have been understood not to be signs of *sickness* at all, and instead are seen as clues to the ways in which troubled individuals have been *wounded*, especially in childhood.

This simple distinction between sickness and wounding is an awareness which has brought great change to the healing process of therapy. In the late 1980s a quiet revolution occurred, as small groups of individuals began to meet in self-help environments. Modeled at first on the Alcoholics Anonymous 12-step program, and encouraged chiefly by human-service and social work professionals, these groups met, not so individuals could analyze each other, but so they could *listen* to and support each other in sharing their most painful experiences and traumas, such as childhood physical and sexual abuse, with others who were hurt in similar ways.

The theoretical implications of a psychological paradigm which arises, not from the opinions of experts, but from the experiences of individuals, have yet to be considered fully. But this idea provides the basis for our exploration of the myth of Psyche and

Eros and, indeed, is the key to the transformation of the myth of Romantic Love. *It is no coincidence that when Psyche and Eros are treated as individuals rather than archetypes of gender, they appear in need of transformation, not because they are evil, sick or incomplete, but because they have been wounded in terrible and deliberate ways.*

Every version of the story of Psyche and Eros begins with an explanation of Psyche's beauty. When Psyche was born it was commonly said that she was as beautiful as Aphrodite. Not everyone would utter this blasphemy, but it was generally agreed that Psyche was a special child. She was the darling of her father the King and her mother the Queen, and though her sisters were fair, they were not so beautiful as Psyche. As she grew to be a young woman she was so lovely that offerings were left in her name before the palace gates. When she walked among the people, flowers were strewn at her feet. Some of her admirers went so far as to proclaim that she was not only *as* beautiful, but *more* beautiful, than the goddess Aphrodite. Eventually this account reached the ears of the goddess herself who reacted with jealousy and rage.

Psyche's father, the King of a wide and fattened land, received a terrible message from the oracles: since Psyche was too beautiful ever to marry a mortal man she must be given to the Dragon on the mountain instead, as a sacrifice to Aphrodite. If this was not accomplished his kingdom would be blighted and destroyed. Psyche offered herself freely and without hesitation. It was not that she did not love life, but she loved her family more. She understood her duty and she also understood her crime. The night before she was to be killed a priest asked Psyche if she knew why she must die. "Because I am beautiful," she said simply. She knew that to name her sin was to commit it again, but she imagined that even a goddess could not kill her twice.

Psyche is made to understand that she is going to be killed, and that this is her fault, not the fault of her admirers for their enthusiasm, nor Aphrodite's for her jealousy, not even her father's for agreeing to let her die, but her own fault, for being so beautiful. Physical beauty is central to the romantic myth for women and so it deserves a closer look. Psyche's story begins in her childhood, but instead of describing *who* she is, it explains *how she is perceived*. That by itself is not strange; children often develop identities based on the traits their parents value. But boy children are recognized for making things, for demonstrating initiative or creativity, while girls are more likely to be given approval for how they look and how they behave.

Studies have shown that gender training begins at birth. Infants who are believed by an observer to be female are perceived to be more fragile, more emotional, more *feminine*, than infants who are believed to be male. As a result, girl babies are handled more tentatively than boy babies, who are expected to be more vigorous and physically coordinated, more *masculine*. As children grow, the process of gender-identification becomes increasingly apparent. In most cultures girls are given dolls to play with and to take care of. It is no wonder that a girl child soon learns that her relationship to others, and in particular, her ability to please and care for them, is the most important part of her identity. Being beautiful, or for girls, being pretty or cute is the easiest way to please.

"I was the 'beautiful child' in my family," says Beauty. "That's why I had to go to the Beast's garden, instead of one of my sisters."

"I was the 'beautiful child' too," says Iseult proudly.

"Me too," admits Guenevere. "I remember I was taught to be a princess as soon as I could walk. That meant being pretty and fragile – and loving and unselfish, too, I suppose."

"And what is wrong with that?" demands Iseult.

Eve replies. "Well, think about it, Iseult. Psyche's beauty didn't get her approval. It made Aphrodite jealous and got her condemned to death!"

"Being beautiful isn't always wonderful," agrees Guenevere. "Maybe you get admired by some people, but other people will just hate you."

Psyche's sisters, like Beauty's, are usually portrayed to be pathologically jealous of her beauty. A favored child like Psyche who naturally fulfills the expectations of her parents and her society provides a really painful comparison for those who do not or those, like Aphrodite, who fall a little short. Aphrodite's need to punish Psyche shows how insecure she is, not how powerful. But she is insecure with good reason. The history of prejudice against those who do not fulfill cultural expectations for femininity is full of atrocities. Women who have been thought of by men as unattractive, women who are not maternal, women who are childless, whether by choice or circumstance, have been stigmatized as evil or cursed. Women past child-bearing age have been considered in many cultures to be useless; they are said in Egypt to have reached *Sin El Ya'as*, literally the age of despair or of no hope.

> "The whole idea of beauty is so twisted," continues Guenevere. "I never felt beautiful. It doesn't mean anything to me at all. If being desirable was supposed to make me so worth-while, why did it always seem to condemn me?"
>
> She is silent for a moment, then continues. "My mother told me that my body made me sinful and there was nothing I could do about it. I remember being sexually admired from a very young age – oh, comments you know, or else being grabbed by my uncles and cousins and the boys I grew up with. I was always accused of teasing them. But I never wanted that kind of attention from them."

Although girls are taught to need approval, and the best way to get it is to be submissive, attentive and attractive to men, approval that is based on physical beauty is double-edged. It is very common that the thing which a girl is taught will bring her approval, her physical attractiveness, brings instead unwanted attention from men and resentment from women. In Psyche's case it also brought a sentence of death. A sexually abused child might be told that she is "only good for sex" but also that she is "a little whore": the one thing that can bring her approval also makes her worthless! Similarly, a rape survivor may be told that she was attacked because she dressed "provocatively." Ironically, after a woman has been raped, her worth is lessened in the eyes of the world: she has been violated, blamed and then stigmatized for the crime of being found attractive by a man.

Dressed as a bride, Psyche was chained to the side of a mountain to be consumed by a shadow beast, servant of the gods. All during the ceremony she displayed no fear. But when she was alone then she did cry, thinking that perhaps the gods would not mind seeing her humbled before their will. She paced the length of the twisted rock with her eyes, since plainly she could not do so with her feet, but she did not try to loosen her chains or to escape. Psyche knew that to be an effective sacrifice the victim must be willing to die.

Psyche's sacrifice is interpreted by Jungians to be an obvious example of the *universal* principle of sacrifice. The first casualty of this interpretation is the awareness that Psyche is being *punished* for her beauty. Instead, her death is perceived romantically, as if she were being *rewarded* for her beauty. Psyche is veiled when she goes to her death, like a bride going to her wedding. Erich Neumann explains the Jungian view, that Psyche's sacrifice is a spiritual event, a *hieros gamos*, a sacred marriage:

Every marriage is an exposure on the mountain's summit in mortal loneliness, and a waiting for the male monster, to whom the bride is surrendered. The veiling of the bride is always the veiling of the mystery, and marriage as the marriage of death is a central archetype of the feminine mysteries. In the profound experience of the feminine, the marriage of doom recounted in innumerable myths and tales, the maiden sacrificed to a monster, dragon, wizard, or evil spirit, is also a hieros gamos. [10]

But if women experience marriage archetypally as death, then what is it like for men? According to Neumann, "for the male – and this is inherent in the essential opposition between the masculine and the feminine – marriage ... is primarily an abduction, an acquisition – a rape."[11] While the sexual encounter of marriage is experienced by the male as "aggression, victory, rape, and the satisfaction of desire," for women it is supposed to be "destiny, transformation, and the profoundest mystery of life." To die, to be sacrificed, *to be raped, is being described as the essential transformative experience for women!*

Robert Johnson, reflecting on the myth of Psyche and Eros, regrets that in modern culture "we do not have a place for a girl's dying experience in the wedding."[12] And it can be argued that within patriarchal culture marriage, for women, *is* experienced as a loss, even as a kind of death. Women traditionally have been raised to take their "proper" role, sacrificing themselves for their families and serving their husbands. It almost sounds noble, except that this service has amounted to culturally sanctioned abuse: sexual submission or habitual assault. This is a matter of cultural history and for many women even today, it is just daily life. But the assumption that a woman's loss of power, identity and autonomy is *inevitable* in marriage *because it is archetypal* is outrageous. It does provide us, however, with an excellent example of how myths which are used to determine human universals disregard the experiences of individuals.

In Ovid's retelling of another Greek myth, he describes Hades' rape of Persephone from the child's point of view as a terrifying and disorienting loss of innocence and joy:

> She plucked white lily and the violet
> Which held her mind as in a childish game
> To outmatch all the girls who played with her,
> Filling her basket, then the hollow of small breasts
> With new-picked flowers. As if at one glance, Death
> Had caught her up, delighted at his choice,
> Had ravished her, so quick was his desire,
> While she in terror called to friends and mother,
> A prayer to mother echoing through her cries.
> Where he had ripped the neckline of her dress,

Her flowers had slipped away – and in her childish
Pure simplicity she wept her new loss now.[13]

When Neumann claims that every marriage enacts the rape of
Persephone, "the virginal bloom, by Hades, the ravishing, earthly
aspect of the hostile male," he obviously never asked Persephone
how *she* felt about being raped, or if it was for her a transformative
experience of "the profoundest mystery of life." If there were
really some *universal* principle at work when Persephone and
Psyche became the objects of sacrificial rape because of their
beauty, what is the implication for other victims of rape? Are they
supposed to feel guilty for being beautiful? Perhaps they should
be flattered at the attention?

Associating rape archetypally with heterosexual sexuality
necessarily discounts the trauma of victims. It also gives rapists
a justification for their crimes, a powerful mandate which
operates even if they are unconscious of the specific myths which
support it. The idea that women want to be "taken" in order to
be "fulfilled" is the *romantic* myth of rape. To counteract the
influence of this myth Ruth Herschberger suggests in her essay
"Is Rape a Myth?" that rape should not be classified as sexual
intercourse at all, but might be named more appropriately
"intravaginal masturbation," a label as *unromantic* as the act.[14]

*Quietly and without fanfare Persephone, Queen of the Underworld,
appears among the others, simply dressed, a somber smile on her
face. The ladies greet her respectfully, but then they are silent, a
little frightened, waiting for her to speak.*

*"I still find myself thinking," Persephone says, "if I hadn't been
beautiful, maybe I wouldn't have been raped."*

*She notices Lilith's expression and smiles. "No, Lilith, I know better.
I know it's not my fault."*

*Persephone looks around at the faces of the other women. "Rape
is in all of our myths, but it's down-played, or disguised."*

*"She's right," says Eve tentatively, breaking the silence. "That's why
Lilith left Adam. And Blodeuedd and Iseult were married when they*

were very young to men they didn't love – men they didn't even know. Guenevere was constantly in danger of being kidnapped and assaulted. By some accounts she was raped by her nephew, Mordred."

"I prefer other versions," says Guenevere reluctantly. "Where I manage to get away."

"Could you rewrite your story?" Beauty asks Persephone. "So that you get away too?"

But Persephone answers, "I'm the Queen of the Underworld. While children are still being raped in the world, my myth has to reflect that, because history won't."

"And even when we get away," adds Lilith grimly, "we've still been violated."

The image of a child sacrificed to a Dragon is a central motif in the myth of Psyche and Eros, as well as the folktale of Beauty and the Beast. If we free it from its romantic role as archetype, as *hieros gamos*, it becomes metaphorical testimony to a brutal drama: it reflects the casualness with which children are abused, with what unconsciousness and righteousness they are "sacrificed." In the well-known story of the Dragon Sacrifice there is always an isolated village or kingdom, peaceful and prosperous, which harbors a terrible secret. For generations beyond memory a Dragon has lived in the woods near the village, a lurking terror, always nearby, but just out of sight.

Long ago a bargain had been struck, a tribute, a tax, so that now once a year the elders of the village order a girl-child, occasionally a youth, to be sacrificed to the Dragon. This is a hardship, yes, but the villagers toughen to the task. Village children are raised to be submissive and obedient. The girls who are chosen (only the beautiful and the pure) are resigned to their fate. More often they are eager to go since they have been told it is a duty, an honor, a prize. No one ever mentions the Dragon.

The ceremony is treated with a reverence that becomes religious, as if the village were making sacrifices to a god. The sacrificed child is garlanded in flowers, like a bride. Then she is chained to a stone in the woods and left alone. Presumably she is devoured; no one ever stays to watch. But the village is made safe – at least until the next time the sacrifice needs to be made. Sometimes Dragon Fighters arrive in the village, eyes full of glory dreams. But none of them ever returns from the Dragon woods and the sacrifices continue in their season.

To suggest that the folktale of the Dragon Village reflects any actual or historical event seems at first to be ridiculous. How could any society conceive of such a bargain? How could parents sacrifice their children? Why would children go willingly? Why would the victims not refuse or run away?

But this story relates an aspect of human experience that is not limited to historical incidents of ritual sacrifice. For thousands of years, in most cultures that we are aware of, children have been considered to be expendable property, possessions which could be exploited at will. In the modern world there may not be fire-breathing Dragons to be appeased, but there are monsters just as terrible that families are unwilling to acknowledge or confront. The price of their denial is almost always a child sacrificed, that is to say, neglected, unloved, shamed, belittled, scapegoated, intimidated, terrorized, verbally assaulted, physically battered, tortured, sexually coerced or raped.

"'Poor Psyche," says Beauty. "Her serenity isn't spiritual at all. It's emotional. She sacrifices herself to be dutiful to her family."

Persephone nods. "Psyche's father would have lost his fattened lands if she had refused. I suspect Psyche never questioned what they asked her to do. How can a child know she has a right to safety and affection?"

"I don't know that now," says Guenevere with a rueful smile. "And I'm grown."

There are as many different Dragon stories as there are dysfunctional families, but one dynamic occurs again and again: a child is sacrificed to protect and maintain a family secret.

Very often the most severely dysfunctional families appear just like the peaceful, prosperous village. They isolate themselves emotionally from the rest of the world, insuring that there will be no witnesses to what goes on in their homes. In these families the abuse is the Dragon and the family is the village which strikes a bargain with the Dragon, a bargain which inevitably involves overlooking the sacrifice and suffering of the young.

Psyche is a *willing sacrifice*, however, a point which intrigued Joseph Campbell in his writings about sacrifice as a universal principle. He describes a ritual ball-game played by the pre-Columbian Mayans in which the *winning* team was sacrificed at the end of the game. This implied to Campbell that the victims were willing to die, perhaps that they accepted death as an honor. He compared their sacrifice to that of the Christ who (according to Augustine) went to the cross as "a bridegroom to a bride."[15] But this conjecture is an unfortunate distortion of the experience of a sacrificial victim.

A child who is chosen for the mythical Dragon Sacrifice is told and *believes* that she has been awarded an honor or a prize. This conviction and her subsequent willingness, perhaps even eagerness, to be a sacrificed "bride to a bridegroom" does not make the honor any less of a lie. Even if those Mayan ball-players were thoroughly convinced that their deaths had momentous symbolic significance, their acceptance of death does not make them any less victims of their culture's religious pathology.

The myth of the willing victim is an extraordinarily misguided one. During Adolf Eichmann's trial for his part in the killing of millions of Jews during World War II, the Jewish witnesses were asked by the defense why they offered so little resistance to their extermination: "'Why did you not protest,' 'Why did you board the train?'"[16] These questions Hannah Arendt dismisses as both "cruel and silly," and reminds us, if an answer is required, of the Dutch Jews in the Jewish quarter of Amsterdam, who "dared to attack a German security police detachment. Four hundred and thirty Jews were arrested in reprisal and they were literally tortured to death."[17] In spite of the obvious fact that non-Jews persecuted by the Nazis behaved no differently from the Jews, the question "Why did millions of Jews walk quietly to their death?"

was asked again and again after the war by psychologists who claimed to have the answer.

As recently as 1960 Bruno Bettelheim attributed the lack of resistance on the part of the Jews to the "fact" that psychologically they were *willing victims*:

> The Jews of Europe could equally have marched as free men against the SS, rather than to first grovel, and then wait to be rounded up for their own extermination, and finally walk themselves to the gas chambers. It was their passive waiting for the SS to knock at their door without first securing a gun to shoot down at least one SS before being shot down themselves that was the first step in a voluntary walk into the Reich's crematoria. [18]

His fascination with the Jews allowed him to pass over the pathological behavior of the Nazis themselves, with little comment:

> The unique feature of the extermination camps is not that the Germans exterminated millions of people ... What was new, unique, terrifying, was that millions, like lemmings, marched themselves to their own death. [19]

According to Bettelheim the Jews were manifesting a "death instinct" en masse: "Freud insisted that human life is one long struggle against what he called the death instinct, and that we must learn to keep these destructive strivings within bounds lest they send us to our destructions." [20] The unspoken implication is that if the Jews were willing victims, culturally masochistic, then the Nazis *were not quite as guilty;* perhaps because of their "death instinct" the Jews brought the Holocaust onto themselves. The same twisted logic appears in rape trials when a rape survivor must bear scars to prove that she resisted the attack. If she did not try to fight off the rapist, no matter that her life was threatened, or that she was paralyzed with terror, she may be judged to have *consented* to the sexual encounter.

But no one is born to be a victim. A boy who is beaten by his parents may be told that his suffering is for "his own good." He is expected to obediently "take his medicine" and he certainly will do so if he has learned through experience that resistance only draws additional punishment. A Victorian guide to child-rearing suggested this method of beating girls:

> Nothing like leather ... cut a strap into strips, let your governess tie your daughter down upon the ottoman after evening prayers; the strap thus cut may be depended upon to inflict acute suffering; you then make her kiss the rod and let her go. [21]

A girl who is forced to kiss the rod that beats her is being trained to accept that idea that her parents are hurting her *because they love her*, that their abuse is "good for her soul." She has, in effect, learned to be a willing sacrifice to her parents' cruelty. [22]

Sexually abused children are sometimes expected by the adult abuser to enjoy the experience. They are told that they want it, even perhaps that they have "asked for it." After the fact, ignorant but well-meaning adults may ask a child why she did not tell anyone what was happening to her, why did she let the abuse continue. Anxious to vindicate the accused adult, the questioner might go even farther: was she sexually precocious? Was she perhaps a *willing* partner? [23] But calling the submission of abused children to their abuse *complicity*, and supposing that it reduces the culpability of the abuser, is an epistemological error of the grossest variety. The Mayan ball-player who goes triumphantly to his death is violated no less by the lies that made him believe his sacrifice was necessary, than by his bloody death itself. He was violated *through* his faith and his loyalty to his culture.

Children maintain loyalty to the most abusive families, in part because even the worst situations are not bad all the time. As in the Dragon village where sacrifice is only given in its season, domestic violence or sexual abuse can be periodic or alcohol-related, which means there is always the chance that it might stop on its own – at least that is the hope. The idea of breaking up a marriage, sending an abusive parent to prison, or even just disturbing the delicate balance of a turbulent home seems more terrible to a child than enduring the fear and pain involved with protecting the secret. Children often feel stronger than the adults they are protecting, but in truth it is their inherent *powerlessness* which forces children into the terrible bargain. They sacrifice their safety, their innocence and their childhood itself so they can be fed, so they can have a family, so they can live.[24]

"We're talking about me now, aren't we?" asks Beauty.

"Well, not specifically," Persephone says with surprise. "But your story and Psyche's have common roots. You might say that mythologically, you're distant relatives."

"It's the idea of the willing sacrifice," says Beauty. "Psyche feels this huge sense of duty to her family. But no one in her family does anything to try to protect her."

"I thought that was strange, too," says Eve.

"No, not strange," says Beauty. "Familiar. When my father told me he'd die unless I gave myself to the Beast, I didn't hesitate. But if it had been me, if it had been me that had to die, unless someone in my family was sacrificed, I never would have asked them. And you know, I don't think they would have volunteered, either." She shakes her head. "I always thought my father would protect me from everything bad in the world, but when it really counted, he didn't. He gave me to the Beast."

Tragically, when children do manage to reveal their terrible secrets, when they try to ask for help, often they are disbelieved, or even if their story is believed, the circumstances of abuse may not change. If there is more than one abuser in a dysfunctional family, the person they ask for help may, and frequently does, abuse them in turn. But sometimes the loyalty of non-abusive family members is simply pulled in two directions. The terror of losing the security of a familiar family structure causes them to deny what they would otherwise be able to recognize. In the end, it is less complicated to let a child be hurt than it is to confront or refuse the Dragon.

> *Persephone recites softly:*
> *"'As Persephone cried to her father Zeus, no one heard her except Hecate in her cave, and the Sun. Zeus was seated in another place, receiving sacrifice from men and did not object to the rape of his child by his brother.'"*
> *"His brother?" asks Eve with dismay.*
> *Persephone nods. "Hades, who raped me, was my uncle."*
> *For a moment no one speaks.*
> *"We shouldn't be surprised," says Lilith, finally. "Myths and folktales are full of incest. At least they used to be."*

Sex and violence, especially in the form of incest and child abuse, were major themes in the Grimms' collection of tales *before they were edited*. When they published the stories, the Grimm brothers had no problem depicting step-mothers as villains, but where they intensified *maternal* malice, they tended to exonerate *paternal* violence. In the story of Hansel and Gretel, for instance, the father is presented as completely unwilling and essentially innocent of his part in the abandonment of the children. In even more straightforward editing the Grimm brothers also removed most of the sexually abusive fathers from the stories, even where fear of incest provided the motive for the actions of the child and was central to the plot. Maria Tatar, in *The Hard Facts of the Grimms' Fairy Tales*, explains:

> When it came to passages colored by sexual details . . . Wilhelm Grimm exhibited extraordinary editorial zeal. Over the years, he systematically purged the collection of references to sexuality and masked depictions of incestuous desire. But lurid portrayal of child abuse, starvation, and exposure, like fastidious descriptions of cruel punishments, on the whole escaped censorship. [25]

Apparently maternal cruelty was socially acceptable in a way that paternal sexual violence was not. This cultural bias was to be an important factor in the development of psychoanalytic theory. Early in his career, Freud's work on "hysteria" led to the presentation of a remarkable and courageous paper, "The Aetiology of Hysteria," in which he concluded, on the basis of interviews with his patients, that the condition was caused by incidents of incest and other childhood abuse. The "Seduction Theory" thus suggested that women were disturbed because they had been sexually abused, or as he said, "seduced" as young children:

> At the bottom of every case of hysteria there are *one or more occurrences of premature sexual experience*, occurrences which belong to the earliest years of childhood but which can be reproduced through the work of psycho-analysis in spite of the intervening decades.[26]

Freud understood that incest was inherently exploitative because of the imbalance of power within the relationship: the adult on one hand, "armed with complete authority and the right to punish," and the child on the other hand, "who in his helplessness is at the mercy of this arbitrary use of power." Freud believed that this disparity would mark the development of the child later in life "with countless permanent effects which deserve to be traced in greatest detail."

Perhaps not surprisingly, this paper was received poorly by the psychiatric community. As Freud wrote to his friend and confidant, Wilhelm Fliess:

> A lecture on the aetiology of hysteria at the Psychiatric Society met with an icy reception from the asses, and from Krafft-Ebing the strange comment: It sounds like a scientific fairy tale. And this after one has demonstrated to them a solution to a more than thousand-year-old problem, a "source of the Nile!" ... They can all go to hell.[27]

In spite of his brave beginning, it was not long until Freud changed his mind about the new theory and claimed instead that most of his patients had lied about the abuse, that their memories were in fact fantasies and repressed desires:

> You will recall an interesting episode in the history of analytic research which caused me many distressing hours. In the period in which the main interest was directed to discovering infantile sexual traumas, almost all of my women patients told me that they had been seduced by their father. I was driven to recognize in the end that these reports were untrue and so came to understand that hysterical symptoms are derived from phantasies and not from real occurrences. It was only later that I was able to recognize in this phantasy of being seduced by the father the expression of the typical Oedipal complex in women. [28]

What occurred in those "distressing hours" that caused Freud to be "driven to recognize" that women's memories of being sexually assaulted by their fathers were fantasies, and that these women actually *desired* their fathers sexually? It has been suggested that Freud had to back down from his original theory because he had endangered his own career by attempting to question the validity of the dominant cultural myth. [29] "I am as isolated as you could wish me to be: the word has been given out to abandon me, and a void is forming around me," he wrote to Fliess. [30]

The Oedipal Complex (which one is tempted to call the real "scientific fairy tale") did not disturb in the least the patriarchal assumptions of his day. Indeed, it restored Freud's career and gave him his place in history as the "father" of modern psychoanalysis. But Freud was also intent on discovering a universal psychology. If *any* father were capable of sexually assaulting his own child that meant that *every* man had that capability, or at least the repressed desire, including his own father. This Freud could not bring himself to accept, and so he chose instead to disbelieve and, ultimately, to blame the victims.

Jung apparently was aware of the blaming going on in Freudian thought: "The fact that mothers bear children is not holy but merely natural. If people say it is holy, then one strongly suspects that something very unholy has to be covered up by it. Freud has said out loud 'what is behind it,' only he has unfortunately blackened the infant instead of the mother." [31]

But even Jung was afraid to blacken the *father*. In any case, he neglected to reclaim what Freud necessarily had to deny: the actual experiences of individuals. Psychoanalyst Alice Miller, examining the denial of the sexual abuse of children in *Thou Shalt Not Be Aware: Society's Betrayal of the Child*, states:

It is meaningful that these two such different intellectual systems are essentially concealing the same situation: the real traumatizations of the first years and the necessity of denying and repressing them by means of childhood amnesia. Freud, the Jewish son, atones for his forbidden insight with his drive theory, and Jung, the Protestant son, is united with his theological forefathers by locating all evil in an abstract and harmless unconscious that is oblivious to the concrete, individual realities of a specific childhood." [32]

It is easy to see the potential for damage when these therapeutic systems are imposed on someone who actually was abused as a child. It was only through denying the experiences of individuals that Freud could believe his own Oedipal complex: the *universal* sexual desire of children for their parents. When his patients could not relate to having such a desire Freud could always claim that they were repressing unconscious material. If this approach seems to lack compassion for the suffering of individuals, it is because Freud lost his compassion for his patients as his theories changed.

In 1897, while Freud still considered that child sexual abuse might be a real occurrence, he proposed for psychoanalysis this motto: "What have they done to you, poor child?" But by the 1930s Freud could write, "Patients are riffraff." He no longer liked sick people. It seems likely that Freud's change of attitude was a byproduct of his abandonment of the Seduction Theory.[33] In any case, it took eighty years for the ideas which Freud proposed in "The Aetiology of Hysteria," and abandoned, to emerge again. Who knows but that the twentieth century might have played out much differently if Freud had not chosen to sacrifice the victims in order to protect the abusers.

The distinction between *illness* (which blames the victim) and *wounding* (which fixes the blame on the perpetrator of harm) is crucial in healing the source of emotional pain, not just the symptoms. But, of course, it is very painful to name the Dragon, to admit who the real perpetrators of violence in our society are. We still tend to blame teenage prostitution on bad kids, for instance, rather than indict the families and adult systems that failed them, even though statistics continue to show that nearly all urban street children who become prostitutes experienced incest or other child sexual abuse before leaving home.

Similarly, the moral questions surrounding abortion disguise a deep denial. Why do protests against abortion not extend with equal fervor against rape and incest or the rights and protection of unwanted children *after they are born*? Real-life tragedies involved with unwanted pregnancy cannot be sentimentalized or over simplified; as a result, they are often forgotten within the debate. It is far easier to label a 14-year-old girl who aborts her own father's child a murderer, than to name her father a rapist, especially if he is an upstanding religious man. Ironically, though abortion restrictions are meant to protect the rights of unborn "children," they simply provide another nightmarish violation (enforced pregnancy or back-alley abortion) for the thousands of sexually abused girls who live on the streets to escape abusive situations at home.

Eve shakes her head. "It makes me sick. The incest taboo doesn't stop it from happening; it only stops the victims from talking about it."

"And the experts from believing it," adds Lilith.

"I believe it," says Beauty, suddenly. All eyes turn towards her, but no one speaks.

"I mean, I think it probably happens. I mean . . ." Beauty begins to cry, noiselessly. "I'm afraid I know what my story is about. I mean I know a version of my story so horrible I don't want to think about it. But I have to think about it or else I'm being dishonest with myself."

Persephone says, "Beauty, you don't have to tell your story this way."

"But it's so obvious," says Beauty. "I was my father's favorite child. He was so devoted to me after my mother died he wouldn't even let me get married. I did all the duties a wife would do. Except one, I think."

She closes her eyes as she speaks. "The idea, of being my father's lover would have been unthinkable – unnatural and just wrong, like bestiality is wrong. And what would he have said to me, when I refused him? He wouldn't have raped me, I think. But he would have asked me again and again and again, telling me he loved me, trying to convince me that if only I could accept the unacceptable, accept – him, that it wouldn't be horrible, that he wouldn't be a beast.

"And he would have begged me. He would have told me he would die, unless I slept with him. And my sisters, their reaction, it fits too, doesn't it?"

Persephone hesitates. "Yes," she says finally. "Sexual abuse isn't always physically violent. Sometimes it's the favorite child who's the target for the sexual attention. Jealous siblings only see their sister or their brother getting something they're not. They can't know they're the lucky ones."

When we think of childhood abuse it is the abuse of girls which most frequently comes to mind; when we think of perpetrators of abuse, we think of men. It is no wonder, since this is the way that myths have traditionally drawn the lines. The truth is that men *and* women abuse children, that girls *and* boys are commonly sacrificed when they are young. It is just the *lie* that is told to girls which differs from the lie told to boys. Girls are taught that *women are naturally victims* and so any abuse they receive is only what they deserve and what they should learn to expect from the world. Boys, on the other hand, are told that *men are not victims* and thus any violence they experience is not actually abuse at all, but a kind of training which will toughen them up, and make them into men.

The same kind of cultural tunnel vision which has denied or distorted the pain experienced by boys in childhood has also hidden the violence perpetrated by women. Although the overwhelming majority of violent crimes are perpetrated by adult males and teenage boys, the pain of those children who have been abused by women should not be ignored simply because the cultural myth says that all men are aggressive and all women are loving. It is ironic that an abusive mother is called an "unnatural mother" but this phrase is not used to describe abusive fathers, as though there were something more natural or acceptable about abusive men.

Sexual abuse is only one extreme example of how girls are sacrificed. They are taught to be responsible to others' needs before their own. They are taught that their identities rest on how well they meet other people's expectations for them. But the specific ways a child learns these lessons can be very different. If a child grows up in an alcoholic home she may believe it is her fault every time her mother takes a drink; if her father has walked away from the family, she may have to carry the burden of adult responsibilities that he has left behind.

Iseult, who has been silent during this conversation, looks at Persephone. Her face is very white. "I must be very lucky. In my childhood no one abused me."

"Then you are lucky," says Guenevere. "That's wonderful."

Iseult is embarrassed, and does not respond. When she finally speaks, her voice is low, and she is staring miserably at the ground.

"I know I have no right to complain. But I have been thinking of what I do remember from my childhood. When everyone around

you drinks, you do not think much about it. My mother would say to me, 'Oh your father did not mean what he said last night. He was drunk. He does not even remember.' Or she would say, 'Your uncle did not mean to frighten you. He has been drinking. He is really a nice man.'"

This self-reflection is so uncharacteristic of Iseult that everyone stares, not wanting to interrupt the train of her thought.

"But when I was small I was frightened of them both, my father and my uncle, because sometimes they were very nice as my mother said, but I never knew when they would turn into the other, the crazy drunk men. But my mother, she would just laugh at my fears. 'Iseult, you are too sensitive,' she would say. She always defended them. She made excuses for them all the time. When my father decided to give me away to King Mark, she did not argue with him. What did she do? She gave me a potion to drink!"

Denial has been the major coping strategy for frightened and damaged adults for thousands of years. By choosing not to confront difficult emotional issues, parents and social systems perpetuate the abuse of children, often wounding them so deeply that the abuse is passed on from generation to generation.

Women have been taught to give up their dreams, their desires and even their freedom for others and to do it willingly, in the name of love. That is what they have been told love is: loyalty and sacrifice, even at the price of their own pain.

6

PSYCHE AND EROS:
The Romance

Romantic Love tries its best to fulfill our longings; it tells us that we are incomplete and what we really need is to be in love. Romantic Love distracts us with glittering hope; it promises that if we find a soulmate we will never be lonely again. And it sounds reasonable enough. If the longing for wholeness which underlies Romantic Love *does not* arise from a primal separation between men and women, then why do we long to be whole? If the longing for love *does not* come from a split in our psyches between masculinity and femininity, then why do men and women idealize each other? If the longings for rescue and sacrifice are *not* evidence of the inherent strength and dominance of men and the corresponding weakness and submission of women, then why do men go out seeking the perfect woman, while women wait at home for the perfect man to come along?

Although Romantic Love does not acknowledge it, *what we really need is to heal our wounds*. Learning how to choose and develop healthy relationships after a childhood of inadequate or inconsistent love is a difficult process. It requires that we *become conscious* that childhood experiences establish the emotional longings that we will carry with us into our adult relationships. Unfortunately, rather than admit that childhood wounds are influencing our adult choices, we usually attribute our feelings of loneliness, rage or frustration to an inadequacy of true Romantic Love in our lives!

Of course not everyone was abused in childhood. There are

many people who have grown up well loved and respected by their families and friends, but they live in the same world as the wounded people and are affected by the same gender conditioning. Cultural myths are so strong and there is so much pressure to conform to them that everyone, healthy or wounded, is affected by them. It may be overzealous to claim that all dominant myths are myths of wounded people, but in the case of the myths of Romantic Love all the popular ones are. Sacrifice, pain, betrayal and suffering, these are the things that have made the stories of Iseult, Guenevere and Beauty exciting. The real *wounding* behind the suffering has been invisible, unacknowledged and irrelevant to the romantic myth.

Childhood wounds can be described as *wounds of gender* since boys and girls are affected differently by the abuse they experience. A girl who is beaten by her father to teach her that she is a worthless female may continue to atone for her sin later in life by accepting abusive relationships, as if that is all she deserves. In contrast, a boy who is beaten by his father to "make him a man" may later demonstrate that definition of manhood with his wife, by verbally or physically abusing her when she defies him.

Still, the question of why some people who are abused in childhood grow up to be abusers while others do not, cannot be explained simply by gender. The belief that men are naturally more brutal than women is inadequate, and ignores the fact that *every persecutor was once a victim*. In *For Your Own Good: Hidden Cruelty in Child-Rearing and the Roots of Violence*, psychoanalyst Alice Miller recognizes the difficulty people have in accepting this idea. People want to believe that Hitler, for instance, committed his atrocities because he was evil or insane, not, as is the case, because he was hideously and continuously abused as a child. When Erich Fromm exonerates Hitler's parents in *The Anatomy of Human Destructiveness*, he fosters the mystery: "How can we explain that these two well-meaning, stable, very normal, and certainly not destructive people gave birth to the future 'monster', Adolph Hitler?"[1] But to Miller, the connection is clear: "It should be very obvious that someone who was allowed to feel free and strong from childhood does not have the need to humiliate another person."[2]

Not every abused child grows up to be Hitler, but those children who do grow up to be healthy adults, according to Miller, do so because they *were aware as children that they were being abused* and thus were able to acknowledge their feelings:

> It is not the trauma itself that is the source of illness but the unconscious, repressed, hopeless despair over not being allowed to give expression to what one has suffered and the fact that one is not allowed to show and is unable to experience feelings of rage, anger, humiliation, despair, helplessness, and sadness.[3]

It is this dynamic of repression that makes abuse seem, coincidentally, to be a gender issue. Women become abusers less often because girls have an easier time recognizing their victimization: they are allowed to cry. The gender conditioning that teaches boys not to feel their pain also predisposes them to abuse. Men have a much harder time than women acknowledging childhood wounds because of this kind of conditioning.

If a man admits to having been a victim, he ceases to be fully masculine in the eyes of the world; as a result men tend to romanticize childhood abuse. Physical and verbal brutality is sentimentalized, thought of as an expected, perhaps even necessary, part of childhood for a boy. Boys who are beaten are not supposed to cry, but to learn to "take it." Boys who are sexually abused are often expected by their abusers to enjoy the experience. So strong are the cultural assumptions which underlie this belief that many men who were abused as children have difficulty even thinking about the experiences as abusive. This phenomenon is described by Mike Lew in *Victims No Longer: Men Recovering from Incest and other Child Sexual Abuse*:

> In general male survivors seem to consistently discount or minimize early sexual abuse. "It was no big deal"; "I enjoyed

it" ... As one man stated, "I guess I was lucky; I got a piece of it early." Men are influenced by our culture to view sex more in terms of whether it was easy or hard to get than whether it was a positive or negative experience.[4]

According to Lew, a major turning point in the healing process for male survivors of sexual abuse is the acceptance that their "seduction" was abusive.

While women who do not fit the culturally sanctioned ideas of femininity have been declared by society to be sick, men who do not fit the model of masculinity are described as something much worse: womanly. The terror for men of being considered to be feminine is a cultural constraint which has been kept aflame by myths of female inferiority; actually it has much less to do with women than with the way men *want* to perceive themselves and the ways in which they *force* themselves and each other into committing acts of dominance and aggression.

If we set Psyche free from her identity as the archetypal female, as we have begun to do, by looking at the events in her life which may have caused her to be submissive enough to be sacrificed, then it is only fair that we also allow Eros to look at himself apart from the brutal expectations of archetypal masculinity. Because childhood wounds lay the groundwork for adult expectations about the nature of love, expectations which are dramatically different for men and women, the transformation of the myth of Romantic Love requires *both* men and women to challenge their most cherished assumptions about what it means to be a man and what it is to be a woman.

Despite the fact that the myth of Psyche and Eros has been cast as a metaphorical woman's journey, Eros' actions and feelings are just as important to examine and they provide for men as much reflection and hope for personal healing and transformation. What happened to Psyche when she was sacrificed on the mountain top? As the long evening waned to a chill and dark night Psyche heard the fluttering of great wings. A shadow passed in front of her eyes, and so great was her fear that she fell into darkness. It was Eros who approached her, the son of Aphrodite. Eros had been commanded by his mother to shoot an arrow into Psyche to make sure, if the Dragon did not consume her, that she would be degraded by falling in love with the vilest outcast of a man.

If we consider Eros as an individual, we have to wonder what happened in his childhood that would make him willing to participate in Psyche's sexual violation and degradation. It does not take much of an examination of the Olympian pantheon to see the dysfunctional family patterns which occur there on the grossest possible scale. The Romans recast Eros, the Greek god of Love, into Cupid, a winged infant who hovers about scenes of lust and rape; there hardly could be a more exaggerated image of a sexualized child. Like Psyche, Eros was sacrificed, but to the expectation of masculine brutality, a brutality that is only disguised but not transformed by the sentimentality of Romantic Love.

Psyche did not die on the mountain. She woke from darkness into darkness to find the rock replaced by a bed, soft, warm and wide. Invisible hands tended her, tucking her bed coverings, smoothing her hair. When she realized that the hands meant no harm, she was not frightened but accepted their unearthliness and waited for what would happen next. So it was that Psyche became a bride. She did not ask her lover who he was. In the darkness, beneath the power of his touch, she was content to be ignorant since he was content to have it so. He forbade her the light so that she could never see his face. She accepted that she loved him because he had decided that she should.

At night Psyche lay with her husband. By day she wandered the palace he had made for her. The halls were endless, turning upon themselves in such a way that she was always and never lost. She walked and dreamed, searching for her lover, but never finding him. Psyche had been sacrificed. She should have been devoured. Her life now belonged to the one who had saved her and if he, in his way, also devoured – was that not his right?

Instead of dying when she was sacrificed, Psyche was rescued by Eros, the god of Love. At this point we know much less about Eros' experience than Psyche's. Her life in the magic castle is full of the dream-like euphoria of Romantic Love. Being in love seems to dissolve all the pain and loneliness of her past. In her happiness Psyche can deny the feelings of terror and abandonment she experienced during the sacrifice. She can tell herself that no one really meant her any harm. She might even feel guilty for having doubted the good will of the gods and her family. It does not matter at the moment that the terms of her marriage necessitate the sacrifice of her power, her identity and her sexual freedom. What matters is that Romantic Love came through for Psyche. She was saved.

"At least Psyche did not get devoured by the shadow beast," says Iseult.

"Oh didn't she?" says Beauty. "I don't think she was saved by Eros at all."

"I don't think so either," agrees Guenevere. "He keeps her in prison, even if it is a beautiful one. The Beast's garden was beautiful, but you were still a prisoner there, Beauty."

"Psyche's story is a lot like mine," says Beauty, nodding. "I had to accept the Beast exactly as he was, and Psyche doesn't even get to see what Eros is. Is he a Beast or a Prince? She just has to accept him."

"But Psyche likes being with Eros," protests Iseult. "Why would she like being his – his – " She struggles for a word.

"Sex-slave?" Lilith suggests.

Iseult laughs. "Is that what you call it in English?"

"No," says Guenevere. "I think we call it 'being in love.'"

Iseult nods. "She likes being with him. Why did I enjoy being with Tristan so much if it was not good for me?"

Guenevere answers. "Well of course romance feels good! There were times with Lancelot when I was deliriously happy. But those times had nothing to do with the rest of my life. The romance distracted me from my problems, but it was not a solution."

She thinks for a moment then adds, "Our love had no healing in it."

Unfortunately, Romantic Love *seems* to be offering to heal us. Romantic attractions are not arbitrary: the abuse which we have forgotten will show itself, invariably, in our romantic and sexual longings. Women whose fathers were alcoholic have a tendency to fall in love with men who are also alcoholic, for instance. Women who were beaten as children may find themselves married to violent men. This phenomenon is not caused by any inherent masochism, but arises from an overwhelming desire to deny our wounds.

We want the pain we experienced as children *never* to have happened. We want those who did not love us adequately or appropriately *to have loved us better.* And so, unconsciously, we may be drawn to those who remind us of the abusers in our past. If these individuals treat us differently, then perhaps (in a flash of sympathetic magic) childhood experiences will also disappear. But healing does not work that way and the childhood wounds that we deny simply recur in our adult relationships, like repeating nightmares trying to get our attention, until we recognize the real sources of our pain.

"I was not abused," says Iseult, "and still I fell into a romantic situation with Tristan."

Persephone recites grimly:

"'Por Deu omnipotent, il ne m'aime pas, ne je lui, fors par un herbe dont je bui et il en but.'"

Iseult is silent for a long moment. "You are right," she says at last. "'By almighty God, he loves me not, nor I him; except for a herb potion which I drank and which he drank.' Just like Maman, I blamed the drink. 'It was not my fault. I am not responsible.'"

She looks at Persephone sadly. "Tristan drank the potion too. What was love and what was the drink? How am I to know?"

As a strategy for denying childhood pain, Romantic Love closely resembles chemical addictions and it is, like all addictions, *non-relational.* When we are "in love" we do not really see the other person; we see something which has symbolic significance to us for the moment, something which meets our needs for the moment, something which makes us forget the longings we have inside of us – for the moment. The addictive nature of Romantic Love makes it very difficult to base lasting relationships upon it:

> The analogy of the drug makes clear the irretrievably solipsistic, narcissistic, and segregative character of passion. Those who 'travel' are always alone. Their passion does not touch the reality of the Other, but loves only its own image. That is why marriage cannot be based on passion.[5]

When we ingest drugs or alcohol to alter our emotional state without pausing to investigate the *roots* of our fear, despair or dissatisfaction, the relief is only temporary; we will be compelled to ingest them again and again. In the same way we fling ourselves into romantic relationships without considering the *source* of our emotional need. Engaging in passionate romance may temporarily alleviate the symptoms of emotional longing, but it will not affect any of the underlying causes. Like drug-induced euphoria the passion of Romantic Love cannot last. It numbs the pain but does not make it go away.[6]

> *Iseult is sitting with her head in her hands. Guenevere asks kindly, "Iseult, dear, are you all right?"*
> *"Me? No," says Iseult, lifting her head. "I am angry. At who? I am not sure. But I tell you, I am glad I changed my story! I never touched the potion! I was not drunk when I made love with Tristan! And he was not! But maybe my father was drunk when he sent me away, and maybe my mother was when she let me go."*

Mature love is not a drug, as Romantic Love so often seems to be. It *confronts* instead of denying, and *clarifies* rather than obscuring painful issues. Only when we become conscious of our wounds and work through whatever emotions the memories evoke, can we stop playing out the pain in our lives and begin to choose relationships in a more deliberate fashion. But Psyche never had the opportunity to choose Eros consciously and her pain is hidden by the romantic euphoria. Although Psyche believed that Aphrodite could not kill her twice, her marriage to Eros will simply reprise the original sacrifice.

Months passed or years in the magic castle, who can say? After a time, through the mists of her existence Psyche began to hear voices. At first the voices were indistinct, but they sharpened into the familiar tones of Psyche's two sisters, left behind in the world of the living. Sometimes the voices chattered, sometimes harangued, but always they spoke in the same vein. "Who is Psyche's lover?" and "Why will he never show his face?" For a while Psyche tried to ignore the voices, thinking, "They are jealous of me," because the voices were often bitter. But other times they were full of love and fear: "Oh Psyche, what if he is a beast?" Then she only wanted to prove his loveliness to them which she knew, even without the evidence of her eyes.

At last she settled on a plan. She concealed a lamp beneath her bed and while he slept she cast the light on his face. So it was that Psyche beheld Eros, the god of Love. Psyche could not help her trembling. From the shaking hand which held the lamp fell a single drop of oil. Eros awoke with a cry of pain, but it turned to rage when he saw Psyche's face in the thin light. He tore the lamp from her hand and threw it on the ground. Darkness dropped like a curtain. The castle dissolved around her. Psyche found herself standing alone on a desolate but earthly plain.

The Beast turns into a prince after I agreed to marry him," says Beauty thoughtfully, "but Psyche loses her prince."

"Her god," corrects Lilith.

Beauty laughs. "Better yet, Psyche loses her god of love as soon as she disobeys him."

"But all she did was look at him!" says Iseult. "I can tell you I would not willingly marry a man I did not look at first!"

"The important word there was 'willingly,'" says Persephone. "Beauty never had a chance to choose the prince. She was supposed to choose the Beast. Psyche doesn't get to see her lover either. She has to accept him, as he is, unseen."

"Or else . . ." says Lilith ominously.

"Or else," Persephone agrees, "she will lose him and the castle too."

"But what is she actually losing?" asks Guenevere. "A man who comes around once in a while when it's convenient for him, but who doesn't let her leave, a man who controls everything in her life but won't even let her see what he looks like!"

"But what was Eros so afraid of?" asks Eve. "Why did he abandon Psyche just because she saw his face?"

"Men, men, men," complains Iseult. "Who knows why they do what they do."

"Who indeed," says Persephone, distracted by movement in the sky. "I believe we are about to find out."

Persephone points upwards and they squint at a speck that has appeared in the sky, growing larger and more distinct as it approaches.

"Is it Psyche?" asks Beauty.

"Afraid not," says Lilith whose eyes are sharpest. She grins. "I hope he's ready for us."

"He? Who?" asks Iseult.

"I think it's probably Eros," says Persephone. "He's coming this way."

They watch in silence as Eros, the winged god of Love, lands gracefully among them.

"Mon Dieu!" Iseult whispers to Eve. "But he is handsome!"

By his rejection of Psyche, Eros finally shows his face, in more senses than one. Until this point in the myth there are few clues about Eros' motives for rescuing Psyche or why he disguises his identity. But ending the relationship when he does communicates explicitly what he requires: control and anonymity. Like a modern male who resists commitment, preferring casual sex to the intimacy of a long-term relationship, Eros departs when Psyche becomes dissatisfied with the terms of the romance and asks for more. Sociobiologists might attribute this to the inherently polygamous and aggressive nature of male sexuality, but if we assume that Eros, like Psyche, expresses the pain of his childhood through his relationships, then Eros' behavior becomes more significant and complex.

Persephone greets Eros warmly, introducing him in turn to all the ladies. He smiles at them beautifully.

"I'm sorry to bother you, Persephone," he says. "I thought you'd be alone." His voice is golden, too.

"Stay," says Iseult. "We were just talking about you."

"Oh-oh," he says. "Then you know about Psyche."

"So why did you abandon Psyche when she looked at your face?" Eve asks abruptly.

Eros' handsome jaw drops. Persephone laughs. "Forgive our curiosity, but we understand Psyche's motives better than we understand yours."

When Eros says nothing, Lilith smiles at him. "You don't have to be frightened. Just because we're a mob of angry women, doesn't mean we're going to take anything out on you. Honest, we just want to ask you a few questions."

Eros looks defensively at Persephone. "I don't know what you're all talking about. I left Psyche because she betrayed me. There's nothing else to tell."

The women exchange a meaningful glance.

"Well, there's a place to start," says Lilith cheerfully. "What did Psyche do to you exactly?"

"It's simple," says Eros. "I told her not to look at me or she would ruin everything. And she disobeyed me."

Eve asks very softly, "So you think if Psyche had just obeyed you, the two of you would have lived happily ever after?"

Detecting irony, Eros says nothing.

But Beauty laughs out loud. "Oh yes, supposedly I had a happy ending. I got the prince. But what was the message? What does a woman have to do to have a happy ending? Be dutiful to her father and submit to the Beast!"

Eros smiles uncomfortably. "Persephone," he says in his golden voice. "I think I'd better come back another time."

Persephone laughs too, but kindly. "Stay where you are, Eros. Sooner or later you're going to have to face up to the nature of the Beast. Do you know the story of Bluebeard?"

Bluebeard went courting a young lady. She was unsure whether or not to accept him because he had been married several times before, and no one seemed to know what had happened to his previous wives. Still he was very rich, and when her parents pressed her, she accepted him. Bluebeard treated her well enough by the standards of the day. They lived in a palatial home. She had the run of the place except for one closet where he forbade her to go. There was a key that he kept above the fireplace which would unlock the door to the forbidden room. He showed her the key and the room, making it clear that under no circumstance should she enter there.

For a while she was content just to explore Bluebeard's wonderful house. But her curiosity grew greater with the passing of time. What could be behind the forbidden door? One day Bluebeard announced that he had to leave on business and that he would not be home until the next day. His wife knew that her chance had finally come. After she was sure that her husband was gone, she went to the fireplace and took the key. She went to the closet and unlocked the door. Then she opened the door and looked inside.

To her horror she discovered the murdered bodies of Bluebeard's previous wives, still dressed in all their finery. The lady slammed the door shut and locked it tight. But in her haste she dropped the key which must have fallen in a pool of blood, for now it was stained, and no amount of cleaning could remove the blood. She hid the key in her room and waited for Bluebeard to return.

The following day when Bluebeard arrived home he discovered that the key was missing from the fireplace. When he questioned his wife she reluctantly gave it up, and from the blood stain on it, he knew that she had seen what was behind the door. "You're just like all the rest," he said. "And now you have to die, too."

The wife begged for her life, but Bluebeard would not be swayed. He did agree to give her 15 minutes to pray before she died. She fled to the highest tower of the house, looked out of the window and prayed – for rescue! She spied the dust of horsemen on the road. Would they come in time? Fifteen minutes passed and Bluebeard called for her to come down and be murdered, "or I'll have to come up after you!" which presently he did. But just as he was about to run her through with a sword, her brothers arrived, killing Bluebeard and saving her life.

"What do you suppose was the moral of Bluebeard's story?" Persephone asks Eros.

Eros looks at his hands and does not reply.

"Talk to a man's ex-wife before you marry him?" suggests Eve, smiling at Lilith.

"How about, when you find dead bodies in your husband's wardrobe – run away," says Guenevere.

"Wrong and wrong," says Persephone. *"The traditional Victorian moral was: 'Don't be curious. There are things a woman is better off not knowing.'"*

"What?" cries Iseult. *"That is ridiculous."*

Lilith laughs. "Well, think about it. It's Beauty and the Beast all over again. Bluebeard is only a Beast if his wife disobeys him. He's a prince when she obeys."

"But that is insane," insists Iseult.

"It's not very healthy," Persephone agrees. *"And actually I think he's still a murderer whether she knows about his past or not. Bluebeard just finds it more convenient to blame his wives' curiosity than to admit maybe he has a problem."*

"Maybe he has a problem?" asks Iseult.

Eros looks up and interrupts them. "Persephone, I don't see what the story has to do with me."

"It didn't matter what Psyche found when she turned on the lamp," says Eve sadly. *"I mean, I caught God in a lie when I disobeyed Him. It's still our disobedience that's the crime."*

Eros behaved like a prince while Psyche obeyed him. He became a beast only when she refused. This interpretation allows Eros to blame Psyche for his violence. Psyche disobeyed Eros out of an impulse for truth, just as Eve disobeyed God for the sake of knowledge. They were punished, like Bluebeard's wife, not because they did not have good reason to be curious, but because they were supposed to accept *unquestioningly* the authority that controlled their lives. Eros is angry because Psyche defied his authority, his right to name the terms of their relationship. By leaving Psyche, he violently reclaimed his right; punishing her, he demonstrated that he still had control over her fate.

Although marriage laws are changing in most Western countries, they traditionally have protected the power of the husband over his wife and children. In the Middle East men can still divorce their wives with a simple declaration before witnesses, while women have no such freedom. In Israel there are thousands of women who are separated from their husbands but cannot be divorced because the husbands refuse to give consent. They are called the *agunot*, the "anchored." But even in regions where divorce is freely available, many women stay in abusive relationships because they are afraid to leave, afraid of violent retribution.

The film *Fatal Attraction* popularized the story of a woman, rejected by her lover, who seeks revenge by attempting to murder him and his family. Statistically, of course, the film has it backwards. Domestic murders committed by women are most often committed in self-defense, to end abuse, while murders committed by men upon wives and girlfriends more often follow the women's attempts to end the relationship. "If I can't have you, nobody can," is a cliche which underlies countless acts of domestic violence. The irony is that, like Bluebeard, these murderers may blame their victims, claiming that the women died *because they had no right to leave* in the first place.[7]

Of course the story of Bluebeard and the real-life examples of domestic homicide are extreme cases. Psyche was not even trying to leave. She just wanted to know who she was having sex with at night. But Romantic Love is not about anyone knowing anyone else, much less anyone knowing themselves. Few romantic relationships can bear the lantern light of truth which Psyche casts on hers. The extent to which many men require control over their relationships is grossly obvious in Bluebeard's case, but harder to see when it gets more familiar. If the wife of an alcoholic tries to encourage her spouse to get help, he might accuse her of "dwelling on the bad," or even "making things worse," as if admitting the problem is somehow worse than ignoring it. The one who insists on intimacy or commitment may be blamed, as Eros blames Psyche, for "ruining everything."

"Look," Eros says. "I'm not Bluebeard. I don't have any terrible secret. Was it too much to expect a little loyalty from Psyche? I mean, I saved her from the Beast."

"I'd like to hear about that," says Beauty.

"What happened," Eros explains, "is that Aphrodite asked me to shoot an arrow into a monster, to make sure it raped a woman named Psyche, and also to shoot an arrow into Psyche to make her want to be raped."

"Hm," says Lilith. "Tell us more."

"I know it's horrible. But you don't understand. When I saw Psyche I couldn't let her be hurt. I fell in love with her and took her to my castle. You know the rest. We were lovers. She saw my face. So I left her."

No one speaks. Finally Guenevere asks, "You say you fell in love with her. Why?"

"Because she was beautiful," says Eros.

"Not because you liked her?" asks Beauty.

"Well, how could I? I didn't know her."

Guenevere continues, curiously, "So you could be in love with a woman you didn't like?"

"Of course."

"How about a woman you disliked, or even hated?"

"I guess so," he says. "As long as she was, you know, good-looking."

"This is really interesting to me," says Beauty. What does desire

feel like for men if it doesn't have emotion in it?"

"Believe me," laughs Guenevere. "Sex is emotional for men. They're just not supposed to admit that!"

"Stop talking about me like I'm not even here," interrupts Eros, defensively. "It's not my fault if men are jerks."

"But don't you see," says Persephone, "that men base their sexual identities on whatever myths of masculinity are available to them."

Lilith laughs. "As the god of lust, you have inspired mortal men to some pretty shallow acts."

Men have been characterized by psychologists, theologians and sociobiologists alike as having an insatiable sex drive which inspires behaviors ranging from infidelity, to the solicitation of prostitution, to rape. Emotional factors are thought to be irrelevant to these natural masculine phenomena. But studies of rape long have shown that it is an act of anger or domination, not of passion, not even of desire: rape is an emotional act with a violent physical manifestation. [8] Likewise the powerful sexual attractions which we associate with Romantic Love are not based on longings which are sexual at all. We interpret these longings as sexual need because our emotional needs are too painful to face. Eros is desperately afraid of being seen by Psyche, but the myth of his masculinity will not let him admit this fear, and so it prevents him from being able to really love her. He can only be "in love."

Eros' need to control his relationship with Psyche, his desire not to be seen, his anger and violence triggered by her act of disobedience, these are symptomatic of a deeper disturbance. Eros' wounds, like Psyche's, are obscured by the euphoria of the romance, but they reveal themselves inevitably when the romance pales. The conditions of his relationship with Psyche gave Eros the illusion of control. Psyche's idealization of her invisible lover, her willingness to defer to his needs and desires, her existence led only for him, gave Eros an elevated sense of his own power and importance in the world. When idealization was no longer enough for Psyche and she wanted to see Eros, when she dared to challenge his authority, when she made a decision, in short, for herself rather than for him, his tenuous illusion was shattered.

Adult male rage and need for control can only be understood in the context of the powerlessness and victimization experienced by boy children. As Miller points out, only a child who has been humiliated will need to humiliate others as an adult; only a child who has been powerless will need to experience control over others; only a child who feels guilty will need to blame.

Eros looks at Persephone. "I'm going to leave now. I didn't come down here to get beat up by a lot of women."

"Is that what it feels like we're doing to you? Beating you up?" asks Persephone.

Eros gives Lilith a sideways glance.

"Wait a minute," says Lilith. "I think he's talking about me in particular. Eros, do you have a problem with me?"

Eros lowers his lids, embarrassed. "I shouldn't expect to get any understanding from you. You don't especially like men, do you, Lilith?"

Lilith laughs. "I must confess I am immune to your peculiar charms, Eros, if that's what you mean. But I don't dislike you. I'm as sympathetic to your misfortunes as I was to Guenevere's."

"It's just not going to feel like sympathy while you're still deceiving yourself," Guenevere says, smiling at Lilith. "Believe me, I know."

"Deceiving myself?" asks Eros, incredulous. "Deceiving myself about what?"

"About Psyche's guilt," says Persephone gently. "We're all prepared to be compassionate about the real source of your pain. But as long as you insist on pitying yourself and blaming Psyche, you'll get no sympathy from any of us – not even from Iseult."

Iseult, who is at this moment staring at Eros' shapely thigh, looks up, and blushes crimson. "Oui. I mean, non. I mean, you cannot blame Psyche for wanting to see you!"

Lilith laughs again. "Iseult means you can't blame Psyche for wanting to know you. And that goes for the biblical sense, too. How come you get to 'have' Psyche, and she doesn't get to 'have' you?"

Eros looks confused now. "Well, I'm the man and . . ."

Persephone interrupts him, "That explanation isn't going to work anymore, Eros. You're going to have to look deeper than that."

"Look deeper?" says Eros, and now it's his turn to blush. "I hope you're not talking about the Oedipal complex. I don't want to sleep with my mother, even if she is Aphrodite."

"Freud had it backwards," says Persephone kindly. "But perhaps your mother wanted to sleep with you – and maybe your father too." Eros looks less shocked than offended. He stretches his wings as if to fly away.

There is a tendency among gay men to think of ancient Greece romantically, as if it had been a golden age for homosexuality. But what we now think of as homosexuality, the consensual involvement of two male adults who are in sexual and emotional relationship to each other, is not what the Greeks were up to. Adult men in ancient Greece were not culturally sanctioned to be involved with each other, but to take pubescent boys as lovers, an arrangement which was hardly conducive to equality since the adult enjoyed every social and sexual advantage over the child:

> This inequality, so like the heterosexual male/female combination, inevitably resulted in men trifling with boys as they did with women. They took them as concubines, bought and sold them in prostitution . . . Some boys were violated, raped and forced into sexual slavery. And since soft femininity was so desired, many boys were castrated, for men found in them the height of pleasure.[9]

Florence Rush chronicles the long history of child sexual abuse in *The Best Kept Secret: Sexual Abuse of Children*. What is most shocking about cultural habits of abuse, from pederasty in ancient Greece, to child prostitution in Victorian England, to child marriage in India (legal until 1955), is how rarely it has been considered to be abuse, much less to be an act of criminal violence. Instead, children have been treated as property to be owned, sold and used. What all manifestations of child abuse have in common is *the absolute powerlessness of the child.*

The Greek philosopher with his adolescent lover, the wealthy Victorian with his virginal whore and the middle-aged Hindu with his 9-year-old bride all believed they were making use of what was theirs. The belief that children are the property of adults is the assumption which underlies most child abuse. In ancient Greece, as indeed everywhere, cultural myths justify the appetites of the powerful. In his myth of the Halved Soul, Plato postulated cynically that humanity was originally dual, and that one of these primal pairs consisted of two males who were split in half. This myth seems to explain homoeroticism, but of course, only as it was acceptable to the Greeks. Plato's fable asserts that because of the primal split, *men naturally desire immature youths, while boys naturally want to be sexual objects of older men!* [10]

In spite of the implied equality of a primal split in *half*, interpretations of the myth of the Halved Soul always attribute greater power and importance to the half that is the adult male, while the lesser half, woman or child, is supposed to be fulfilled through domination by the male. Greek poetry is full of romantic descriptions of the feminine charms of young boys. "Oddly enough," Rush notes, "we hear nothing from youths admiring the hairy thighs and bristling lips of their bearded lovers." [11] Apparently Plato eventually came to perceive this imbalance: "As wolves for lambs," he said, "so lovers lust for boys."

Aristotle described women as impotent males long before Freud defined them as "castrated." But Aristotle elaborated his metaphor by declaring that "a boy is like a woman in form." Of course the description is not literally true. Boys have male genitalia. They do not have breasts. So what is it about boys that makes them like women? Sexually, it is their vulnerability to assault and socially, it is their powerlessness. The sexual violation of boys in the modern world might be appropriately described as the "best-kept secret" of all. The fact that it is reported to occur significantly less frequently than sexual abuse of girls may be misleading, since it is more ambiguous and misunderstood, both by society and the victims themselves. Although it is men who usually target boys sexually, homosexual men attack children much less frequently than heterosexual men; in fact, men who target boys for sexual attack do not necessarily consider themselves to be homosexual at all.[12] This is an important point which has to do with cultural definitions of masculinity. Once a youth matured in ancient Greece he was expected to abandon his dalliances with older men and turn to women and boys himself, moving from the passive "female" role to the active "male" role. A man who kept to these guidelines could rest assured of his masculinity. A man who did not, a man who continued to demonstrate "feminine" characteristics and to seek adult lovers, was ridiculed and despised. This division of masculine and feminine roles in male homoeroticism has appeared in many diverse cultural contexts. The ultimate result is that a dominant male can "possess" a submissive male or a boy child without threatening his masculinity or being considered to be less than a man.[13]

The type of homosexual behavior that is prevalent among incarcerated men often plays by these rules. In Manuel Puig's novel, *Kiss of the Spider Woman*, two men share a prison cell. As their friendship develops one of the men, who is a "feminine" homosexual, "gives" himself to the other man whose masculinity and heterosexuality are never in doubt, even after the act. According to the myths and expectations of our society, it is only the "object" of a homosexual act who (having been used "as a woman") must question his masculinity. Mike Lew reports that boys who are assaulted frequently worry that the experience has *made them gay* or perhaps even *proves* that they are gay.[14] In order to demonstrate that they are not (or if they are, to show that in any case it does not make them feminine), some boys may become abusive themselves. In ancient Greece this transformation from victim to abuser was a cultural rite of passage.[15]

The brutality that boys routinely experience as they grow up is not confined to sexual abuse, nor does it come only from parents, but is part of a process of male socialization which is carried out by siblings and peers. Colin Turnbull turned his anthropologist's eye to his own childhood within the British public school system, describing how sexual brutality was accepted as part of the normal, perhaps even necessary development of masculinity:

> Sex became something private and shameful, unnatural and debasing rather than public and joyful, responsible and ennobling. Sex was sullied by the same values we learned in other ways; deceit, violence, and competition ... Within my first week in a school dormitory, I saw everything, starting with the gang rape of a friend of mine who did not yell for help or scream as I would have done. As he fought silently, he just cried. [16]

What is particularly twisted about this type of violent act is that the first sexual experiences of Turnbull and his fellow students were "systematically divorced from normal human relationships." Brutal homosexual attack was acceptable behavior because it was perceived to be masculine, while ordinary affection between boys was suspect:

> If two boys formed a liaison because of mutual affection and respect, whether such a liaison was accompanied by sexual interaction or not, the two were condemned publicly and accused of all manner of perversions. Yet gang rape or splattering sperm on walls was just "good clean fun." [17]

Not all boys become victims or witnesses of sexual assault, but most boys will experience the powerlessness and terror of being persecuted by older boys, siblings or peers. No boy escapes the barrage of propaganda from books, television, films, toys and games which teach him what a real man and male sexuality is supposed to be. What separates "the men from the boys" has traditionally been simple to determine: who stands up under attack, who submits, who cries, who runs away, who gets revenge.

Locker room boasting about sexual exploits is a cliché which illustrates the extent to which boys must *prove to each other that they are men*, or to say it another way, to prove that they are not *women*.

The familiar childhood experience of being treated as the property of adults is no less painful for girls than for boys, but the myths of femininity are designed to make girls accept their powerlessness. In order to distinguish themselves from girls and to become men, boys are supposed to demonstrate power (or at least the illusion of power) by abusing the powerless and "possessing" others rather than being "possessed" by them.

"You can leave if you want to, Eros," says Lilith. "You've done it before."

Eros turns angrily to Lilith, "I know what your problem is. You hate men. All of you, you're angry at men and you're taking it out on me. Well, I've never done anything to any of you."

"Cousin," says Persephone softly. "Once you shot an arrow at Hades and Hades raped a child."

Eros looks away from Persephone. He is silent for a long moment.

"I'm sorry, Persephone. I've always felt bad about that. You know how Zeus and Aphrodite involved me in their affairs. I had to shoot arrows at whoever they wanted to curse with sexual desire."

"What a terrible thing they asked you to do," says Beauty. "Did they treat you in a sexual way too?"

Eros looks uncomfortable. He hesitates, then shrugs. "You know my mother, Aphrodite. I guess she always treated me more like a lover than a son. Oh she never – we never – you know, but she always wanted me to be close to her. And of course, it was my job to bring her lovers. I did that for Zeus too."

"Was Zeus your father?" asks Beauty.

"Aphrodite was never sure who my father was, but Zeus was my father figure, I guess you would call it."

"Well, Zeus was my father," says Persephone. "I know what he's like. Not exactly a healthy role model for a child."

"You mean his sexual habits?" Eros asks.

"She means, he's a rapist," says Lilith.

After a moment, Eros nods. "Yes. He's a rapist. I suppose you think I'm one too, because I shot arrows for him."

Persephone shakes her head. "Zeus and Hades are responsible for their own actions just as you are responsible for yours."

"Listen," says Eros. "I'm the god of sexual desire. I've had to live up to that. My reputation depends on the number of women I can – " he coughs, " – captivate."

"So Psyche was just another conquest for you?" asks Guenevere with distaste.

"No," says Eros quickly, "Psyche was different."

"How, different?" asks Beauty.

"I already said. I was in love with her. She was the most beautiful woman I'd ever seen. And there was something else about her too, something pure."

The myth of Romantic Love is often used by men to deny the myth of brutal male sexuality which they have internalized. Men concoct wild idealizations of female virginity to distance themselves from their own sexuality and the beastliness they fear must be within them. The belief that all men are potentially monstrous can be described as the myth of the "beast within." It is an idea which is at the heart of the myth of the Halved Soul, and has been echoed again and again by the experts. What was theology to Augustine and psychology to Freud became a matter of science to sociobiologists:

Over and over again in recent years, popular accounts of sociobiology have reverted to a secular version of the doctrine of original sin. By replacing the legendary past of the Garden of Eden with the prehistoric past of our evolutionary ancestry, these accounts reproduce the dualism of nature and grace in Christianity as the opposition between an ancient core of biological impulses and a modern overlay of cultural constraints. This transformation amounts to the replacement of one myth by another, which may be termed the myth of the beast within.[18]

Some sociobiologists have gone so far as to claim that the ability to rape is not only a natural biological function, but an evolutionary strategy:

> We suggest that *all* men are potential rapists . . . We expect that the probability of a particular individual raping will be a function of the average genetic cost/benefit ratio associated with the particular conditions he faces. [19]

The myth of the "beast within" also maintains that a women's appearance or behavior can entice or civilize the beast; some women are "good" and those are the women you marry; other women are "bad" and those are the women you sleep with. This is the logic behind the veiling of Arab women. Since men are not supposed to be able to control their sexual desires, a woman who exposes her face or her arms is a bad woman and no virile man should be expected to refrain from violating her. American history provides another dramatic example of this attitude. Southern white "gentlemen," who took pride in the courtesy and respect they showed to southern white "ladies," thought nothing of raping black women, an attitude which lasted long after slavery had been abolished:

> From emancipation through more than two-thirds of the twentieth century, no Southern white male was convicted of raping or attempting to rape a black woman. Yet the crime was so widespread that the staff of the National Commission on the Causes and Prevention of Violence admitted in 1969 that the few reported instances of the crime reflected not the crime's low incidence but the fact that 'white males have long had nearly institutionalized access to Negro women with relatively little fear of being reported.' [20]

Judgments about the goodness or badness of women, their purity or immorality, are all fantasies and projections which relate to the myth of the "beast within." It was inevitable that Psyche should stray from the narrow definitions that Eros required of her. Psyche began as a good woman, a virgin, a willing sacrifice, but became a bad woman when she desired to know her husband, and disobeyed him. Eros' treatment of Psyche varies accordingly. When *she* is good, he is a prince; when *she* is bad, he is a beast.

"If you loved Psyche so much, why did you abandon her?" asks Guenevere pointedly.

Eros shakes his head. "You make it sound like I wanted to leave her. I didn't. That's why it hurt me so much when she betrayed me."

"Stop saying she betrayed you," says Eve angrily. "She did what she had to do and she did it for you, too."

Eros looks at Eve with surprise. "But our relationship was fine the way it was."

"Oh yes?" asks Lilith. "What did you like about it?"

"Well, we always had great sex. And it wasn't just me," Eros adds quickly. "Psyche liked it too."

"Did it ever occur to you that maybe sex wasn't enough for her?" asks Guenevere dryly.

"But I gave her everything else she needed too – food, clothes, an exotic place to live. What else did she need?"

"How about a life?" mutters Guenevere.

After Eros left Psyche alone in the wastes she wandered without direction, giving no notice to hunger or weariness, to aching limbs or bleeding feet. She paused only when her path was blocked by a swiftly flowing river. Without a moment's thought she began to wade into the water, meaning to end her terrible despair in death. But Psyche's suicidal depression is rooted less in Eros' abandonment of her than in the older pain, the abandonment and betrayal of her family. Why else would Psyche have been able to accept the inequitable terms of her marriage so easily, and why would it be such a terrible loss when it was gone? Psyche was powerless, without identity. She invested so much of her own identity into her invisible god, that when he was gone she lost herself as well. Since romantic relationships often serve as a smokescreen, a way to deny our childhood wounds, the loss of romantic love may throw us into a despair that is out of proportion to what we are actually losing at the moment.

Fortunately Psyche's suicide was interrupted by the sound of laughter behind her. The river rushed so furiously around her knees it was only with difficulty that she managed to turn. She saw the god Pan sitting on the bank with a nymph on his lap. Somehow she could not drown herself while he was watching her. She found herself wiping her eyes and walking back towards him. Pan seemed to know all of her story already and his kind words soothed her aching grief. When he eventually leaped up to chase the playful nymph he called to Psyche over his shoulder, "Don't kill yourself. Pray to Eros. Pray to the god of Love!" The idea of praying to the lover who had abandoned her struck Psyche as so funny that she actually laughed – and her wasting despair was ended.

But Psyche also knew now that she was pregnant. There was nothing left for her but to visit Aphrodite's shrine and beg for mercy and forgiveness. Aphrodite was furious with Psyche for having survived. She declared to the weeping girl another sentence of death for her and her bastard child, with only one condition of mercy. If Psyche could complete four tasks in just four nights, she might live.

"Seems like you neglected to tell us something," says Guenevere.

"What do you mean?" says Eros defensively. "I swear I didn't know Psyche was pregnant when I left."

"We're not accusing you," says Persephone. "But you must know how common it is for abandoment to follow pregnancy. In fact, it's often unexpected pregnancy that shines the lantern light on a romantic affair."

"How frightened Psyche must be," says Iseult, "to be having a child all alone, and to be poor and want to die."

Lilith nods. "Everyone knows that a pregnant woman without a husband is a whore. And her kid is a bastard unless some man will claim it."

"It's not my fault the world won't accept her," says Eros. He ignores a glare from Guenevere and continues. "And what was I supposed to do anyway? Live openly with a mortal?"

Persephone shrugs. "What do you think?"

He looks around at the expectant faces. He takes a deep breath. "OK, maybe it was a heartless thing to do, leaving Psyche the way I did. But I'm the god of erotic love. Staying with Psyche would have ruined my reputation."

"Love-'em-and-leave-'em Eros," says Lilith. "What a guy."

"Persephone!" protests Eros. "I didn't come here to be – "

Persephone interrupts him. "What did you come here for?"

Eros looks down. "I miss Psyche," he says quietly. "I wanted you to help me get her back."

Persephone shakes her head. "I'm sorry, Eros. You can't get Psyche back. She's not yours anymore."

If men are truly driven by a psychological need to dominate others, and a biological urge for personal gratification so intense that it is natural for them to disregard the feelings, the needs and even the rights of the women they sleep with, then the myth of the Halved Soul provides an accurate explanation for human longing and Romantic Love should be an effective strategy for fulfilling the longing. But precisely because the myth of masculine sexuality is *not* a natural psychological or biological condition of being male, *the expectation that men must demonstrate sexuality "divorced from human relationship" to prove that they are men is a terrible wound that all men carry,* much as women carry the burden of collective female inferiority.

The way that individual men are affected by this wound can differ widely. Some men will internalize the brutality as part of their own sexual identity. So familiar is the myth that women have a desire to be raped, overpowered or otherwise claimed, that many men sincerely believe if they do not act in such a way women will not consider them to be attractive. Other men will reject the traditional images of male sexuality with horror, but then will be at a loss to find healthy images with which to replace them.[21]

These wounds of gender, for women, the myth of the willing sacrifice and for men, the myth of the beast within, are also romantic myths. Men and women try to ease their longings by engaging in romantic relationships. The attempts will invariably fail. The longings for love, for wholeness and for rescue have all arisen from wounding, but the traditional myth of Romantic Love will never acknowledge the wounds.

7

PSYCHE AND EROS:
The Tasks

The romantic myth of the Halved Soul is inadequate as a strategy for healing precisely because it reinforces the gender distinctions which underlie our wounds. It is difficult to heal childhood wounds without recognizing that the stereotypes we internalized when we were children appear dysfunctionally and sometimes pathologically in our adult relationships. While Eve believes that women are guilty of causing the suffering of men, she will always be submissive to Adam; while Guenevere believes that women are responsible for the sexual desires they inspire in men, she will never have a sexuality of her own; while Beauty believes it is the duty of women to sacrifice themselves for men, she will remain a victim, in need of rescue.

Fortunately healing *is* possible for these characters and for all of us. When myths of femininity are unmasked and released, healing follows as a matter of course. When Eve refused to be Adam's scapegoat she became his equal instead; when Guenevere refused to be defined by physical attractiveness she gained personal identity; when Beauty refused to be sacrificed she was able to set herself free. In the same way, by challenging the myths of masculinity Eros has the opportunity to heal his wounds as well.

From the outside it looks as if the Jungian myth of the Halved Soul could help a man do just that, by encouraging him to integrate his *anima*, his "feminine" side, in order to have access to qualities of emotional sensitivity and intuition, qualities which men and patriarchal culture in general have undervalued and rejected. Likewise, a woman is advised to integrate her *animus*, in order to develop the "masculine" qualities of logic, justice and rationality. Just as Romantic Love advises us to seek wholeness through union with another person, Jung suggests that we unite with the "other half" that is within us and become more psychically androgynous.

But androgyny is a frightening concept for many people, conjuring up images of a world filled with passionless neuters. This may be why Jung insisted that a healthy woman should remain mostly feminine: more emotional and less rational, and that a healthy man should remain mostly masculine: more logical and less intuitive. The Jungian myth never intended to allow men and women to have these attributes in equal measure. According to Jung, a man should recognize and *integrate* his feminine side, but he should never cease to be masculine in his active conscious life:

> Since masculine and feminine elements are united in our human nature, a man can live in the feminine part of himself, and a woman in her masculine part. None the less the feminine element in man is only something in the background, as is the masculine element in woman. If one lives out the opposite sex in oneself one is living in one's own background, and one's real individuality suffers. A man should live as a man and a woman as a woman. [1]

Unfortunately, not only polarization but *inequality* between the sexes is implicit in Jungian thought. It is certainly true that many men lack empathy and that many women lack independence, but, as we have seen, the limitation of the Jungian paradigm rests in its insistence upon the *archetypal* nature of gender distinctions. Robert Johnson defined archetypes as "those ancient, embedded patterns of thought and behavior laid down in the unconscious of the human psyche through countless years of evolution." [2] But when human *behavior* is used to define human *nature*, without taking into account the cultural and social influences which may affect it, the resulting arguments are tendentious and occasionally absurd.

In the pre-civil war American south, for instance, whites believed that Africans were innately "slavish" because of the obsequious behavior of slaves. This circular logic has been used again and again to support both sexism and racism. Women are raised to be "feminine," and when they learn their lessons well, they certainly can be observed to act in a "feminine" manner. But in spite of the explicit conditioning, their actions are still taken as *proof* that women are *naturally feminine*. In Schopenhauer's essay "On Women" he confidently declares:

> That woman is by nature meant to obey may be seen by the fact that every woman who is placed in the unnatural position of complete independence, immediately attaches herself to some man, by whom she allows herself to be guided and ruled. It is because she needs a lord and master.[3]

The belief in women's natural subservience has had a long history. According to Aristotle, "The male is by nature superior, and the female inferior; and the one rules and the other is ruled." He uses this judgment to support not only sexism, but slavery as well: "that some should rule, and others be ruled is a thing, not only necessary, but expedient; from the hour of their birth, some are marked out for subjection, others for rule." The idea that women incarnate into a subservient feminine psychology because they are biologically female is an assumption which is similar in principle to historical justifications of slavery and the racism of caste systems in general. In India, an individual who is born into a family of low caste is expected to demonstrate specific personality characteristics. Of course, surrounded by those of his own caste and given few opportunities to be other than his caste allows, it is likely that he will exhibit the expected traits. His own behavior can be used easily (and unfairly) to justify and reinforce the inequalities of the caste system.

In the famous nineteenth-century treatise, *The Subjection of Women*, John Stuart Mill recognized that both sexism and racism rely on the premise of *universal* qualities of human nature:

> Of all the vulgar modes of escaping from the consideration of the effect of social and moral influences upon the human mind, the most vulgar is that of attributing the diversities of conduct and character to inherent natural differences.[4]

Mill's willingness to denounce the economic and sexual bias of the traditional marriage contract which institutionalized the slavery of women, and his very non-traditional marriage to the strong-willed Harriet Taylor, stood in contrast to the attitudes and behaviors of the men of his day. Significantly, Mill's critics would eventually attack not his arguments, but his masculinity: "For though he could not be argued down by reason even after he was dead, it could be asserted that he was more a woman than a man, and as a woman, need not be listened to."[5]

That Mill's critics should judge him to be *feminine* for refusing to condone abusive behavior in men is a revealing indication of the emotional difficulties men have in accepting women as social equals. When Qasim Amin, an Egyptian lawyer and judge, published *The Liberation of Women* in 1899, claiming that Islam did not require women to wear the veil or remain in seclusion and that, in fact, these traditions denied women the basic rights and privileges that Islam granted to them, more than 30 books were published to refute him.[6] The violent emotional reactions that men experience when faced with the social equality of women cannot be blamed on religious devotion, even if it is cloaked in religious terms.

Recognizing the link between masculine aggression and sexist attitudes, Eli Sagan explains that non-aggressive qualities have been named "feminine" by frightened men and it is this fear which makes it so difficult for men to revise their judgments of female inferiority:

Men have used the various forms of sexism to defend their fragile masculine identity. When one asks a man to give up sexism, one is not just appealing to him to welcome half of humankind as his equal. One is also insisting that he take the enormous risk of losing his own gender identity. It is no wonder that he is willing to do almost anything else before assuming that hazard.[7]

By describing certain human traits as feminine, rather than referring to them in gender-neutral terms, Jung effectively ensured that men would never be able to accept them. The fear of being considered to be womanly is too powerful a cultural constraint. As Demaris Wehr explains, "Jung's intention with the anima concept was to encourage men to claim this image as part of themselves, but the symbolic feminine language functions at the same time to keep men one step removed from a full realization of their human frailty, emotionality, and vulnerability."[8] Fortunately social equality does not require that men and women blend into sexless androgynes, and wholeness does not need to be a question of gender. In order to become whole individuals, every one of us needs to be emotional *and* rational, intuitive *and* logical, nurturing *and* just. Arbitrarily classifying these characteristics as masculine or feminine is unnecessary and self-defeating. When it is *masculine* to be intuitive and nurturing men will be able to develop these traits: "If men felt these qualities fully as theirs, rather than as belonging to their animas, they would be closer to the truth. They would also be closer to feeling generally, and would be less alienated and afraid of women, the anima, and the 'feminine.'"[9] When it is *feminine* to be rational and strong more women will be able to claim these characteristics as well. But there is already less of a stigma for women who exhibit "masculine" traits, than for men who appear "feminine." There is no equivalent of the "tomboy" for girlish boys, for instance: being called a "sissy" is never a compliment to a boy. Many girls will shed "boyish" ways when they discover that femininity is necessary to gain approval from men, but they do not *fear* masculinity in themselves and other women the way men fear femininity in men. For this reason one suspects that the polarization of masculine and feminine traits which Jung observed is more distinct in men than it is in women, perhaps because it is more zealously enforced. Women may not be as dissociated from the supposedly "masculine" traits as men are from the "feminine" ones. Jung himself noted:

So far as my experience goes, a man always understands fairly easily what is meant by the anima . . . But I have, as a rule, found it very difficult to make a woman understand what the animus is, and I have never met any woman who could tell me anything definite about his personality. [10]

It is obvious that both men and women are in need of healing, but it may not be accurate to assume that what each sex needs to be whole is the mirror image of what the other needs. Men and women are wounded in *parallel*, rather than opposite, ways. If the specific nature of their wounding is taken into account, rather than being explained away by the myth of the Halved Soul, the emotional adventure of Psyche and Eros provides a remarkable approach to healing that leads away from traditional gender distinctions and towards a transformation of Romantic Love. The healing begins where the romance ends.

Rejected by her lover, pregnant and all alone in the world, Psyche faced the first of four impossible tasks. Aphrodite demanded that she sort through an enormous pile of seeds, wheat, millet and barley, putting each into its own pile, and she must finish before the dawn. The task was so daunting Psyche lay down on the ground and cried herself to sleep. But during the night a group of ants who were investigating the seeds sorted them into neat and separate piles. In the morning, expecting death, Psyche awoke to see that her task was complete.

The act of sorting seeds is an obvious metaphor for the reasoning capacities of the human mind, one realm in which women have been perceived to be deficient. The assumption of men's superiority over women has been used as the basis for traditional divisions of work roles by gender. What is designated to be exclusively men's work or women's work has differed widely from culture to culture. But the work done by men tends to be perceived as being more difficult and confers a higher status than the work done by women.

When it has suited men to use their greater physical strength as an indication of their masculine superiority, for instance, they have done so. For most of the world physical strength has come to be defined by upper body strength and muscular mass, which favors the anatomical structure of men, rather than lower body strength and general endurance, which favors the physical structure of women. But ironically, in cultures where physical labor (especially the carrying of burdens) is regularly performed by women, physical strength is seen as a mark of inferiority.[11]

The judgment of the intellectual superiority of men has, likewise, not risen from any objective test, but from observation of the behavior of men and women which has seemed to reveal that men are more rational than women and women are more emotional than men. These observations have been used as justification for the traditional divisions of work by gender. Women are supposed to be intellectually suited for relational tasks which involve nurturing and caretaking. According to Schopenhauer:

Women are directly fitted for acting as the nurses and teachers of our early childhood by the fact that they are themselves childish, frivolous and short-sighted; in a word, they are big children all their life long – a kind of intermediate stage between the child and the full-grown man, who is man in the strict sense of the word. See how a girl will fondle a child for days together, dance with it and sing to it; and then think what a man, with the best will in the world, could do if he were put in her place.[12]

This attitude ridicules "women's work" to the point that it

appears to be not work at all, but extravagant childishness. It is important to note that although the work of women has been judged by men as having little value, the value it does have arises from its element of *service* to a man, usually the bearing and caretaking of a man's children. Francis Bacon even left out the children when he explained that "wives are young men's mistresses, companions for middle age and old men's nurses," a tidy summation of the worth of women, which was later reiterated by Freud in nearly the same words.

The unselfish care that women the world over have provided to their families has nearly always been taken for granted. The women of Khajuron in India, for instance, still lead thankless lives. Women belonging to the upper or middle castes are kept in total seclusion at home, occupied from morning until night with housework and the care and feeding of men, children and extended relations. Generally, their husbands will not consider what they do to be work. A woman of lower caste is expected to work in the fields all day and still perform all the housework and childcare as well. One Western observer noted, "It may be too strident to say that a woman in Khajuron was either a prisoner or a slave, but whatever one wants to call her, she could never hope to escape from her fate nor determine it herself."[13] The tragic implications for a woman whose identity is based solely on service to her family is that when her children are raised, her life is qualitatively over. El Saadawi describes the experience of a woman in Egypt after her childbearing years are past:

The very time when she reaches the peak of her intellectual, physical and emotional maturity and activity, is designated by society as the moment of decline, when she is transformed by social and familial pressure into an old barren woman, whose functions in life are over and who is ready to be buried by society while still alive.[14]

Women receive scant recognition for the intelligence it takes to accomplish the multitudinous tasks involved with maintaining a household and raising children. Their work has had little mention in history and until recently, not much attention in anthropological ethnographies compared to the extensive studies of the activities of men. So habitual is this lack of respect (in contrast to the shameless aggrandizement of "*Man's* Great Achievements in the Rise of Human Civilization") that biologists and evolutionists studying the life of the earliest humans long assumed that it had to have been a man who invented humanity's first tools. More recent work by scientists who are aware of the preconceptions which arise from an unconscious androcentric perspective have concluded that a *woman* was probably the first toolmaker, innovating for the benefit of her children.[15]

In spite of objective evidence to the contrary women have been perceived to be purely emotional creatures, lacking the rational and logical nature of men. As a practical result of this assumption men are commonly believed to have a natural advantage in the hard sciences like mathematics, physics and engineering. Scientific studies which have attempted to determine whether or not the male brain has an inherent mathematical edge over the female are not only inconclusive, but reveal the extent to which girls are *encouraged not to pursue* the traditionally male-dominated careers which require abstract, non-emotive reasoning. Because this kind of academic pressure is nearly invisible, intellectual differences between the sexes will appear to be innate.[16]

When Psyche looks at the pile of seeds to be sorted she decides, without even trying, that the task is impossible. Her lack of confidence is no surprise since she was trained for incompetence. Her beauty was all she was ever supposed to need. Gender-based work roles for women disguise a message more subtle and damaging than explicit inferiority. Since many women are still dependent on their fathers and husbands (and in many places in the world, their sons) to give them identity, women learn that they cannot and may not sort out what is true in the world for themselves. They are not allowed to define their own identity or make their own life choices.

Eros says, "You know, Persephone, when I heard that Aphrodite was making Psyche sort that pile of seeds, I felt terrible and I wanted to help her. But when I got there, the seeds were already sorted. She didn't even need my help."

"That's right. She didn't," says Persephone, smiling. "She had to sort the seeds by herself."

"But she didn't do it herself," says Eros. "The ants did it for her."

"Well I grant you she was unconscious," says Persephone. "But most of us do our best healing in that state. The ants were a dream image, a metaphor. Psyche had to be as intrepid as the ants. She had to sort out the truth in her past from what she had been told to believe."

"That's what I did too," says Eve happily, "when I took my story apart, bit by bit, and put it back together again."

Persephone nods. "You were sorting seeds."

In her autobiography, nineteenth-century American feminist Charlotte Perkins Gilman describes the incapacitating depression she experienced after her marriage and the birth of her child. Her doctor advised her to "live as domestic a life as possible. Have your child with you all the time ... Have but two hours intellectual life a day. And never touch pen, brush or pencil as long as you live."[17] She reports that following this advice deepened her depression and nearly killed her. Eventually she decided to ignore the doctor and act on her own authority. She left the marriage, taking along the baby *and* her pens in search of peace and her own identity. Because Psyche never had the opportunity within her family or in her relationship with Eros to reflect on her life and her identity, the first stage of healing for Psyche is the recognition that she has the right to define her identity for herself. She must tell the story of her life the way she experienced it to be, not the way others told her that it was.

"How could the ants be part of Psyche's dream if I saw them too?" asks Eros. "Mindlessly running around the anthill, staying up all night sorting seeds ..."

"The ants mean one thing to Psyche," says Persephone, "but obviously they mean something entirely different to you."

Eros shakes his head. "They don't mean anything to me. I just thought they were strange."

"Not so strange," says Persephone. "Men are supposed to have a high tolerance for mindless drudgery."

Eve nods. "When I was cursed with childbearing, Adam was cursed with sweat. Work was God's punishment on mankind."

"On womankind too," protests Beauty. "Cleaning, cooking, washing clothes, and no escape except to get rich enough to hire other women to do the work."

"But women aren't the only ones who have roles forced on them," says Persephone. "Isn't that true, Eros?"

"A man does what he has to," says Eros with a shrug.

"Come on, Eros," laughs Lilith. "Men are only supposed to flex their muscles, sleep with women and make money. Did I miss anything?"

Eros turns an angry face towards Lilith but Persephone intervenes. "She's right, Eros. A man 'does what he has to' and usually that means fulfilling the romantic myth."

"I understand the muscles and the sex," says Eve. "But what's romantic about making money?"

"Think about it," says Beauty. "Aren't we all supposed to want to marry the richest man?"

While women are expected to be able to provide *emotional* care for their families, men are expected to be *financial* providers for their wives, children and other dependent family members. According to this myth of masculinity a man either has value or he does not, depending on how much money he makes. Traditionally, it hardly matters if a man cheats on his wife and beats his children, as long as he is a "good provider." The anxiety caused by the intense pressure to make money and the corresponding fear of professional failure are very close to the surface for many men, but they may be less conscious of the resentment they feel towards those who are dependent on them.

Few men have the opportunity to choose the role of bread-winner; the choice was made for them by the prevalent social myths.

Because men are not allowed to express their feelings of resentment, which could allow them to cope with the situation in a healthy fashion, it emerges in more destructive ways. A man might treat his wife and children as possessions, for instance. Since he works hard to feed and clothe them, that means he has paid for them: he owns them. He can tell them what to do and can even abuse them if he wants to. If he drinks in response to the stress of his work (or the lack of work), his family will probably bear the brunt of his frustration.

Another man might accept the role of provider, working, making money and acquiring possessions, to the extent that financial security becomes more important than anything else. He can be as mindless as the ants, or at least, without conscience. He can cheat the poor and destroy the environment without any problem because he is still fulfilling the mythical expectations of what a man is: his actions are justified and his self-worth is intact because *his own* family is fed. A third reaction, the choice that Eros makes after Psyche is pregnant, is for the man to abandon his responsibilities, to refuse the role that his culture demands of him.

It is interesting to note that in his utopian novel, *The Republic*, Plato imagined full equality between the sexes, but only because the society would have dispensed with personal ownership, and most importantly, the ownership of children and wives: "they will not tear the city in pieces by differing about 'mine' and 'not mine'; each man dragging any acquisition which he has made into a separate house of his own, where he has a separate wife and children and private pleasures and pains." As a result of men's freedom from having to support their wives, and women's freedom from having to care for children, Plato hypothesizes that gender distinctions would disappear:

Men and women are to have a common way of life much as we have described – common education, common children; and they are to watch over the citizens in common whether abiding in the city or going out to war. They are to keep watch together, and to hunt together like dogs; and always and in all things, as far as they are able, women are to share with the men . . . In so doing they will do what is best, and will not violate, but preserve the natural relation of the sexes.[18]

Based on similar visions, Socialist theories also critiqued the oppression of women in marriage and in society and, theoretically, offered women economic equality with men. But in practice, instead of being liberated by a social system which encouraged them to work outside of their homes, many women in communist countries (who were not being effectively relieved of the duties of housework and caring for their children) found themselves, like lower caste villagers in Khajuron, doing it all.[19] In the light of such compounded burdens, being able to work *only* at home seems like a privilege, as in fact it is becoming in Western countries where the two-income family is more necessary than revolutionary.

Because the entrance of women into the male work force does not usually demonstrate social equality between the sexes, but rises from economic necessity, the myth of masculinity will inevitably judge the rising unemployment rates and falling wages which make it necessary for women to work as *the failure of men to provide adequately* for their families. Male resentment towards the professional success of women is an expression of the myth of masculinity which attaches a man's self-worth to his ability to make money; by the logic of the myth a woman who makes more money than her husband is more of a *man* than he is.

Women are not served by lobbying for the right to engage in mindless drudgery outside the home as well as in it. What is needed is a transformation of the work ethic for both men and women which focuses on meaning rather than tradition and choice rather than duty.

Eros emits a weary sigh. "OK, Persephone, I guess you're right about what a man is supposed to do. But I have no idea what I want to do with my life."

"Leaving the sex-business might be a start," laughs Beauty.

"Even if it means making my mother angry?" asks Eros. "What about duty and obedience to my parents?"

"I think it's more important to have a meaningful life," says Beauty. "If Aphrodite gets mad, well, let her be mad."

"How do you feel about babies?" asks Eve.

One of our deepest wounds of gender is being given an identity based on our biology rather than our own inclinations, an identity which we will spend our whole lives trying to live up to, especially within our adult relationships. If we can examine ourselves as individuals apart from the influential judgments of our society about what men and women are supposed to be, we will have begun to transform the myth of Romantic Love.

Having fully expected Psyche to fail, Aphrodite was furious to discover that Psyche had completed the first task. She now ordered Psyche to collect fleece from the golden rams which grazed by the river side. Psyche knew very well that these rams were so fierce they would gore anyone who dared to touch them. She fled to the river again, thinking that death by drowning might be better for her and her child than being torn apart by wild beasts.

But as Psyche drew near the water, she fancied that she heard words in the whispering of the breeze through a slim green reed. "Wait until the rams are asleep," said the wind, "then collect the fleece from the briars." Amazed, Psyche hid herself until nightfall. Then she approached the sleeping rams and did as the wind had said. In the morning she brought the fleece to Aphrodite and her task was complete.

The image of the rams, which often has been associated with male sexuality and aggression, provides the clue to unraveling the meaning of Psyche's second task. The term "aggression" has been defined so broadly that positive and negative associations have become confused. A corporate executive who closes an ambitious deal is admired for his "aggressive" tactics; one nation that invades another is described as having committed an "act of aggression"; a woman who takes the sexual initiative with a man is said to have behaved "aggressively." So natural these phrases sound, we are rarely conscious that the blending of associations between professional competence, acts of war and sexual behavior is a cultural myth and not a biological truth:

> The very fact that we possess a single term in our language that is capable of being applied to anything and everything from stag fights to star-wars is a trap for the unwary. For it tempts them to regard aggression, not as a category of convenience, but rather as a natural class of phenomena . . . It is but a short step to the conclusion that beneath the superficially diverse range of phenomena embraced by the term there lies a unitary biological 'base' – an aggressive 'instinct,' perhaps, whose origins may be traced far back in animal evolution.[20]

The myth of the beast within argues that violent aggression, including corporate take-over, rape and war, are all inevitable expressions of the male sex drive. But studies which have examined the link between the male hormone testosterone and aggressive hostility in humans, as well as other primates, have demonstrated no significant correlation. In fact, research with American soldiers in Vietnam showed a *drop* in their testosterone levels before they went into battle, and a study of rhesus monkeys revealed the *lowest* testosterone level in the dominant male.[21] But because they are firmly linked in the popular imagination, the *myth* of masculinity which associates hostile aggression and sexual aggression has had powerful implications for human society.

Many sociological and psychological theorists have taken this view including, most notoriously, Freud:

> Dismissing as an 'untenable illusion' the idea that humans are fundamentally good but corrupted by circumstance, he portrayed aggression as 'an innate, independent instinctual disposition'; and the sombre question with which he left his

readers was whether and to what extent humankind would succeed in mastering the beast within.[22]

Ironically, because sexual aggression in men has generally been perceived as a positive attribute and sexual "prowess" has been so applauded and admired, acts of violent aggression, like cut-throat business deals and "successful" wars, have come to share in the admiration. It is important to note that the romanticization of aggression which so many cultures have actively encouraged is not, in fact, a universal phenomenon.

Anthropologist Jean Briggs, who studied Utku Eskimo society in 1970, reported that "the Utku never find what we term aggressiveness a good quality; bad temper is always disapproved of, and even personal intensity or dominance that involves no temper at all are considered either amusing or frightening."[23]

In cultures like our own, displays of aggression which the Utku would judge to be "childish" are instead perceived as masterful demonstrations of adult masculinity and power! The term "power," unlike "strength" or "vitality" usually implies *power over* someone or something else, which is why the dominance and control of an abuser *over* his victim is an essential element of aggression. If the victim can be terrorized or humiliated to the point of willing submission, the abuser's feeling of domination is heightened. In a cultural sense, men have needed women to be powerless so that they could feel powerful. To this end, the romantic myth has encouraged women to submit themselves to the supposedly overwhelming sexual power of men.

Although J.J. Bachofen was one of the first mythologists to acknowledge the significance of images of women in religion and mythology he, like Jung, insisted on interpreting gender images in traditional ways, allowing women to be strong, but not so strong that they threaten the dominance of men. Describing the fate of an archetypal Amazon, Bachofen rhapsodizes:

The woman recognizes the higher strength and beauty of the man and gladly inclines to the victorious hero. Weary of her

Amazonian grandeur, which she can sustain only for a short time, she willingly bows down to the man who gives her back her natural vocation. She realizes that not warfare against man but love and fertility are her calling. Thus she willingly follows him who has redeemed her by his victory.[24]

Romanticizing female passivity at the same time as masculine aggression reveals what can only be called practical strategy from the abuser's point of view. The anti-heroic dragonslayer in Tanith Lee's short story, "Draco Draco," wisely observes, "In legends it's always the loveliest and the most gentle gets picked for the Dragon's dinner. You perceive the sense in the gentle part. A girl with a temper might start a ruckus."[25]

> *Eve says, "Doesn't it seem strange to you, Persephone, that Lilith was the first woman and they replaced her with me?"*
>
> *Persephone nods. "They replaced a strong woman with one who would accept blame."*
>
> *"Psyche was raised to be a victim," says Eve, "like me, like I used to be. That's why she has to do this task."*
>
> *Persephone agrees. "Psyche needs to develop the personal strength that Lilith always had."*
>
> *"I also knew what sexual consent meant," says Lilith, "even if Adam didn't. I hope he's learned it by now, Eve."*
>
> *Eve shrugs. "I always have sex with him whenever he wants it, so he's never had to force me. I don't think he would, but I don't know for sure."*
>
> *"Does Adam have sex with you whenever you want it?" asks Iseult.*
>
> *Eve gives Iseult a strange look. "When I want it? How am I supposed to know when I want it?"*
>
> *Iseult stares back at her. "But how do you not know?"*

When Aphrodite asks Psyche to do the impossible, to gather fleece from the golden rams, the unstated implication is that if a woman attempts to acquire what men have in abundance, namely power and sexuality, she will fail, she will die. This inequality of power between the sexes has been established and enforced so effectively that it almost seems natural. Men have been able to deny women control over their own sexuality by enforcing their virginity and arranging their marriages. On a more subtle level, women have been denied their sexuality itself, except as it is expressed passively in relationship to men. German philosopher Johann Fichte declared that "in the uncorrupted woman no sex drive expresses itself and there dwells no sex drive, but only love, and this love is the natural drive of the woman to satisfy a man." David Hume was somewhat more candid about the mythmaking manipulations of men upon the sexuality of women in his "Treatise on Human Nature." Since providing for children is such an awesome task, according to Hume, men will only be able to do it if they are sure they are not supporting some other man's child, and so they require absolute confidence in the chastity of their wives. They accomplish this by means of mythical behavior modification: "In order, therefore, to impose due restraint on the female sex, we must attach a peculiar degree of shame to their infidelity, above what arises merely from its injustice and must bestow proportionable praises on their chastity." [26]

To keep women uncorrupted, and to prevent their straying into any aggressive sexuality of their own, women have been well educated in sexual shame. Chastity has been universally praised, but so has marital obedience. Although Plutarch championed kindness and companionship in marriage, he also lessoned that, "it behooves an honest woman to behave herself toward her husband, never to shun nor to disdain the caresses and dalliances of his amorous inclinations, when he himself begins; but never herself to offer the first occasion of provocation." That it is a woman's duty to acquiesce to all of her husband's sexual demands, while never making any of her own, is the classic power relationship in the traditional marriage.

When a woman refuses to deliver a man his conjugal rights she is definitely straying from the terms of the romantic myth; the myth, however, is prepared for this event and advocates the use of force. It is nothing else but Romantic Love in Margaret

Mitchell's *Gone With the Wind* when Rhett Butler carries a screaming Scarlett O'Hara up the stairs and forces himself upon her. In the morning she is smiling and fulfilled: "He had humbled her, hurt her, used her brutally through a wild mad night, and she had gloried in it."[27]

The truth of marital rape is, of course, somewhat different. The experience has been judged by some to be *more* traumatic for the woman than rape by a stranger because, like incest, it is a betrayal of trust within a family relationship, but also because a survivor of marital rape will usually continue to live with her abuser, vulnerable to future assault. Like all acts of sexual violation the motive for marital rape is not sexual desire *for a woman*, but power *over a victim*:

> The typical marital rapist is a man who still believes that husbands are supposed to 'rule' their wives. This extends, he feels, to sexual matters: when he wants her, she should be glad, or at least willing; if she isn't he has the right to force her. But in forcing her he gains far more than a few minutes of sexual pleasure. He humbles her and reasserts, in the most emotionally powerful way possible, that he is the ruler and she the subject.[28]

To enforce the sexual passivity of women many cultures have not been content with culturally sanctioned rape, but have performed routine circumcision: mutilation or amputation of the external female genitalia. While traditional rites of circumcision for boys (which will not leave them sexually impaired) symbolize the attainment of adult power and identity, initiation rites for girls are intended to enforce subservience and obedience. Clitoridectomies are still performed in some areas of Saudi Arabia, Egypt, Pakistan, Sudan, Somalia, Ethiopia, Ghana, Congo, Zaire, Nigeria, Kenya, Burkina Faso, Sierra Leone, Mali, Senegal, Mozambique and in the Central African Republic, and are intended, universally, to impair or destroy women's capacity to feel pleasurable sexual sensations during sexual intercourse.

Clitoridectomies were also performed surgically in Europe and

America in the nineteenth and early twentieth centuries, ostensibly as a treatment for "hysteria" in women. But the philosophical assumptions upon which the diagnoses were made are no different from those which inspire ritual removal of the clitoris in Africa to this day:

> According to Freud, this organ had to disappear from the consciousness of mature women, just as if they had never possessed it; otherwise they are no longer controllable sexual objects but sexual subjects full of their own desires and impulses, full of curiosity.[29]

The idea that a man's sexual pleasure depends on the utter passivity of a woman also underlies the tradition of foot-binding which was practiced upon women for centuries in China. The deformed foot and the helplessness of a woman who was too crippled to walk unaided were exquisitely arousing to Chinese men. Although extreme in its sadism this sexual preference is no more bizarre than the prevailing Western attitude that a woman's leg is more attractive when she is perched precariously on two-inch spiked heels, than when she is wearing "sensible" shoes which allow her to run. Part of Psyche's task is to discover her own sexuality, not as an object of male desire, but as a spontaneous sexual being of her own.

"Iseult," says Guenevere uncomfortably. "There's a question that I've been wanting to ask you for a long time."

"Is it about sex?" asks Iseult.

"Well, yes," Guenevere admits. "Did you really like having sex with Tristan? The reason I ask," she adds quickly, "is that I didn't have sex with Lancelot very often, and I was usually too scared of being discovered to enjoy it much. And with Arthur, it was a duty. I'm like Eve. I don't even know if I like sex or not."

Iseult laughs. "Guenevere, if you ask me, did I enjoy sleeping with my husband, that would be a different question. But for Tristan and me, of course, the sex was very nice, very exciting."

Guenevere persists, "But do you think the sex with Tristan will still be as good when he's your husband? What if he starts to treat you like Mark did. What if he thinks he can rape you, or have you killed if you disobey him?"

"Well," says Iseult, "then he will not be my husband for very long."

Psyche's only alternative to violent death, seemingly, is to kill herself. By going sideways to either of these choices Psyche rejects the role of willing sacrifice within the myth of masculine power. It did not immediately occur to Psyche that she could get the fleece without making the rams mad, in much the same way that Iseult did not know that she could refuse to marry King Mark. But the truths which are sorted out in the first task are useless without the strength discovered in the second. Iseult decided to tell King Mark that she loved Tristan; Beauty told her father she considered his expectations of her to be abusive; Guenevere told Arthur what she required of him for the relationship to continue.

Psyche's refusal to be victimized by the rams is a powerful act, although *vital act* would probably be a more appropriate description, since Psyche did not kill the rams nor overpower them to acquire the fleece: *she did not have to become dominant, to cease being submissive.* Brunehilde, who imitated the most wounded male image she could find, is a different case. Being powerful in such a distorted way did not make her as strong as Iseult was when she rewrote her story or as vital as Psyche was when she got the fleece.

Eros breaks into the conversation, "But if women get to be powerful, what are men for?"

"Was that a rhetorical question," asks Persephone, "or did you mean it?"

"I would have fought those rams with my bare hands to protect Psyche," says Eros. "But she waited until dark and got the fleece without ever putting herself into danger."

"Does that bother you?" asks Lilith.

"Well, it makes me feel useless. I went there to help her and she didn't need my help."

"You're just used to thinking women can't take care of themselves," says Lilith. *"And that we're – no offense intended of course – weaker than men and kind of stupid, too."*

"I never said that!" Eros protests. *"But it's upsetting to hear you talk about women getting more powerful."*

"I see," says Lilith. *"You think that if Psyche gets stronger, you must have gotten weaker."*

"Not exactly," says Eros, flustered. *"Well, I don't know, maybe something like that."*

The association of femininity with weakness has served the interests of the masculine myth very well. Men have been able to feel powerful in contrast to women, children and any men who could be dismissed as being not fully men: pacifists, priests or artists. In their persecution of homosexuals, white supremacists can also be described as masculine supremacists, since they seek to destroy what is not strictly gender identified in traditional ways. Racism offers men the same feeling of superiority that sexism does. As German feminist Marielouise Jannsen-Jurreit has pointed out:

> All the qualities that are ascribed to women in a Christian patriarchal culture – incessant sexual seducibility, childishness, negligible intellectual powers, unoriginality, ample emotional life, and limited self-discipline – have time and again been applied to ethnic minorities as well as to oppressed majorities. [30]

Not only did Nazis consider Jews, Slavs, Gypsies, Africans, Italians, the English and the French to have feminine attributes, their disdain for American men would have been a profound shock to the average American G.I. had he known. According to a German correspondent to America during World War Two, "the excessive feminism in America is adverse to culture and a national disgrace. What is more, it could threaten the continued existence of the people if America ever had to fight a serious war and were forced to pit effeminate males against an enemy with uncorrupted men." [31]

Because the prevalent myth of masculinity depends on a belief in the inferiority and weakness of others, giving up racist and sexist beliefs is terrifying for many men because it means losing their tenuous grip on self-esteem and personal power. Eli Sagan suggests that this is the dynamic behind both patriarchal aggression and political tyranny:

> One cannot comprehend the causes of psychological and moral regression within the family in the nineteenth century – sexual repression of children and women, the reconstruction of authoritarian patriarchy – without understanding the acute panic that men felt as women advanced toward equality. Nor can one comprehend those causes without being aware of how powerful the exercise of domination is as a defense against anxiety. Men are capable of any degree of tyranny or destruction in the attempt to overcome inner terror. The twentieth century has surely taught us that.[32]

Rather than acknowledging the fear that underlies acts of political and social "aggression," we tend to romanticize criminals and tyrants, perceiving them to be *powerful* (in contrast to women, children and victims of assault), because in their dominance and aggression, *they have proved themselves to be men*. Bruno Bettelheim reveals an unconscious admiration for the Nazis by expressing less distaste for their acts than for what he perceived to be the femininity of the Jews. "Why did so few of the millions of prisoners die like men?" he asks. Bettelheim's association of femininity with weakness and victimization is blatant. More than half of the murdered Jews were women and children who were already, from the traditional psychological perspective, willing victims, and so could not have been expected to "die like men." Bettelheim's scorn is for Jewish men who, by falling prey to the terror and humiliation of Nazi oppression and concentration camps, showed themselves to be, as the Nazis had claimed all along, "womanly."

In an essay entitled "Some Psychical Consequences of the

Anatomical Distinctions Between the Sexes," Freud explained
that the difference between the sexes arises from the woman's
lack of a penis. Because women are already castrated, they never
suffer the *fear* of castration which inspires the Oedipal Complex
in men, and the development of the superego. In other words,
according to Freud, women can *never* attain the intellectual and
moral development of men. By this logic, only underdeveloped
men are equal to women:

> We must not allow ourselves to be deflected from such
> conclusions by the denial of the feminists, who are anxious to
> force us to regard the two sexes as completely equal in position
> and worth; but we shall, of course, willingly agree that the
> majority of men are also far behind the masculine ideal.[33]

The fear that men who have "feminine" traits are no longer fully
men, and the corresponding fear of "masculine" (or as Freud said,
"castrating") women, is still a perceptible influence in Jungian
psychology. Johnson's interpretation of Psyche's second task
includes the admonition that Psyche only needs a "bit of the
fleece," only a small portion of the characteristics that men have
in full, in order to be whole:

> When we talk of a woman's acquiring fleece, or masculinity, we
> must understand that we are not striving for an equal amount
> of masculinity and femininity within ourselves. Many women
> say they want just as much focused consciousness as a man. This
> is not reasonable or safe . . . The masculinity in a woman is a
> minority. We all have such limits dictated by biological limits
> or functions.[34]

But in her history of love relationships between women,
Surpassing the Love of Men, Lillian Faderman reports that
"masculine" women only seem unreasonable and unsafe to the
men who fear that their own territory is being threatened: "It
was not the sexual aspect of lesbianism as much as the attempted

usurpation of male prerogative by women who behaved like men that many societies appeared to find most disturbing."[35] Men have claimed both power and sexuality as their own domain, and Jungian psychology has validated the claim by designating the fleece in Psyche's second task to represent masculinity itself. It may be more accurate to judge the *distortions* of sex and aggression as belonging to the myth of masculinity.

"Aggression is biological," says Eros. "Men have always fought wars. It's in our nature."

Persephone shakes her head. "War is a pathology that can't be blamed on nature."

"All right then," Eros says. "Men fight wars to protect women."

There is a general uproar and everyone tries to speak at once.

Guenevere breaks through the clamor and says angrily, "Men always think up noble reasons for fighting wars, just to hide the real motives."

"Greed," says Iseult. "War always means someone is getting land, money, power."

"Women are raped," says Beauty.

"Children die," says Eve.

"But there have been female warriors . . ." Eros begins.

Lilith laughs. "Yeah, I've met one. But she's not going to help your argument."

"Trying to defend war is not going to work, Eros," says Persephone. "When men go out and kill each other and call it glorious, they're caught in the most pathological expression of Romantic Love there is."

"Romantic Love?" asks Eros, and a few of the ladies turn their heads to look at her in surprise.

It is no coincidence that conquering armies traditionally have raped the women of the conquered land as part of their victory prize.[36] Possession of land through military victory is part of the same myths that allow a man to claim the woman he loves. Lancelot demonstrated love and devotion to Guenevere by killing monsters and performing other "manly" deeds. To win, to possess, to kill, to rape, these things are all romanticized in myths of war. Many wars are fought ostensibly to defend an ideal like "Freedom" or "Democracy" or "Racial Purity." But whenever a political system or a philosophical belief is idealized it becomes romantic in the same way a relationship would be, and all of the same distortions occur.

A military or religious leader who commands fanatical devotion is in a romantic relationship with his followers. He dominates, controls and saves them. They love, sentimentalize and obey him. Or "it" in the case of an ideal; people will commit atrocities in the name of an ideal only if they are, in some sense, in love with it. In contrast to the Nazis, who justified their killing of Jews with idealistic rhetoric and racist generalizations, those who risked their lives to protect Jews under the third Reich seemed to have no correspondingly romantic motives. They simply looked at the Jews as *individuals*. In many cases they helped people they had known before the laws changed, people they knew very well did not deserve to die. [37]

Eros sighs, "I'm willing to admit there's something unhealthy in war, but I was always taught to glorify it."

"Sounds like you've been taken in," says Lilith sympathetically.

"What?" Eros turns his head, startled.

"There are ways to make bitter pills easier to swallow," says Persephone. "Think about it. If you want to encourage women to be submissive, what do you do? You romanticize myths of duty and submission."

"Right," says Lilith. "So if you want young boys to commit horrifying acts, how do you get them to do it?"

When Eros hesitates Guenevere answers for him.

"You create a romantic myth about it! The Round Table is the best example I can think of. For nearly one thousand years boys have wanted to grow up to be knights because of King Arthur."

In the same way that girls are raised to be submissive so that they can be sacrificed to sexual encounters they do not choose, boys are raised to be brutal so that they can be sacrificed as soldiers to wars they do not understand. The romantic myth of war exploits the misunderstood tangle of biological aggression and wounded rage. It is only *wounded* men who feel the need to demonstrate power by establishing domination over those they consider to be weaker than themselves. Men are not innately violent any more than woman are inherently servile. The strength and determination a man expresses pathologically in war appears in a healthy way in a firefighter, for instance. Boys have to be desensitized to violence; they learn gradually to accept the idea that they can kill. But they are helped along in their lessons by experiences of powerlessness and humiliation, and the understanding that eventually they will be able to redeem their masculinity by demonstrating power over others.

After the First World War Freud encountered men with all the symptoms which he associated with "hysteria" in women: depression, nightmares, uncontrollable weeping. Because he had chosen to deny that trauma was the source of these women's pain, he could not bring himself to acknowledge the link between the suffering of young men and the trauma they experienced during the war. The Oedipal Complex, which hypothesized that women who believed that they had been assaulted by their fathers actually desired them sexually, had its counterpart in the "Death Instinct": Freud maintained that men suffered from "hysteria" only because unconsciously they really wanted to die.

The Vietnam War, whose soldiers committed no more atrocities than soldiers in other wars, hid its wounded veterans less well, perhaps because the war propaganda had worn so thin. But as a result "post-traumatic stress disorder," the very same "hysteria" which Freud had observed in the veterans of his day, was understood to be the inevitable wounding of war. A man who is forced by the myths of masculinity into witnessing or performing a brutal act in war will be as traumatized as a woman who is the victim of a brutal act at home.

Beauty says, "It's horrible to tell a man that he has to kill, that he should be good at it, that he might even enjoy it. It's just like telling a woman she wants to be raped."

Eros is very pale. "You make it sound like men are victims too." There is silence in the group.

"I guess I know the answer to that," says Eros, "but if there's something wrong with what they told me I was supposed to be, what am I supposed to be instead?"

"Very simple," says Iseult. "Men should be more like women. You need to be more like a woman, Eros." Then she whispers to Beauty, "But not too much like a woman, eh?"

Lilith laughs. "You'll never get men to change by telling them that, Iseult! I could chase Brunehilde back to Valhalla because I'm strong, not because I'm masculine. If Eros figures this task out, he'll be a loving man, not a feminine one."

"One thing I understand now," Eros admits. "When Psyche turned that lamp in my face, it was like she won the game and I lost. I was angry, and I got back at her the best way I could, by leaving her. So I won and now I'm alone. But I don't feel powerful at all."

In a world where masculinity and femininity have lost their pathological distinctions, Adam will no longer dominate Lilith or blame Eve, and Tristan will accept Iseult as his sexual equal. The second task of Psyche and Eros is to heal the wounds of misunderstood power. Men must change the way they view themselves, trading power over others for strength in themselves. Women in turn must become strong and *vital*, refusing to be cast in the victim's role (not becoming like Brunehilde, abusers instead), but setting up the boundaries they need within which to develop a sexuality and a life of their own.

8

PSYCHE AND EROS:
The Wedding

Psyche's first two tasks represent the initial stages of healing in which we sort through the lies and truths of our past, acknowledge our wounds, claim the right to determine our own identity and sexuality apart from traditional gender roles, and then develop the personal strength to protect that right.

As women begin to enforce their boundaries, men must learn to distinguish between strength and dominance, recognizing that the need to feel powerful is a distortion, rather than a natural expression, of masculinity. These two tasks represent a significant challenge to the traditional romantic myth which granted to men the right to define the identity and sexuality of women and required women to accept their subservient role. But in order to effect the complete transformation of the myth of Romantic Love, Psyche must now complete two very different tasks.

Aphrodite gave Psyche a jar of polished crystal and commanded her to collect water from the mouth of the river Styx. Psyche knew it to be an impossible demand. The river was defended by terrible monsters who would destroy anyone who came near. Terrified at the sight of the sleepless dragons, Psyche was about to return to Aphrodite and admit defeat when a giant eagle appeared in the sky. It swooped down towards her and grabbed the jar. Then it wheeled off in the direction of the river. When it returned it carefully dropped into her hands the jar, full of precious water. Her task was complete.

Psyche's need for water from the sacred river and the manner in which she receives it suggests that the third task represents her religious or spiritual life. When we allow biology or tradition to define our identities, then we also give up the opportunity for a personal reckoning with the universe, and as many would say, with God. More than anything else, Psyche needs to determine a sense of purpose for herself, a reason for being. The purpose she was given by her parents, to be beautiful and dutiful, did not serve her very well. A man is sometimes encouraged to consider his life's purpose when he chooses his occupation, but the choices are much narrower for a woman. Being a wife and raising children is the only spiritual purpose many women have ever been allowed.

Eve looks troubled. "There isn't anything wrong with being a mother, is there?"

"Of course not," Persephone answers. "But it isn't the only purpose a woman can have. Living in the Underworld, I've found a purpose in paying attention to what goes on up there in the Upperearth, trying to help the people who make the journey down here."

She continues, thoughtfully, "Of course, I didn't have that sense of purpose when Hades first brought me here. My beauty had betrayed me, or at least that's how it felt. But you don't see him here now, do you, the man who raped me – my uncle – my husband."

"Your husband!" says Eve. "You don't mean you married him after what he did to you."

"What other choice did I have? After I lost my virginity, I was unfit for anyone else. At least, that's what he told me. But I figured it out eventually, that I couldn't heal while I was still married to him. After I sorted out enough truth to tell Hades to leave, and after I made sure he'd leave me alone, then I began to question who I was and what I wanted to do with my life. It was a spiritual process for me, even though it didn't involve the gods."

Guenevere nods. "That's what I was trying to say when I told Arthur I'd be happy to live without him in the convent. It's for spiritual reasons, not religious ones that I want to go there. I need to spend time alone. I need to figure out who I am, and what I want and what I believe."

Issues of religion and spirituality are a factor in the transformation of Romantic Love in the Western world because the relationship between a man and a woman, and marriage in particular, is expected to parallel the relationship between God and men. Just as virtuous men must submit to the laws of God, so women have been expected to "love, honor and obey" their husbands. The result of this expectation is the heightening of spiritual and moral *authority* of men over their wives and children, and the lessening of women's control over their own beliefs. Plutarch's description of a "virtuous woman" makes this clear: "It behooves her to worship and adore only those Deities which her husband reputes and reverences . . . Phidias made the statue of Venus at Elis with one foot upon the shell of a tortoise, to signify two great duties of a virtuous woman, which are to keep at home and be silent."[1]

The Christian tradition of silence as a virtue in women was justified by biblical teachings which declared that women could neither preach nor prophesy: "It is shameful for a woman to speak in church."[2] The equality that had been granted to women by Gnostic sects which encouraged them to pursue their own mystical communications with God, and to participate beside men in the religious community, was condemned as heresy by the early Church fathers. Tertullian was explicit:

It is not permitted for a woman to speak in the church, nor is it permitted for her to teach, nor to baptize, nor to offer [the eucharist], nor to claim for herself a share in any *masculine* function.[3]

By denying women direct access to God and requiring them to experience His authority through the intercession of a priest, the Church reserved for men the exclusive right to communicate and interpret God's word, insuring that women would never be able to interpret the word of God for themselves. This has been the state of affairs within most Christian churches for the last two thousand years, a traditional arrangement which Judaism had long supported and Islam was to choose in turn.

With the revealed word of God behind them, men within many of the world's organized religions have claimed the authority to control every aspect of the lives of women, including what they should believe, how they should behave and with whom and how often they should bear children. But ironically, even though it is men who diminish the identity of women down to womb-size, they still cite motherhood as *proof* of the moral inferiority of women.

According to Schopenhauer, "since women exist in the main solely for the propagation of the species, and are not destined for anything else," their whole life and being has "a certain levity," a triviality compared to the significant lives of men, and thus an inferiority in reasoning, justice and honor. The nurturing qualities of motherhood supposedly reduce a women's ability to make "hard" decisions in the world:

> The weakness of their reasoning faculty also explains why it is that women show more sympathy for the unfortunate than men do, and so treat them with more kindness and interest; and why it is that, on the contrary, they are inferior to men in point of justice, and less honorable and conscientious. [4]

This lack of justice was further explained by Freud who attributed it to women's lack of penises, this perpetual state of castration hindering the normal development of the superego (as it is defined, of course, by the behavior of the male):

> I cannot evade the notion (though I hesitate to give it expression) that for women the level of what is ethically normal is different from what it is in men . . . Character-traits which critics of every epoch have brought up against women – that they show less sense of justice than men, that they are less ready

to submit to the great experience of life, that they are more often influenced in their judgments by feelings of affection or hostility – all this would be amply accounted for by the modifications in the formation of their superego.[5]

The charge that women are unable to act with authority because of their reproductive functions and genitalia does not disappear when women *do* act with authority. Instead, behaviors which would be considered to be positive if performed by men are stigmatized in women. When El Saadawi asked her father, "How is it that Eve who was born of a rib in Adam's body and was much weaker than him, should have suddenly acquired an unusual strength that permitted her to convince Adam, so that he listened to her and disobeyed the orders of Allah?" her father answered, "Eve was positive only where evil was concerned."[6] The association of the "masculine" acts of women with *evil* reveals the fear that underlies the judgment. "Let man be afraid of woman when she hates," wrote Nietzsche, "for man in the depth of his soul is only evil, but a woman is base in her soul." If women are inherently corrupt, then the use of force to preserve their powerlessness is crucial: "Do you go to women? Do not forget the whip!"[7]

The whip has not been the only weapon used by male authority to control women. Witch-burning was practiced over several hundred years in both Europe and America. Although its misogyny eventually spared neither the young, nor the married, nor the devout, this sentence of torture and death was at first directed at female herbalists whose gift of healing was believed to come from Satan, since it was not controlled by the Church. A close examination of the crimes for which women were burned reveal that what was truly at issue was spiritual authority. Just as women had no right to choose their beliefs for themselves, they were not allowed to control what happened to their own bodies:

The charges leveled against the "witches" included every misogynist fantasy harbored by the monks and priests who officiated over the witch hunts: witches copulated with the devil, rendered men impotent . . . devoured newborn babies . . . But again and again the "crimes" included what would now be recognized as legitimate medical acts – providing contraceptive measures, performing abortions, offering drugs to ease the pain of labor.[8]

Because pregnancy and motherhood can be used so effectively to enforce female subservience, a woman's right to decide for herself when and by whom she should become pregnant has traditionally been denied to her. It is no coincidence that when Lilith left Adam, *refusing intercourse with him*, she was slandered as an unnatural mother, a baby-killing demon who let her own children be murdered. When women have a measure of control over their own reproductive functioning, male authority, both religious and social, is threatened. The politics of reproductive rights to this day are inseparably linked to questions of gender and authority. In most places in the world how often a woman bears a child is not within her own conscious control, but determined by her religion, her government and her husband.

The reproductive services of midwives in the Western world diminished in the nineteenth and twentieth centuries as the authority of the male physician increased, a shift in power which began with the witch-burnings hundreds of years before. According to Barbara Ehrenreich and Deirdre English in *For Her Own Good: 150 Years of the Experts' Advice to Women*, it was female herbalists who understood the workings of the human anatomy and the efficacy of drugs and herbs at a time when male physicians were still treating leprosy with "broth made from a black snake caught in dry land among stones." Paracelsus, the father of modern medicine, confessed in 1527 that he had learned from a Sorceress "everything he knew." The conflict between male physicians and female healers was not about healing, but authority:

Through the witch hunts, the Church lent its authority to the doctor's professionalism, denouncing non-professional healing as equivalent to heresy: "If a woman dare to cure *without having studied* she is a witch and must die." (Of course, there wasn't any way for a woman to attend a university and go through the appropriate study.) The witch trials established the male physician on a moral and intellectual plane vastly above the female healer. It placed him on the side of God and Law, a professional on par with lawyers and theologians, while it placed her on the side of darkness, evil and magic.[9]

The connection between healing and spirituality has been made by many different cultures. Among the Ojibwe Indians of the Great Lakes and Canada, for instance, the major religious community is the Midewiwin, or the "Grand Medicine Society." The major focus of the Midewiwin is healing, both physical and spiritual. This traditional spiritual system encouraged adolescent boys and girls to participate in a *vision fast*, a ritual in which direct contact between the fasting children and the world of the spirits was expected to occur. As a result of this communication, the children would become aware of the nature of their specific spiritual purpose in the world, which might involve lore-keeping, protection of the tribe or healing.[10]

Because religious myths directly reflect cultural myths, those cultures with strict gender distinctions will enforce them through the use of religious authority, while the spiritual systems of those whose customs allow wider, overlapping definitions of purpose for men and women will reflect that tendency as well. For the Ojibwe, the revelation of a purpose which is determined through a vision would supersede other customs which might otherwise discourage a woman or a man from becoming involved in a certain activity.

Psyche's third task is very much like a vision fast, the eagle who comes to help her like the guardian spirit who visits an Ojibwe child, representing the benevolence of the universe, and the knowledge that she is not alone, existing in some isolated human reality, but that she is understood and loved by something greater and more complicated than herself. This task does not imply that women must adopt a religious belief, or even believe in God at all, but only that they must be free to decide what they believe, and determine the nature of their purpose in the world, for themselves.

Psyche was prevented from drawing water from the sacred river because the monsters which protected it threatened to destroy her; women in the Western world often have been prevented from direct contact with "spirit" by the religious authority of men who have assumed the right to deny it to them. But religious authority also has been used to control the economic and reproductive rights of women. In *Radical Spirits: Spiritualism and Women's Rights in Nineteenth-Century America*, Ann Braude explores the fascinating history of nineteenth-century spiritualist mediums, women who actively sought direct mystical experiences and who claimed to receive messages from spirits of the deceased. According to Braude, although not all nineteenth-century feminists were spiritualists, all the spiritualists were feminists.

Active in the abolitionist movement, spiritualists recognized the social oppression of women to be a kind of economic and sexual slavery. One spiritualist recorded her protest "against all forms of slavery, against the sale of my black brother and sister . . . against the education and sale of maidens for the marriage altar . . . against the tyranny of labor, as it is enjoined in our northern cities, in our factories, in our households."[11] But it was the inequities of the traditional marriage which drew the fiercest criticism from spiritualists, particularly the conjugal rights that the law and the Church granted to men. Another woman frankly charged:

Wives are brutalized by their husband's passions, until threatened with death from physical drain of repeated pregnancy. Unwanted maternity turns mothers into murderers and abortionists. [The husband] pleads his legal rights, and the priest, the law, and the marriage institution sustain him . . . Nothing short of giving woman the right to control her own person, and to say when and under what circumstances she is willing to take upon herself the maternal relation, will remedy this great evil. [12]

The beliefs of spiritualist women, who claimed the right to receive and interpret spiritual truths directly rather than consulting male authority, were radically different from the prevalent attitudes of the women of their day. Those who claim to have spiritual authority can exert an extraordinary influence on social customs and behaviors, which is why it is so important, from a patriarchal point of view, to deny women the right to such authority. Historically, the one who reveals the will of God tends to be favored by that will. Islamic tradition includes the humorous story of Aisha, the prophet Mohammed's favorite wife, who challenged one of the Koranic teachings which had descended to him from heaven:

> The Prophet of Allah, Allah's blessings and peace be upon him, did not die before Allah had bestowed upon him the right to have as many wives as he desired, and said unto him "Take to yourself as many as you wish of them." And when this verse descended, Aisha said: "Indeed Allah responds immediately to your needs." [13]

It is obvious that our estimations of the nature of God are influenced by our emotional needs and cultural expectations. When Lilith uttered the unpronounceable name of God she was taken to safety by His mercy – but then God responded to Adam's complaint as well, dispatching angels to punish Lilith. How could this be? Which God was the real God, Lilith's or Adam's? Objectively, it would be difficult to say, but the need to determine *absolute* truths is not itself a universal need, and the question would make no sense in a culture which accepts the relativity of spiritual truth and grants to everyone equal religious authority. Although the visions experienced by individuals in many traditional Native American religions are *personal* truths which may or may not be relevant or useful to others, *the relativity of the visions does not in any way reduce their significance or efficacy.* Religious intolerance arises only among those who have a social or economic interest in limiting spiritual authority to a chosen few.

Eros interrupts the conversation. "Maybe Psyche didn't know where the eagle came from, but I did. That was Zeus' eagle."

"Where the eagle came from was less important to Psyche than the fact that it came," says Persephone.

"But you don't understand," insists Eros. "I knew Zeus didn't care what happened to Psyche. When I saw the eagle come to help her, I knew he must have been watching me. He only sent the eagle as a favor to me."

"The eagle can represent one thing to Psyche and another to you," says Persephone. "The contradiction doesn't make either one less true."

"I do not understand," says Iseult. "If your father was trying to help you why did that not make you feel good?"

"It would have made me happy," says Eros, "if I could have trusted it. But I know Zeus too well. He'd never do me a favor without expecting something back. Probably he had some new victim he wanted me to stick with an arrow."

The difficulty women have had gaining access to religious authority reflects the social authority of "the fathers" in our patriarchal culture. For men the issues involved with spiritual healing are more complicated, involving the wounds they received because of the way in which they were (or were not) fathered. By linking God with the image of a father our emotional associations with fatherhood become entwined with our feelings about religion. Where else would arise portrayals of God the father, a vengeful and jealous God, who wants to be respected and feared, who punishes disobedience without mercy and who demands that faith be confirmed through sacrifice?

Traditionally, the role of the father has been to provide for his children and to discipline them, but not to love them. Aristotle proclaimed that fathers should rule over their children, who in turn owe him the respect they would give to a king or a god. But children learn empathy or cruelty through identification with their parents. Fathers will teach their sons to be decent human beings more effectively by loving them than by merely providing for them well or demanding their respect. In his book *Freud, Women and Morality*, Eli Sagan explores the causal connection between the quality of care received by children in a society and its social ills, suggesting that morality originates in the basic situation of nurturing between a child and its parents:

> So much of the world's misery results from the fact that when politically empowered, he who cannot identify with his fellow human beings becomes a killer. The capacity to make these crucial identifications is fundamentally dependent on the quality of the nurturing that a child receives.[14]

As Alice Miller pointed out, Hitler's diatribes resembled nothing so much as the bombastic lectures of his own father, who insisted on being called "Herr Vater" by his children. But the importance of nurturing by the father in the emotional development of children has been acknowledged by society and the experts only very recently. A once influential reference, the *Manual of Child Psychology*, published in 1954, never found it necessary to use the word "father" at all! In some cultures men have been actively prevented from involving themselves in child care:

> The Ossets would call a man a very insulting name – "Baba" (that is, old woman) – if he ever milked a cow or took care of the children. A father of the South Caucasian tribes may never carry his child in the presence of others or even say a friendly word to it.[15]

Not all women want to give up caring for children, but many women would be glad to share the job. For men, the act of *loving* children is distinct from *providing* for them, because it is a choice, not a duty. Recently, social myths of gender have shifted to allow men to begin to care for their children without shame and as a result "there is now more nurturing of infants and small children by fathers in our culture than possibly at any time since the transcending of "primitive" society." Sagan sees cause for great hope that human society itself may heal its wounds as individuals heal their own: "If one considers how our fathers were raised, and how we have raised our own children, and then how they, in turn, will nurture theirs, this development represents a veritable revolution in the degree to which fathers are involved with caring."[16]

"But if I wait for Zeus to change," says Eros, "it would take forever."

Beauty nods. "I let my father hurt me for a long time. I mean, I let him give me to the Beast! But when I retold my story I stopped waiting for him to protect me. I just left."

Eros asks, "You mean I'm supposed to forgive Zeus? I'm not sure I can do that."

Lilith shakes her head. "Not if forgiveness means letting him off the hook, as if you deserved to be treated badly."

"My father let Hades rape me," Persephone says bluntly. "I've made peace with the grief and anger, but I can't ever say what he did to me was all right."

Lilith nods. "If you accept the horrible things Zeus does to women and children as if it's normal behavior, you risk ending up exactly like him – you might even treat your children the way he treated his."

Eros says, "That's always frightened me, that I could ever be like Zeus. I'm already an absent father, but I don't want to be like him!"

"You don't have to be," says Persephone simply.

The attitudes and abuses of patriarchal culture are just as wounding for men as for women. Psyche's third task is different for men and women only because women have not been allowed to identify with "the fathers": their own and, of course, God the father. As a result, organized religious systems have withheld from women the moral authority they granted to men. Fathers, husbands, Church officials and medical doctors consistently have denied women the right to decide what constitutes moral behavior and to control their own sexual and reproductive functions. A woman's purity and her sanity both have been thought to rest in how well she matches the decrees of the moral authority of her society.

The healing task for a woman, then, is to consult *her own authority*, both as it regards her spiritual purpose and her reproductive life. Because men identify with "the fathers" as a matter of course, their task is to rethink God the father, in order to acknowledge and then heal the abuses they have experienced at the hands of men. Men must also begin to bring to fatherhood the nurturing and empathy that has for so long been denied it by the myths of masculinity. According to Eli Sagan this is the key to the creation of a new and moral society:

> Such a society would be more nurturing and caring; it would substitute a sense of community for the pathologically competitive, isolated individualism of our current form of life; it would bear witness to the love we carry for our children by leaving them a world to live in; it would emphasize equality over tyranny in every human relationship. For men, this means abandoning a fragile masculine identity that has to be reinforced with a multitude of aggressive defense mechanisms that pronounce "I am not a woman" – because I preside over twenty thousand nuclear missiles. [17]

Having received the water from the sacred river, Psyche still faced her final task, which was the most difficult of all. She had to travel to the Underworld to visit Persephone, the Queen of the Underworld, and ask her for a gift to bring back to Aphrodite. Psyche was sure that the task itself was a sentence of death since no mortal could journey to the Underworld and return alive. Psyche fled to the top of a tower, intending to throw herself from

its heights. But a voice which spoke from the tower made her
hesitate. The voice explained to Psyche how she might go to the
Underworld and return unharmed: she must take two coins in
her mouth to pay the boatman; she must carry bread for the
dreadful hell hound, Cerberus; she must not stop to aid anyone
on the journey.

Everything unfolded as the Tower had said. On her journey to
the Underworld she gave a coin to the boatman and was ferried
across the dark river. She saw a body floating in the water and
as the boat passed by, a piteous voice rose from it, begging Psyche
to pull it into the boat with her. But Psyche turned her face away.
On the farther shore she was once again assailed by pathetic
creatures, begging her to postpone her journey and aid them.
Though it broke her heart to pass them by, she continued on her
path.

Eros says, "Just before I came to see you, Persephone, I watched
Psyche start on her journey to the Underworld. This task frightened
me more than the others did. There's so much danger for a mortal
coming down here. I tried to stop her, to tell her it wasn't worth
the risk. I even told her we could go back to where we were before,
in my castle."

He shakes his head sadly, "But she thought I was one of the voices
trying to deceive her. She didn't even turn her head."

"Well, weren't you one of them?" asks Lilith.

"What are you talking about?"

"Women don't always get support from their friends and their
families when they try to change," says Persephone. "Sometimes
they're actively discouraged by the people who would stand to lose
the most."

Eros protests, "But what would I lose if Psyche changes?"

"It was the wounded Psyche who was entranced by you," says
Lilith. "Healed, she's not going to let you dominate her anymore."

"She's not going to laugh at all your jokes," says Beauty.

Guenevere nods. "A lot of the attention she gave to you, she's going
to keep for herself."

"She's not going to follow you around like a puppy either," says Eve.

Iseult laughs. "And she will not make love with you whenever and however *you* want it!"

"Well, Eros?" Persephone asks. "You can't take Psyche back to your magic castle. Are you ready to accept her as an equal?"

After a pause Eros says, "My mother would never approve. She was furious when she found out I'd gotten involved with a mortal – especially the mortal she told me to punish."

"But why should it matter what your mother thinks of her?" asks Iseult. "If you really love her . . ."

Eros runs his fingers through his beautiful hair. "I have a hard time standing up to my mother. She still treats me like a child."

The ladies exchange a significant glance. Lilith looks as if she were about to comment, but Eros' expression is suddenly resolute.

"All right," he says. "I know what I have to do."

With that announcement, Eros launches himself into the sky.

Psyche's final task is deceptively simple. She must journey to the Underworld all alone. She must seek healing without being deterred by the needs of others. She must put herself first. This crucial selfishness is nearly impossible for many women to achieve because the romantic myth declares that a good woman puts the needs of others before her own. But relationships which do not allow women to take care of themselves and to receive care from others will never be fully equal. Women must be given the opportunity to understand themselves and to heal.

The fourth task for men is correspondingly simple. Men must heal their own wounds and mature emotionally rather than looking to women to provide them with the emotional life that the myths of masculinity have denied them. Men must *want* women who will be their equals, instead of their mistresses, nurses or mothers. Women, in turn, must stop romanticizing brutal and dominant men. The transformation of the myth of Romantic Love depends on the transformation of our *expectations* about what the nature of love relationships should be.

When Eros is out of sight, Beauty asks, "What in the world does Psyche still need from you, Persephone?"

"To tell you the truth, I'm not sure what she's going to ask me for," Persephone admits.

"What I want to know is why Psyche has to go through all of these dangerous tasks and Eros doesn't," says Guenevere. "As if things are actually going to improve between them if only she changes."

"I don't know, Guenevere," says Persephone. "It seemed to me the tasks were difficult for Eros, too. The ants, the rams, the eagle – they all challenged him in one way or another."

Lilith grins. "He even made a perilous journey to the Underworld."

Guenevere smiles. "I guess that's true. We didn't exactly give him an easy time."

"I suspect that Psyche . . ." Persephone's words are interrupted by Psyche herself, who suddenly enters the circle of women. The initial flurry of excitement gives way to expectation as they wait to hear the purpose of Psyche's visit.

"If you would be so kind, Persephone," says Psyche at last, "Aphrodite sent me here to ask you for the secret of your beauty. I'm sorry," she adds quickly. "I know it's presumptuous."

"It is perfectly sensible," says Iseult in the startled silence that follows. "Persephone is a lovely woman."

Psyche's final task is to journey to the Underworld to discover the secret of Persephone's beauty. Beauty has always been the central issue of the romantic myth for women. How beautiful a woman is, by the standards of her day, will affect her whole life: who she is, what she does, who she loves. It is a difficult task for women to shift their estimation of self-worth from this arbitrary physical standard to a more intimate and truthful knowledge of self. As long as women allow physical appearance to dictate their identity and self-esteem they will be objects rather than subjects in the world, dependent on others to find them attractive and give them worth. It is an equally difficult but critical task for men to interact with women as equals, rather than assigning them value based on physical appearance and treating them accordingly.

When a man marries a woman exclusively because of her beauty and his sexual desire for her, he is treating her like a prostitute, but one he does not have to pay, an insight that prostitutes have made again and again regarding the lot of married women. Romantic Love encourages men to search for the most beautiful woman in the world, but it remains mute on the subject of nearly every other characteristic a woman may have. It is no wonder that a man might be taken aback when the beautiful body in bed next to him starts to speak, with opinions and feelings and needs of her own, *just like a man*. The dichotomy of the "dumb blond" and the "mousey schoolteacher" is an artificial construct of the cult of female beauty. If sexual desirability to men is the *only* important element in a woman's identity, then it makes sense that her beauty should be judged to be flawed if she is anything other than beautiful, if she is, for instance, intelligent or capable or strong.

The connection between female beauty and helplessness is self-evident. While men still find female powerlessness attractive, millions of Islamic and African girls will continue to have their genitalia amputated to "protect" their virginity and make them acceptable to their husbands. Young Chinese girls' feet are no longer deformed by bindings perhaps, and Western women's spines no longer distorted by whale-bone corsets, but women will starve themselves literally to death to achieve the wraithlike thinness that defines beauty today. They will continue to do so as long as they believe that women must be beautiful in order to be worth anything at all.

Persephone looks perplexed. "The secret to my beauty? You've given us another riddle, Psyche."

"Another one?" asks Psyche. "But I just arrived."

Lilith smiles. "Well, actually you've been with us for a while now. While you were sorting seeds, we were sorting too."

Eve nods. "Lilith helped me sort out my story and then I retold it myself."

"And in your second task, when you got the fleece . . ." continues

Lilith, giving Iseult a nudge.

"I taught them it is good for women to have sexual desire!" says Iseult proudly.

Lilith nods. "And when the eagle brought you water from the river Styx . . ."

Guenevere looks up and smiles at Lilith. "I suppose I listened to the spirit inside of me, rather than accepting the word of the Church and my husband."

"And now you are here in the Underworld to find out the secret of Persephone's Beauty," says Lilith mysteriously. "What could it mean?"

Persephone laughs. "That's enough clues, Lilith," she says. "Of course I can't give Psyche the secret of my Beauty – without asking Beauty what it is."

"What?" exclaims Beauty, as all eyes turn towards her. "Persephone, I don't have any secrets."

"Please Beauty," entreats Psyche. "It is very important that I bring something to Aphrodite."

Beauty looks helplessly at the others. She takes a deep breath. "All right. If Eve did Psyche's first task when she retold her story, and Iseult did the second and Guenevere did the third when they retold their stories, then what did I do when I retold mine?"

Beauty ponders this, and after a moment begins to smile. She unfolds her hand to reveal a tiny petal that she has been holding there.

"You can give this petal to Aphrodite," says Beauty, suddenly confident that she has answered the riddle correctly.

"Is this your secret?" asks Psyche.

Beauty nods. "There once was a woman who was made from flowers. She was very beautiful, but that was all she was ever made to be. She was a prisoner of her beauty. When she became herself again, she turned back to flowers." Beauty strokes the petal gently, as she continues.

"Beauty was the only name my father ever called me. All I was ever supposed to be was beautiful and useful to men. And so my task was to become myself – to stop paying attention to the pitiful voices of my father and the Beast, and to live my own life." She offers the petal to Psyche.

Psyche takes the petal from Beauty and breathes in its lingering fragrance. As she does, a look of startled comprehension crosses her face. Her eyes close, and she begins to fall, disappearing even before she touches the ground.

"Is she dead?" asks Eve in a horrified whisper.

"Yes," says Persephone, "and no." She points up at the sky.

When Psyche left the Underworld, she carried a cask filled with Persephone's beauty ointment to give to Aphrodite: her fourth task was complete. Though Persephone had warned Psyche not to open the cask on her journey home, her curiosity was stronger than her caution. Psyche lifted the lid of the cask in order to see for herself the secret of Persephone's beauty. But the moment that she set eyes on Persephone's gift, her mortal spirit left her and she fell to the ground, dead.

Psyche awoke from death, by the grace of the gods, to find herself in the heavens. Eros stood beside her, smiling, holding out his hand. The other gods were gathered too, festive and laughing. There seemed to be a wedding going on. Psyche felt a sharp kick in her womb and knew with a shock of joy that the child she had carried with her through her trials would be born not mortal, but divine. And so Psyche the goddess was wed to Eros the god and their daughter was named Delight.

Psyche dies after visiting Persephone in the Underworld and then marries Eros in Heaven, but this death is not a metaphorical sacrifice and rescue like the one she experienced as a child. Her marriage is not a *hieros gamos*, because she has also become a god. Tanith Lee makes this point (and reveals the connection between the folktale of Beauty and the Beast and the myth of Psyche and Eros) in her short story "Beauty." Beauty's character, named Estar, discovers that far from being monstrous the Beast is actually a "god"; more importantly she discovers that she is a "god" as well. In Lee's story Beauty's union with the Beast is a relationship of equals, but it requires that Beauty leave her mortal life behind her: "In any form of death, the soul – Psyche, Estar, (well-named) – refinds a freedom and a beauty lost with birth."[18]

When we experience profound personal transformation it is impossible to be the person we were before, and so it can seem to be a kind of death. But what dies is only what we were forced to become by circumstance; what we lose are the masks of cruel necessity. What we gain, like the silkie who found her skin and disappeared into the sea, like the crane who found her robe of feathers and flew into the heavens, is nothing other than ourselves. When we heal our wounds, we come closer to being who we would have been, had we not been wounded in the first place. When Blodeuedd turned herself back to flowers, she ceased to be a woman, but her spirit did not die just because she left the old form behind. Likewise, Psyche did not transform into something new through her death experience; she simply assumed her original (divine) nature.

"But it is so romantic!" sighs Iseult, as they watch the wedding playing out in the sky above them.

"That depends on what you mean by romance," laughs Beauty. "You'd think it would be more romantic for Eros to save Psyche and take her back to his magic castle."

"Or she should die of grief," says Guenevere.

Persephone nods. "But those things could only have happened before Psyche and Eros were conscious of their wounds. Now that they've completed their tasks, the old romantic myths won't fit anymore."

She looks at Beauty, curiously. "Could you go live with the Beast now?" Beauty shakes her head.

"I don't believe Adam is my soulmate either," says Eve.

Persephone smiles. "Eve, you and Adam can't possibly be halves of one soul – because human beings aren't incomplete! We're just wounded so badly our suffering seems to be human nature."

"That's how the myth started that all woman really want to be raped," says Guenevere.

"And that all men are capable of rape," agrees Lilith.

"That children should be beaten for their own good!" says Beauty.
"That war is noble," adds Iseult.
"Or that anyone can be evil," says Eve at last. "Psyche and Eros
had to work really hard at all their tasks to figure out the truth."

By accepting Psyche as a god, Eros demonstrates his acceptance
of her strength, her sexuality and her authority as equal to his
own. In order to do this, he had to make a conscious decision
to defy the expectations of the dominant cultural myths of his
world. When John Stuart Mill became romantically involved with
Harriet Taylor she was married to another man, but the unusual
circumstances of their affair allowed him a glimpse into the
experience of a Victorian wife. Harriet was continuously forced
into unwanted sexual intercourse with her husband, but she was
sufficiently strong-minded and self-aware to resent her
victimization. She perceived marriage as a sexual contract "in
which one of the parties, the necessarily virginal woman, could
have no idea of what she was committing herself to."[19] Because
of his empathy for Harriet's experience, when John and Harriet
finally married he wrote the following disclaimer:

I, having no means of legally divesting myself of these odious
powers ... feel it my duty to put on record a formal protest
against the existing law of marriage, in so far as conferring such
powers; and a solemn promise never in any case or under any
circumstances to use them ... I absolutely disclaim and
repudiate all pretension to have acquired any *rights* whatever
by virtue of such marriage.[20]

An equitable relationship between a man and a woman does not
come about normally while the social and economic dynamic
between them is unequal. In her novel *Jane Eyre*, Charlotte Brontë
delayed the reconciliation of the characters Jane and Rochester
until Jane had become financially independent and Rochester had
lost his house, one of his hands and the use of his sight.[21] From
a mythological point of view *Jane Eyre* is a retelling of the myth

of Psyche and Eros. The fact that Brontë felt the need for such extreme measures to equalize these characters simply reflects the extent of the sexual inequality in Victorian society. But Brontë demonstrated a remarkably intuitive understanding of the transformation of Romantic Love which is necessary for real love to flourish.

Just as Psyche was abandoned and sacrificed by her family, Jane Eyre was orphaned as a child, abused by the relatives who were supposed to care for her and mistreated at the school where she became a charity ward. Just as Psyche was rescued by Eros and taken to his magic castle, Jane found herself rescued and caught up in a fairy tale as well: Rochester, the lord of the Manor where she was employed as a governess, falls in love with her and asks her to marry him. But just as Eros will not allow Psyche to see his face, Rochester demands that Jane not pry into the secrets of his house or his past.

When the terrible secret is revealed, that Rochester is already married to a madwoman, he begs Jane to accept the circumstances and stay with him as his mistress. Like Psyche, Jane refuses to accept love within a life of shadow and lies, and as a result of this decision ends up alone and penniless. But when her tasks and adventures are complete, Jane returns to Rochester to declare, "I am independent, sir, as well as rich; I am my own mistress." Rochester's tasks are at least as dramatic, changing his character as well as his physical condition. Jane tells Rochester that she loves him, vulnerable and sensitive, more than she did when he was roaring and brutal: "I love you better now, than I did in your state of proud independence, when you disdained every part but that of the giver and protector."

The transformation of the romantic myth *does* require men to stop romanticizing beauty and powerlessness in women but it also requires women to give up the romantic expectation that the perfect man is rich, successful and powerful. When Jane and Rochester marry they do so, like Psyche and Eros, as equals; as the book ends Rochester recovers his sight in time to witness the birth of their son.

Brontë is not the only novelist to incorporate the healing transformations of Psyche and Eros. Thomas Hardy fell just short of retelling the myth in *Tess of the D'Urbervilles*.[22] In Hardy's story the character of Tess is sacrificed by her family and raped by a nominative relative, Alec D'Urberville, which results in pregnancy and the death of her illegitimate child. She is rescued from her unfortunate fate by Angel Clare, but their idyllic romance and brief marriage dissolves like Eros' magic castle when she reveals to Angel the truth of her past. After he abandons her in horror, Tess is forced by poverty, and the emotional circumstances of her own deep wounding, to become dependent on Alec D'Urberville, the man who had originally violated her.

Although Hardy follows Tess' transformation from the woundings of childhood, to the illusion of Romantic Love, through the tasks of healing, he could not see his way clear to allow Tess to leave Alec without murdering him, or alternately to have her escape her crime unpunished. The death that Psyche experiences metaphorically, Tess experiences in fact, when she is hanged for her crime. The authorities catch up to Tess after she has reconciled with Angel, who is now able to love and accept her, murder, illegitimate child and all. Tess begs Angel to marry her sister Liza-Lu who is "good and simple and pure," and apparently this is what Angel does, after Tess is gone. If Liza-Lu lacks Tess' sin and shame, she also lacks the understanding Tess gained through her transformations and tasks. Liza-Lu, simple and pure, cannot replace Tess, nor can she be compared to Psyche who after her death became a god. Tess simply dies. Liza-Lu gets married.

The most astonishing (though perhaps unconscious) retelling of the myth of Psyche and Eros may be found in John Fowles' *The French Lieutenant's Woman*.[23] Fowles offers two endings to his story which hinge upon Charles Smithson's ability to accept the independence of Sarah Woodruff, a woman with whom he had shared an obsessive affair years before and who had disappeared from his life. "I wish to be what I am, not what a husband, however kind, however indulgent, must expect me to become in marriage," Sarah explains when they finally meet again. What Charles believes that he requires from Sarah, her submissive acceptance of marriage, she will not give. Because of the anger he feels towards her, and this final bitter rejection, he turns to depart. It is here that the two endings to the story diverge.

In the first ending, Charles allows himself to be detained by Sarah, restraining his anger in order to fully understand her motives. What he discovers then is a child – his own child that he had never known had been conceived; mother, father and child reconcile in love. But in the second ending Charles departs angrily, brushing past his child on the stairs, never learning of her existence. Sarah does not try to stop him. She does not want Charles if he cannot accept her independence, even if this decision leaves her child without a father. *She does not want for her child the father he would be.*

In all of its retellings in literature and lore, the myth of Psyche and Eros provides us with this final insight: the child of Psyche and Eros will be born mortal, and perhaps will not live at all, if her parents do not succeed in their equality. She will be divine only when her parents both are gods.

"The child of Psyche and Eros is named Delight," explains Persephone. *"She'll inherit her parents' joy, not their wounds."*

Iseult nods. "That is very good. Tristan was named 'sadness' because of his mother's terrible life."

Eve says, wonderingly, "I just thought of something. Persephone, Iseult, Beauty, Guenevere, Blodeuedd – none of you had children!"

"Having a child would have been a disaster for me," says Guenevere. *"I wouldn't have known whose child it was, and it would have been in danger all its life."*

"Wailing babies are not supposed to be romantic," laughs Iseult. *"But they are in my story now."*

"I remember," says Eve. *"I was going to ask you about it."*

"To love Tristan took all my strength," says Iseult. *"I had nothing left to give to a child. But now I feel different."*

The marriage of Psyche and Eros is a union of two whole people, not a reunion of two halves of one soul. As a consequence, Psyche and Eros will not have to use their daughter to make up for whatever is missing in their relationship, or to play out their own childhood pain in their treatment of her. Although children had no place in the traditional myth of Romantic Love, they become an important part of the myth after it has been transformed. The child of Psyche and Eros will experience and internalize a father's loving behavior, a mother's self-respect. She will develop a positive sense about what it means to be female. She, and all the other children who are born to lovers such as these, will be free of the wounds which caused their parents so much pain.

As the myths of Romantic Love shift, the prospects for the future of these children and the world, according to Alice Miller, will be very bright:

> People whose integrity has not been damaged in childhood, who were protected, respected, and treated with honesty by their parents, will be – both in their youth and in adulthood – intelligent, responsive, empathic, and highly sensitive. They will take pleasure in life and will not feel any need to kill or even hurt others or themselves . . . Such people will be incapable of understanding why earlier generations had to build up a gigantic war industry in order to feel comfortable and safe in this world.[24]

To some the transformation of the myth of Romantic Love would be a tragedy – no more swooning ladies being rescued by heroic men – but what is lost is nothing compared to what will be gained by this transformation: changes in the quality of interactions between men and women, in the way that children are raised and, ultimately, the way the nations of the world choose to relate to each other and to the Earth itself. This is the future that Denis de Rougement imagined as well: "Beyond tragedy another happiness waits. A happiness resembling the old, but no longer belonging to the form of the world, for this new happiness transforms the world."[25]

The healing implicit within the myth of Psyche and Eros is available to us in our own lives if we examine our romantic experiences and expectations for clues to unraveling the ways in which we were wounded as children. For some of us this will mean recalling specific acts of abuse. But for many others the deepest wounding was caused by the myths and expectations of our gender. Few of us were *asked* who we were as boys and girls; we were *told* who we were, and then punished if we strayed. The first three tasks of Psyche and Eros we can accomplish by identifying who we are as individuals, transforming the way that we think about the work that we do, the nature of our sexuality and our spiritual beliefs.

The fourth task is the most difficult task of all: to leave all romantic expectations behind us, to cease looking for wholeness through our relationships, but to seek wholeness in ourselves. Only then will we be attracted to relationships with other whole individuals. Contrary to the claims made by the traditional myth of Romantic Love, the union of two Halved Souls will never produce one whole person, much less two. According to Rilke, accepting and celebrating the individuality of the other, rather than longing for union with the beloved, is the most profound experience of marriage:

> Once the realization is accepted that even between the *closest* human beings infinite distances continue to exist, a wonderful living side by side can grow up, if they succeed in loving the distance between them which makes it possible for each to see the other whole and against a wide sky.[26]

The new romantic myth, in which children are conceived in equitable unions between two whole people and raised with love, is a far cry from Plato's description of halved souls who frantically couple in order to *feel* whole. But transformed by the healing of individuals, the myth of Romantic Love will become more poignant and lovely than the traditional myth ever hoped to be. The myth of Romantic Love is neither universal nor eternal.

Romantic Love is mortal like Psyche and must die, to reveal the real Love waiting beneath, which is divine.

"I don't know about you," says Eve, *"but I'm exhausted. I guess I've been here longer than any of you."*

"Well, you are *the first woman,"* laughs Guenevere.

Eve smiles at Lilith. *"The second one, anyway."*

"Are you going to go back to Adam?" asks Persephone curiously.

"Oh yes," says Eve. *"Ever since God cursed him with hard work, Adam has resented me, but I think that's going to change now."*

"I am going to go back to Tristan," says Iseult happily. *"But to be his wife, not his lover. It will make all the difference for us."*

Beauty looks troubled. *"Did I give up my happy ending when I turned down the Beast?"*

"I hope not," says Guenevere. *"I can't settle for what I had before, either."*

"Happy ever after starts when you're alone," says Persephone, *"and it's a beginning, not an ending. Anything can happen after that."*

She indicates each of the women in turn: *"Eve and Adam have been together for millennia. Iseult and Tristan are finally choosing each other after years of Romantic Love. Guenevere has ended her affair with Lancelot and has separated from Arthur. Maybe they'll get back together and maybe not.*

"Lilith –" here she stops.

Iseult reddens. *"I am sorry for what I called you."*

"But I am a lesbian!" says Lilith. *"At least, the twentieth century gave me that choice."*

Persephone smiles. *"You may find it easier to accept Lilith's road than mine. I'm celibate. I'm not waiting for a husband or a lover."*

"But surely you will have a lover someday," says Iseult. *"You are a very beautiful woman."*

Persephone shakes her head. *"Attractiveness has nothing to do with it."*

"I think the point," says Eve to Iseult, *"is that for healthy people the romantic myth has all these choices in it."*

"Of course," laughs Iseult. *"But I am passionate, you know?"* And

she kisses everyone twice as one by one the ladies fade from sight.

Imagine that you are standing on the vast plain of an Underworld. In that expanse of twilit land, legendary heroes bring peace to the wars they have always fought; mythical women challenge those they have always loved; children learn new games. The sky displays a restless Upperearth where history continuously is made. If you persevere, you can see both worlds wheeling in their opposite extremes: the Upperearth rushing through time, the Underworld changing, but slow. You can see myths created and recast by the history of men and women, above. You can see men and women influenced in turn by the myths below.

Afterword

In order to retell the myths of Romantic Love it has been necessary to disperse much of the spiritual awe which surrounds them. Although psychological and religious myths typically enjoy a status of inviolability which we have been taught not to question, the fact is that mythical images and their meanings change dramatically as the needs of history, religion and politics change.

Carl Jung, of course, coined the term *archetype* to refer to mythic images which "are not disseminated only by tradition, language, and migration, but . . . rearise spontaneously, at any time, at any place, and without any outside influence." However, this *commonality* of cross-cultural mythical images (which has been extensively catalogued by Mircea Eliade and Joseph Campbell, among others) does not necessarily indicate that the *meanings* of the images are universal.

Believing that Jungian scholars often ignore this important distinction, Levi-Strauss maintained that any meaning found in mythology cannot derive from the isolated images, but only in the highly contextual and individual way the images are interpreted and combined.[1] Jung clearly did understand the difference, agreeing that mythical symbols are not universal in their content, only in their form, and then "only to a limited degree." In practice, however, archetypes tend to acquire certain specific meanings, and Jungian interpretations of myths and dreams often follow predictable lines.

The moment the image of a mother becomes the "Great Mother archetype" it has content which reveals the interpreter's prejudices about feminine principles, mothering qualities and the nature of women in general. Jung's imagery, like that of any mythmaker, cannot help but embody his own values and beliefs.

In the same way that psychological theorists choose to view themselves as scientists uncovering facts rather than mythmakers creating myths, religious authorities declare certain truths to be divinely inspired and thus beyond all question or doubt.

In *Alone of All Her Sex*, a comprehensive look at the history of the cult of the Virgin Mary, Marina Warner observes that when psychological and religious myths happen to overlap, the universal nature of their symbolism can be simply taken for granted: "Many people accept unquestioningly that the Virgin is an inevitable expression of the archetype of the Great Mother ... While the Vatican proclaims that the Virgin Mother of God always existed, the Jungian determines that all men want a virgin mother, at least in symbolic form, and that the symbol is so powerful it has a dynamic and irrepressible life of its own."[2] Warner believes that this kind of mythmaking by the Church and by psychological theorists is an attempt to make universally true for all what are actually the interpretations of a few. But when the cultural contexts which give rise to a symbol are ignored, Warner cautions, "the distortions and assumptions the symbol perpetuates in our lives become invisible."

There have been many religious, philosophical and psychological systems which are meant to apply to everyone, regardless of cultural background or personal history. Not only do these systems require that we find within ourselves the qualities or motivations that the authorities describe, but once found they cannot be altered or declined. Throughout history, myths have been used by the powerful to influence social custom: mythmaking is a political process which disguises itself in the sacred. When we set ourselves free from the tyranny of these myths *there is nothing to stop us from retelling our lives.*

Notes

CHAPTER 1: EVE

1 Rabbi Samuel bar Nachman, *Genesis Rabba*, cited by Elaine Pagels in "The Gnostic Vision," *Parabola* 3–4, November, 1978.

2 Genesis 2:21–23.

3 Louis Ginzberg, *The Legends of the Jews* vol. 3 (Philadelphia: Jewish Publication Society of America, 1913), p. 66.

4 1 Corinthians 11:7–9.

5 The voice of Aristophanes in Plato's *Symposium* from *The Dialogues of Plato*, ed. B. Jowett (New York: Random House, 1937).

6 Erich Fromm, *The Art of Loving* (New York: Harper Colophon, 1956), p. 33.

7 John Sanford, *The Invisible Partners* (New York: Paulist Press, 1980), p. 4.

8 Julius Evola from *The Metaphysics of Sex*, cited by John Welwood in *Challenge of the Heart* (Boston: Shambhala, 1985) p. 215.

9 Matthew Fox, *Breakthrough: Meister Eckhart's Creation Spirituality in New Translation* (New York: Doubleday, 1980), p. 41.

10 1 Timothy 2:11-15.

11 Nawal El Saadawi, *The Hidden Face of Eve*, trans. S. Hetata (Boston: Beacon Press, 1982), p. 104.

12 Demaris Wehr, *Jung and Feminism: Liberating Archetypes* (Boston: Beacon Press, 1987), p. 16.

13 Cited by Susanne Campbell-Jones in *In Habit: A Study of Working Nuns* (New York: Pantheon Books, 1978), p. 173.

14 See Elaine Pagels, *The Gnostic Gospels* (New York: Random

House, 1979), particularly "God the Father/God the Mother," pp. 48–69.

15 *Gospel of Philip* 67.9–12, from *The Nag Hammadi Library*, ed. James Robinson (San Francisco: HarperCollins, 1988), p. 150.

16 *On the Origin of the World* 116.20-25, from *The Nag Hammadi Library*, p. 182.

17 Alfa Beta di Sira, *Gates to the Old City: A Book of Jewish Legends*, ed. Raphael Patai (Detroit: Wayne State University Press, 1981), pp. 407–408.

18 Swami Nikhilananda, *The Upanishads* (New York: Harper & Row, 1963), p. 190.

19 Sondra Henry and Emily Taitz, *Written Out of History: Our Jewish Foremothers* (Fresh Meadows, New York: Biblio Press, 1983), p. 15.

20 Tertullian, from *De Cultu Feminarum*, cited by Pagels in *The Gnostic Gospels*, p. 63.

21 *The Hypostatis of the Archons* 89.31–90.12, from *The Nag Hammadi Library*, pp. 164–165.

22 *C.G. Jung: Psychological Reflections*, ed. Jolande Jacobi and R.F.C. Hull (Princeton: Princeton University Press, 1973), p. 16.

23 Augustine, from *Opus Imperfectum*, cited by Elaine Pagels in *Adam, Eve and the Serpent* (New York: Random House, 1988), p. 133.

24 Augustine, from *Contra Julianum*, cited by Pagels in *Adam, Eve and the Serpent*, p. 141.

25 Augustine candidly discusses his own sexual history in his autobiographical account, *Confessions*.

26 El Saadawi, *Hidden Face of Eve*, pp. 136–7.

27 *The Thunder: Perfect Mind* 16–31, from *The Nag Hammadi Library*, pp. 297–298. This tract contains no specifically Jewish, Christian or Gnostic allusions. It has been suggested that the female voice may belong to Sophia or perhaps, Eve.

28 Wehr, *Jung & Feminism*, p. 24.

29 Ibid., p. 24.

30 *On the Origin of the World* 115.30–116.7, from *The Nag Hammadi Library*, p. 182.

CHAPTER 2: ISEULT

1   Petrarch, from *Canzoniere*, trans. A. Mortimer (University of Alabama Press, 1977), p. 63.

2   C.S. Lewis, *The Allegory of Love* (London: Oxford University Press, 1936), p. 11.

3   Ibid., p. 13.

4   Georges Duby, *The Knight, the Lady and the Priest*, trans. Barbara Bray (New York: Random House, 1983), p. 220.

5   Robert Johnson, *We: Understanding the Psychology of Romantic Love* (New York: Harper & Row, 1983), p. 52.

6   Ibn Hazm, from *Tok El Hamama*, cited by El Saadawi in *The Hidden Face of Eve*, p. 149.

7   C.S. Lewis addresses this troubling definition of love in his fable of the afterlife *The Great Divorce* (New York: Macmillan, 1946).

8   Denis de Rougement, *Love in the Western World* (Princeton: Princeton University Press, 1983), p. 24.

9   From the introduction to Strassbourg's *Tristan and Isolt*, in *Medieval Romances*, ed. R. S. Loomis and L. H. Loomis (New York: Random House, 1957), p. 88.

10 De Rougement, *Love in the Western World*, pp. 41–42.

11 Rainer Maria Rilke, cited by Welwood in *Challenge of the Heart*, p. 258.

12 M. Scott Peck, *The Road Less Traveled* (New York: Simon & Schuster, 1978), p. 89.

13 Johnson, *We*, p. 198.

14 D.H. Lawrence, cited by Welwood in *Challenge of the Heart*, p. 50.

15 Martin Buber, *I and Thou*, trans. Walter Kaufmann (New York: Charles Scribner's Sons, 1970), p. 58.

16 Fromm, *The Art of Loving*, p. 20.

17 El Saadawi, *The Hidden Face of Eve*, p. 74.

18 Peck, *The Road Less Traveled*, p. 120.

19 Andreas Capellanus, *The Art of Courtly Love*, cited by Warner in *Alone of All Her Sex*, p. 139.

20 El Saadawi, *The Hidden Face of Eve*, p. 85.

21 De Rougement, *Love in the Western World*, p. 45.

22 Ibid., p. 284.

23 Ibid., p. 209.

24   D.H. Lawrence, cited by Welwood in *Challenge of the Heart*, p. 55.

25   See "How Trystan Won Esyllt" in *A Celtic Miscellany* (London: Penguin, 1971), p. 97.

CHAPTER 3: GUENEVERE

1   All excerpts of Alfred Lord Tennyson's "Idylls of the King," from *Poetic and Dramatic Works of Alfred Lord Tennyson*, Cambridge edition, ed. W.J. Rolfe (New York: Houghton Mifflin, 1898).

2   Geoffrey of Monmouth, *History of the Kings of Britain*, trans. Sebastian Evans (New York: E.P. Dutton, 1958). pp. 232–234.

3   *The Death of King Arthur*, trans. James Cable (London: Penguin, 1971), p. 197.

4   Thomas Malory, *La Morte D'Arthur* Vol 2, ed. Janet Cowen (London: Penguin, 1969), p. 523.

5   El Saadawi, *The Hidden Face of Eve*, p. 84.

6   Thomas Malory's personal attitude towards women may have found its way into his story; it is likely that he was imprisoned at one point in his life on charges of armed assault and rape.

7   See *Poems of the Vikings*, trans. Patricia Terry (Indianapolis: Bobbs-Merrill, 1969), pp 166-209, for several different versions of this story, some which glorify Brunehilde and others which sympathize with Gudrun, the grieving widow.

8   See Marina Warner, *Alone of All Her Sex*, "Virgins and Martyrs," (New York: Random House, 1983), pp. 68–78.

9   De Rougement, *Love in the Western World*, p. 229.

10   Ibid., p. 244.

11   Simone de Beauvoir, *The Second Sex*, trans. H.M. Parshley (New York: Random House, 1989), p. 171.

12   Ibid., p. 156.

13   See Joan Evans, *John Ruskin* (New York: Oxford University Press, 1955), pp. 317–334.

14   Warner, *Alone of All Her Sex*, p. 78.

15   Ernest Becker from *The Denial of Death*, cited by Wehr in *Jung & Feminism*, p. 111.

16   De Rougement, *Love in the Western World*, p. 52.

17   See Theodore Sturgeon, "The Silken Swift," in *E Pluribus Unicorn* (New York: Ballantine, 1953), reprinted in

Phantasmagoria, ed. Jane Mobley (New York: Doubleday, Anchor Books, 1977).

18 Tanith Lee, "Hunting of Death: The Unicorn," from *The Gorgon* (New York: Daw Books, 1985), p. 69.
19 Ibid., p. 71.
20 Ibid., p. 86.
21 Warner, *Alone of All Her Sex*, pp. 77–78.

CHAPTER 4: BEAUTY

1 *The Mabinogi*, trans. Patrick K. Ford (Los Angeles: University of California Press, 1977), p. 103.
2 Ibid., p. 104.
3 Ibid., p. 108.
4 Deuteronomy 22:28–30.
5 The legality of marital rape in Arab countries should not be construed to be intrinsically *Islamic*. The Moslem philosopher, El Ghazali, quotes the Prophet as saying, "No one amongst you should throw himself on his wife, as beasts do. Before you join with your wife in intercourse, let there be a message running backwards and forwards between you and her . . . a message of kisses and tender words." (Cited by El Saadawi, in *Hidden Face of Eve*, p. 129).
6 Marielouise Janssen-Jurreit, *Sexism: The Male Monopoly on History and Thought*, trans. Verne Moberg (New York: Farrar, Strauss Giroux, 1982), p. 232.
7 The Silkie/Crane story has analogues in many cultures. See Edward Armstrong, *Folklore of Birds* (New York: Dover, 1958), p. 56.
8 Diana Russell, *Rape in Marriage* (Bloomington: Indiana University Press, 1990), p. 243.
9 Ibid., p. 18.
10 Ibid., p. xxviii.
11 C.S. Lewis, *The Great Divorce* (New York: Macmillan, 1946), p. 121.

CHAPTER 5: SACRIFICE

1 C.G. Jung, *Collected Works*, 14:89, trans. R.F.C. Hull, Bollingen Series 20 (Princeton: Princeton University Press, 1904).

2 C.G. Jung, *Psychological Reflections*, 72:192, p. 106.

3 Ibid., 112:60, p. 112.

4 Freudian anthropologist Geza Roheim, interpreting the significance of rape within certain indigenous Australian tribes, cited by Janssen-Jurreit, in *Sexism: The Male Monopoly on History and Thought*, p. 253.

5 Steven Goldberg, *The Inevitability of Patriarchy* (New York: Morrow, 1973), pp. 233–34.

6 Anne Fausto-Sterling, *Myths of Gender: Biological Theories About Men and Women* (New York: Basic Books, 1985). For a wide overview of gender research, see also Cynthia Fuchs Epstein, *Deceptive Distinctions: Sex, Gender and the Social Order* (New Haven: Yale University Press, 1988).

7 Prejudice is still prejudice, however. Some feminists find in the innate differences model a way to claim superiority over men, denying men the ability to have a deep personal relationship with 'Mother Earth,' for instance, because they have no wombs.

8 Wehr, *Jung & Feminism*, p. 122.

9 See Barbara Sapinsley, *The Private War of Mrs. Packard* (New York: Paragon Books, 1991). Elizabeth Packard was committed to an insane asylum by her Calvinist husband in 1860 because her religious beliefs differed from his. She went on to become a successful writer and lobbyist for legislation to protect women from husbands who could commit them to institutions without legitimate cause.

10 Erich Neumann, *Amor and Psyche: The Psychic Development of the Feminine*, trans. Ralph Manheim, Bollingen Series 54 (Princeton: Princeton University Press, 1956), p. 62.

11 Ibid., p. 63.

12 Robert Johnson, *She: Understanding Feminine Psychology* (New York: Harper & Row, 1977), p. 12.

13 Ovid, *The Metamorphoses*, trans. Horace Gregory (New York, Viking Press, 1985), p. 151.

14 See Ruth Herschberger, "Is Rape a Myth," in *Masculine/Feminine: Readings in Sexual Mythology and the Liberation of Women*, ed. B. Roszak and T. Roszak (New York: Harper Colophon, 1969), pp. 122–129.

15 Joseph Campbell, *Way of the Seeded Earth*, Part 1, "The Sacrifice" (New York: Harper & Row, 1988), p. 39.

16   Hannah Arendt, *Eichmann in Jerusalem: A Report on the Banality of Evil* (New York: Viking Press, 1964), p. 11.

17   Ibid., p. 12.

18   Bruno Bettelheim, in his introduction to M. Nyiszli's *Auschwitz* (New York: Fawcett Crest, 1960), p. xii.

19   Ibid., p. vi.

20   Ibid., p. vii.

21   A correspondent to "The Englishwoman's Domestic Magazine," 1868, cited by Campbell-Jones in *In Habit*, p. 87.

22   See Alice Miller, *For Your Own Good: Hidden Cruelty in Child-rearing and the Roots of Violence* (New York: Farrar, Strauss, Giroux, 1984).

23   See Sandra Butler, *The Conspiracy of Silence: The Trauma of Incest* (San Francisco: Volcano Press, 1985).

24   See *I Never Told Anyone: Writings by Women Survivors of Child Sexual Abuse*, eds Ellen Bass and Louise Thornton (New York: Harper & Row, 1983).

25   Maria Tatar, *The Hard Facts of the Grimm's Fairy Tales* (Princeton: Princeton University Press, 1987), p. 10.

26   Sigmund Freud, "The Aetiology of Hysteria," trans. James Strachey, reprinted in J.M. Masson's *Freud: The Assault on Truth: Freud's Suppression of the Seduction Theory* (London: Faber & Faber, 1984), pp. 251–282.

27   Cited by Masson in *Freud: The Assault on Truth*, p. 9.

28   Sigmund Freud, *New Introductory Lectures on Psychoanalysis*, trans. James Strachey (New York: W.W. Norton, 1965), lecture 33.

29   See Florence Rush, *The Best Kept Secret: Sexual Abuse of Children*, "A Freudian Coverup" (New York: McGraw-Hill, 1980) pp. 80–104.

30   Masson, *Freud: The Assault on Truth*, p. 10. In 1973, Fliess' son revealed that he had been sexually abused by his father. It would appear that Freud was making his revelations to the wrong man.

31   Jung, *Psychological Reflections*, 88:50, p. 101.

32   Alice Miller, trans. H. and H. Hannum, *Though Shalt Not Be Aware: Society's Betrayal of the Child* (New York: Meridian, 1984), p. 200.

33   This is the opinion of Freud's friend and pupil Sandor Ferenczi

who broke with Freud when he chose to believe the stories his patients told him about being sexually abused. As a result Ferenczi was ostracized by the Freudian community and after his death his final paper, "Confusion of Tongues Between Adults and the Child," which dealt with the sexual abuse of children by adults, was suppressed by Freud himself. This paper is translated and reprinted by Masson in *Freud: The Assault on Truth*.

Although Masson's work on Freud has been controversial, most of the criticism has been aimed towards Jeffrey Masson personally, and not towards the content of his research. Ironically, he has been accused of betraying the psychoanalytic community by refusing to protect its symbolic father.

CHAPTER 6: ROMANCE

1 Erich Fromm, *The Anatomy of Human Destructiveness* (New York: Holt, Rinehart & Winston, 1973), p. 374.
2 Miller, *For Your Own Good*, p. 249.
3 Ibid., p. 259.
4 Mike Lew, *Victims No Longer: Men Recovering from Incest and other Child Sexual Abuse* (San Francisco: Harper & Row, 1990), p. 144.
5 De Rougement, *Love in the Western World*, p. 375.
6 See Stanton Peele, *Love and Addiction* (New York: New American Library, 1975).
7 See Russell, *Rape in Marriage*, "Husbands Who Won't Let Their Wives Go," pp. 237–245.
8 See Susan Brownmiller, *Against Our Will: Men, Woman and Rape* (New York: Simon & Schuster, 1975).
9 Rush, *The Best Kept Secret*, p. 53.
10 For the range of views about homosexuality in the ancient world, see J. Boswell, "Revolutions, Universals and Sexual Categories," and D. Halperin, "Sex Before Sexuality: Pederasty, Politics and Power in Classical Athens," in *Hidden from History: Reclaiming the Gay & Lesbian Past*, eds. M. Duberman, M. Vicinus & G. Chauncey (New York: Meridian, 1990), pp. 17–53.
11 Rush, *The Best Kept Secret*, p. 52.
12 Lew, *Victims No Longer*, p. 61.

13   See *Hidden from History: Reclaiming the Gay & Lesbian Past*, for
     historical instances: George Chauncey, "Christian Brotherhood
     or Sexual Perversion? Homosexual Identities and the
     Construction of Sexual Boundaries in the World War I Era,"
     pp. 294–317; and T. Dunbar Moodie, "Migrancy and Male
     Sexuality on the South Africa Gold Mines," pp. 411–415.

14   See Lew, *Victims No Longer*, "Sexuality, Homophobia and
     Shame", pp. 54–61.

15   See Raphael Patai, *The Arab Mind* (New York: Charles
     Schribner's Sons, 1976). Patai discusses this attitude toward
     homosexuality in the Arab world.

16   Colin M. Turnbull, *The Human Cycle* (New York: Simon &
     Schuster, 1983), p. 115.

17   Ibid., p. 116.

18   John Durant, Peter Klopfer and Susan Oyama, *Aggression: The
     Myth of the Beast Within* (New York: John Wiley & Sons, Inc.,
     1988), p. 18.

19   Shields and Shields, "Forcible Rape: An Evolutionary
     Perspective," cited by Fausto-Sterling in *Myths of Gender*, p. 193.
     Fausto-Sterling critiques the study which gave rise to this
     conclusion, and similar work by sociobiologists in Chapter 6,
     "Putting Woman in her (Evolutionary) Place."

20   Deborah Gray White, *Ar'n't I a Woman?/Female Slaves in the
     Plantation South* (New York: W.W. Norton, 1985), p. 164.

21   See Wendy Maltz and Beverly Holman, *Incest and Sexuality*,
     Appencix A, "Sexuality Concerns of Male Incest Survivors."
     Many of the difficulties described by Maltz and Holman would
     also be familiar to men who were not sexually abused.

CHAPTER 7: TASKS

 1   Jung, *Psychological Reflections*, 114:243, pp. 111–112.

 2   Johnson, *She*, p. 13.

 3   Arthur Schopenhauer, "On Women," from *Studies in Pessimism*,
     trans. T. Bailey Saunders, cited by Rosemary Agonito in *History
     of Ideas on Women* (New York: G.P. Putnam's Sons, 1977).

 4   See John Stuart Mill, *The Subjection of Women* (Bungay, Suffolk:
     Richard Clay, Ltd, 1869).

 5   Michael St. John Packe, *The Life of John Stuart Mill* (New York:

Macmillan, 1954), pp. 318–319.

6   Huda Shaarawi, *Harem Years: The Memoirs of an Egyptian Feminist*, trans. Margot Badran (New York: The Feminist Press, 1986), p. 15.

7   Eli Sagan, *Freud, Women and Morality: The Psychology of Good and Evil* (New York: Basic Books, 1988), p. 237.

8   Wehr, *Jung & Feminism*, p. 113.

9   Ibid., p. 113.

10 Jung, *Collected Works*, 10:41.

11 For instance, L. Luzbetak reports in *Marriage and the Family in Caucasia*, (cited by Janssen-Jurreit, in *Sexism*), that among the Ossets, a man would never help his wife carry heavy burdens and risk being considered 'womanly.'

12 Schopenhauer, "On Women," cited by Agonito in *History of Ideas On Women*.

13 Elizabeth Bumiller, *May You Be the Mother of a Hundred Sons: A Journey Among the Women of India* (New York: Random House, 1990), p. 79.

14 El Saadawi, *The Hidden Face of Eve*, p. 78.

15 See Nancy Makepeace Tanner, *On Becoming Human* (Cambridge: Cambridge University Press, 1981).

16 See Fausto-Sterling, *Myths of Gender*, "A Question of Genius," pp. 13–60.

17 Charlotte Perkins Gilman, *The Living of Charlotte Perkins Gilman* (Madison: University of Wisconsin Press, 1990), p. 96.

18 Plato, *The Republic*, from *The Dialogues of Plato* Vol 3, Book 5, trans. B. Jowett (Oxford: Clarendon Press, 1892).

19 See Hilda Scott, *Does Socialism Liberate Women?* (Boston: Beacon Press, 1974).

20 Durant, Klopfer and Oyama, *Aggression: The Myth of the Beast Within*, p. 6.

21 See Fausto-Sterling, *Myths of Gender*, "Hormones and Aggression: An Explanation of Power," pp. 123–154.

22 Durant, Klopfer and Oyama, *Aggression: The Myth of the Beast Within*, p. 25. On the subject of the 'beast within' the authors conclude: "The idea of the beast within is at best a crudely distorted rendering of the conclusions of evolutionary biology; at worst, it is just plain wrong."

23 Ibid., p. 66.

24 J.J. Bachofen, *Myth, Religion and Mother Right*, trans. Ralph
    Manheim, Bollingen Series 84 (Princeton: Princeton University
    Press, 1967), p. 130.
25 Tanith Lee, "Draco Draco," in *Gorgon* (New York: Daw Books,
    1985), p. 258.
26 David Hume, "A Treatise on Human Nature," cited by Agonito
    in *History of Ideas on Women*, pp. 123–128.
27 Margaret Mitchell, *Gone With the Wind* (New York: Macmillan,
    1964), p. 783.
28 Morton Hunt, from "Legal Rape," cited by Russell, *Rape In
    Marriage*, p. 151.
29 Ibid., p. 243.
30 Janssen-Jurreit, *Sexism*, p. 243.
    31 Ibid., p. 47.
32 Sagan, *Freud, Women and Morality*, p. 60.
33 Freud, "Some Physical Consequences of the Anatomical
    Distinctions Between the Sexes," cited bt Sagan in *Freud,
    Woman and Morality*, p.117.
34 Johnson, *She*, p. 54.
35 Lillian Faderman, *Surpassing the Love of Men: Romantic
    Friendship and Love between Women from the Renaissance to the
    Present* (New York: William Morrow, 1981), p. 17.
36 See Brownmiller, *Against Our Will*, "War," pp. 23–87.
37 Claudia Koonz, *Mothers in the Fatherland: Women, the Family
    and Nazi Politics* (New York: St. Martin's Press, 1987), p. 343.

CHAPTER 8: WEDDING

1 Plutarch, "Conjugal Precepts," from *Moralia*, trans. William
   Goodwin (Boston: Little Brown & Co, 1906).
2 1 Corinthians 14.
3 Tertullian, cited by Pagels in *The Gnostic Gospels*, p. 60.
4 Schopenhauer, "On Women," cited by Agonito in *History of
   Ideas on Women*.
5 Freud, "Some Psychical Consequences of the Anatomical
   Distinctions Between the Sexes," cited by Sagan in *Freud,
   Women and Morality*, p. 117.
6 El Saadawi, *The Hidden Face of Eve*, p. 104.
7 Friedrich Nietzsche, *Thus Spake Zarathustra* Part 1, Chapter 18,

trans. Thomas Common (New York: Random House, 1960).

8 Barbara Ehrenreich and Deirdre English, *For Her Own Good: 150 Years of the Experts' Advice to Women* (New York: Doubleday, Anchor Press, 1978), p. 31.

9 Ibid., p. 35.

10 See Judith Pintar, *A Voice From the Earth* (London: Unwin Hyman, 1990), and (New York: Sterling, 1990).

11 Cora Wilburn, cited by Ann Braude in *Radical Spirits: Spiritualism and Women's Rights in Nineteenth-Century America* (Boston: Beacon Press, 1989), p. 135.

12 Ibid., p. 126.

13 Mohammed Ibn Saad, cited by El Saadawi in *The Hidden Face of Eve*, p. 131.

14 Sagan, *Freud, Women and Morality*, p. 168.

15 Luzbetak, *Marriage and the Family in Caucasia*, cited by Janssen-Jurreit in *Sexism*.

16 Sagan, *Freud, Women and Morality*, p. 245.

17 Ibid., p. 244.

18 Tanith Lee, "Beauty," in *Red As Blood or Tales from the Sisters Grimmer* (New York: Daw Books, 1983), p. 208.

19 Cited by Phyllis Rose in *Parallel Lives: Five Victorian Marriages* (New York: Vintage, 1984), p. 103.

20 Ibid., p. 120.

21 Charlotte Bronte, *Jane Eyre* (New York: Signet, 1960).

22 Thomas Hardy, *Tess of the D'Urbervilles* (London: Penguin, 1981).

23 John Fowles, *The French Lieutenant's Woman* (New York: Signet, 1969).

24 Alice Miller, *The Untouched Key: Tracing Childhood Trauma in Creativity and Destructiveness* (Doubleday, Anchor Books: 1990), p. 170.

25 De Rougement, *Love in the Western World*, p. 323.

26 Rilke, cited by Welwood in *Challenge of the Heart*, p. 258.

AFTERWORD

1 See Claude Levi-Strauss, *Structural Anthropology* (New York: Doubleday, Anchor Books, 1967), p. 206.

2 Marina Warner, *Alone of All Her Sex* (New York: Random House, 1983), p. 335.